Party People

COMPARATIVE POLITICS

Comparative Politics is a series for researchers, teachers, and students of political science that deals with contemporary government and politics. Global in scope, books in the series are characterized by a stress on comparative analysis and strong methodological rigour. The series is published in association with the European Consortium for Political Research. For more information visit www.ecprnet.eu

The series is edited by Nicole Bolleyer, Chair of Comparative Political Science, Geschwister Scholl Institute, LMU Munich, and Jonathan Slapin, Professor of Political Institutions and European Politics, University of Zurich.

OTHER TITLES IN THIS SERIES

Coalition Agreements as Control Devices
Coalition Governance in Western and Eastern Europe
Heike Klüver, Hanna Bäck, and Svenja Krauss

Voters Under Pressure
Group-Based Cross-Pressure and Electoral Volatility
Ruth Dassonneville

The Government Party
Political Dominance in Democracy
R. Kenneth Carty

Party System Closure
Party Alliances, Government Alternatives, and Democracy in Europe
Fernando Casal Bértoa and Zsolt Enyedi

The New Party Challenge
Changing Cycles of Party Birth and Death in Central Europe and Beyond
Tim Haughton and Kevin Deegan-Krause

Multi-Level Democracy
Integration and Independence Among Party Systems, Parties, and Voters in Seven Federal Systems
Lori Thorlakson

Coalition Governance in Central Eastern Europe
Edited by Torbjörn Bergman, Gabriella Ilonszki, and Wolfgang C. Müller

Party People

Candidates and Party Evolution

ALLAN SIKK
AND
PHILIPP KÖKER

Great Clarendon Street, Oxford, OX2 6DP,
United Kingdom

Oxford University Press is a department of the University of Oxford.
It furthers the University's objective of excellence in research, scholarship,
and education by publishing worldwide. Oxford is a registered trade mark of
Oxford University Press in the UK and in certain other countries

© Allan Sikk and Philipp Köker 2023

The moral rights of the authors have been asserted

All rights reserved. No part of this publication may be reproduced, stored in
a retrieval system, or transmitted, in any form or by any means, without the
prior permission in writing of Oxford University Press, or as expressly permitted
by law, by licence or under terms agreed with the appropriate reprographics
rights organization. Enquiries concerning reproduction outside the scope of the
above should be sent to the Rights Department, Oxford University Press, at the
address above

You must not circulate this work in any other form
and you must impose this same condition on any acquirer

Published in the United States of America by Oxford University Press
198 Madison Avenue, New York, NY 10016, United States of America

British Library Cataloguing in Publication Data

Data available

Library of Congress Control Number: 2023936259

ISBN 9780198868125

DOI: 10.1093/oso/9780198868125.001.0001

Printed and bound by
CPI Group (UK) Ltd, Croydon, CR0 4YY

Links to third party websites are provided by Oxford in good faith and
for information only. Oxford disclaims any responsibility for the materials
contained in any third party website referenced in this work.

Für unsere Familien

Pühendusega meie peredele

Contents

List of figures viii
List of tables xi
Preface and acknowledgements xii

1. Introduction: Candidates and party evolution 1
2. A conceptual model of candidate and party change 18
3. Measures matter: New concepts, methods, and big data 45
4. Determinants of candidate change 68
5. Old, new, and partially new parties 90
6. Getting volatility right 117
7. Fission and fusion 151
8. Leadership change 180
9. Programmatic change 199
10. Conclusion 220

Bibliography 229
Index 247

List of figures

1.1. Albatrosses of Southern African waters, Gough Island, and the Prince Edward Islands — 9
2.1. Multidimensional party change — 23
2.2. The levels of party people — 25
2.3. A conceptual model of candidate entry, exit, and return — 35
3.1. Hypothetical standardized weights — 52
3.2. Overall weighted candidate novelty over time — 55
3.3. Congruence and list placement — 57
3.4. Fidesz and MDF 1998 candidates in Fidesz–MDF 2002 — 59
3.5. Pairwise slate congruences: Estonia 1992–5 and Hungary 1998–2002 — 60
3.6. Tree of party evolution, Poland 1991–2015 — 62
3.7. Candidate novelty by list position: Estonia 1995–2015 — 65
3.8. Candidate novelty and relative list position, by weighted candidate novelty and party size — 66
3.9. Candidate novelty and relative list position ratio to party vote share, by weighted candidate novelty and party size — 67
4.1. Electoral support and raw candidate turnover — 70
4.2. Electoral support and weighted candidate turnover — 72
4.3. Electoral support change and weighted candidate turnover — 74
4.4. Weighted candidate turnover and change in corruption perception — 82
4.5. Predicted effect of CPI change and vote change on weighted dropout in governing parties — 85
4.6. Predicted effect of CPI change and vote change on weighted novelty in non-governing parties — 86
5.1. Hypothetical relationship between support for new/exiting parties and overall candidate novelty/dropout — 93
5.2. Party entry/exit (Powell & Tucker) and weighted candidate turnover — 94
5.3. Party entry according to different data sets — 96
5.4. Scatterplot matrix of party entry in various data sets — 98
5.5. Party exit according to different data sets — 99
5.6. Distribution of candidate turnover among continuing and not continuing parties — 110

5.7.	Party entry: candidate novelty approach in comparison	111
5.8.	Party exit: candidate novelty approach in comparison	113
5.9.	Probability of agreement between classifications of party entry over slate size and country size	116
6.1.	Volatility scores for Estonia 1992–5 compared to CEE means	121
6.2.	A simple example of split-by-congruence volatility	127
6.3.	Fission and split-by-congruence volatility	128
6.4.	Collective defection and split-by-congruence volatility	129
6.5.	Virtual slates, Estonia 1992–5	131
6.6.	Virtual slates, the Czech Republic 2002–6	132
6.7.	Split-by-congruence volatility compared to indices from other sources	134
6.8.	Virtual slates, Lithuania 2000–4	135
6.9.	The effect of GDP change on electoral volatility	139
6.10.	Trees of party evolution	142
7.1.	Electoral slate fission and fusion	154
7.2.	The evolution of successors to For Human Rights in a United Latvia (PCTVL)	156
7.3.	Expected relationship between candidate congruences, turnover, and fission and fusion	158
7.4.	Distribution of the fragmentation of successors: fissions vs other slates	160
7.5.	Candidate novelty: post-fission slates and other slates	160
7.6.	Fragmentation of successors: fissions vs other slates	162
7.7.	Fission detected based on candidate movement	167
7.8.	Successor fragmentation over time	169
7.9.	Distribution of component congruence and novelty: fusions and non-fusions	171
7.10.	Candidate dropout: pre-fusion slates and other slates	171
7.11.	Fragmentation of predecessors: fusion and other slates	172
7.12.	Fusion detected based on candidate movement	176
7.13.	Predecessor fragmentation over time	177
8.1.	Leadership novelty in new and continuing slates	189
8.2.	Leadership and candidate novelty	190
8.3.	Leadership and candidate novelty: the effect of slates' vote share	192
8.4.	Fusion: candidate and leadership congruence	193
8.5.	Fission: candidate and leadership congruence	195
9.1.	MARPOR RILE and CHES general left–right	202
9.2.	Distribution of programmatic change variables	206

9.3. Development of Ü and MCPP over time — 206
9.4. Programmatic change and weighted candidate novelty and dropout — 211
9.5. Programmatic change and candidate change including moves between parties — 212
9.6. Regression models for candidate turnover: policy change and control variables — 213
9.7. Regression models for candidate turnover: policy change and control variables (individual continuing parties) — 215
9.8. Programmatic and candidate congruence under fission and fusion — 216

List of tables

3.1. The origin of Fidesz–MDF (2002) candidates	60
4.1. Electoral support and raw candidate turnover	70
4.2. Electoral support change and weighted candidate turnover	75
4.3. Descriptive statistics	81
4.4. Determinants of weighted candidate turnover	84
5.1. Candidate novelty: the largest entering parties	101
5.2. High candidate novelty slates	103
5.3. Candidate novelty: the largest continuing parties	104
5.4. Candidate dropout: the largest exiting parties	106
5.5. Slates with the highest candidate dropout ($v \geq 5\%$)	107
5.6. Candidate dropout: the largest continuing parties	109
6.1. Electoral results in Philistia, 950–948 BC	119
6.2. Elections to Riigikogu, Estonia 1992–5	123
6.3. Descriptive statistics	138
6.4. Determinants of electoral volatility	139
8.1. The scale of slate leadership novelty	185
8.2. Candidate novelty and leadership novelty	191
9.1. Aggregate programmatic change: Polish Civic Platform 2006–10 in CHES	203
9.2. Parties with highest and lowest Ü	207
9.3. Parties with highest and lowest MCPP	208

Preface and acknowledgements

Party politics is increasingly in flux across political regimes. Frequent political change and party system instability are no longer confined to countries that have undergone seismic transformations in recent decades, such as in Central and Eastern Europe (CEE), or to a handful of outliers, but have become commonplace in traditionally more stable (Western) democracies. Several major democracies have undergone fundamental changes: from France, where the success of Emmanuel Macron and his En Marche! turned the political landscape upside down in 2017, to the United States, where political competition since the 2016 presidential election has been fundamentally altered not by the emergence of new challengers but by a shift in the balance of power within the Republican Party. In other words, party politics is becoming more complex—or perhaps the potential for complexity that was always there has been unleashed.

This increasing complexity challenges established theories and analytical approaches, often developed on the basis of the relatively stable Western (European) party systems of the 1960s and 1970s. At the same time, it poses new methodological challenges for researchers, especially (but not only) for those seeking to study several countries comparatively. How can we make sense of this increasing (party) political complexity? How can we conceptualize and measure political change in parties and party systems? These are the questions that motivate this book. Our aim is to introduce a new way of understanding and analysing party and party system change that examines such processes by focusing on 'party people'. Political parties are nothing without the people involved—therefore, we propose to study party evolution by focusing on the people who make up these organizations and cause them to change, rather than using the party as a monolithic unit of observation.

We argue for using a 'genetic approach' for the analysis of party change and evolution. In this approach, electoral candidates—the most visible and perhaps the most important stratum of 'party people'—are conceptualised as 'party DNA' that ultimately determines signals what parties stand for. Thus, analysing the change in candidates, their movement between parties as well as their entry and exit from the political scene, presents a highly useful indicator of overall party change. The primary purpose of this book is to explicate this new approach and show how it can be used to provide valid and reliable analyses, both nuanced and extremely large-scale, of party and party system change. We do so by applying our approach to the democracies of CEE, a set of countries long characterised by constant political change and great variation in party system innovation (including periods of apparent stability/institutionalization).

Throughout the book, we show how the change in electoral candidates can be used to finetune existing approaches (such as the electoral volatility index) and relate it to other commonly discussed features of party change such as changes to programmes, organization and leadership. Thereby, our quantitative analyses are based on our novel data set Electoral Candidates in Central and Eastern Europe (ECCEE), which covers sixty elections in nine countries from 1990 to 2016 and comprises more than 200,000 candidacies from more than 1,400 parties. Furthermore, our quantitative insights are complemented and validated by 'thick' qualitative insights and in-depth analysis. Nevertheless, this is not a book only about party politics in CEE. Our aim is to highlight how an approach based on electoral candidate data can aid the analysis of past, present, and future developments in democratic (and non-democratic) regimes around the world.

The ideas at the heart of our approach 'evolved' over time—often only slowly, but occasionally interspersed with rapid transformations of our thinking. More than eight years ago, we started to collect data on candidates in CEE and began to think about how changes among 'party people' were indicative of greater political trends and changes, and how a candidate-centred view of party politics could be used to improve existing measures. Now, with progress delayed by Philipp moving between universities twice (and countries once), Brexit, and a global pandemic, the final product looks very different from what we initially imagined. Therefore, we do not claim that this book is the last word on candidate change and party evolution. Yet, we hope that it will inspire and engage others to use our 'genetic approach' and to make sense of complexity elsewhere by studying the evolution of the 'big' through change in the 'small'.

Although only our two names appear on the cover, writing a book always involves many more (party) people. Throughout our work on this book, we have benefited from generous feedback from many colleagues and friends. We are indebted to all those who read drafts of chapters, particularly Tim Haughton, Raimondas Ibenskas, Kaili Järv, Neil Prime, Sherrill Stroschein, Frederik Springer, and Rein Taagepera. Furthermore, our gratitude extends

xiv   PREFACE AND ACKNOWLEDGEMENTS

to everyone who offered comments in personal discussions or at our presentations at conferences, workshops, and seminars in Belfast, Brighton, Canterbury, Florence, Glasgow, Hamburg, Mainz, Montreal, Nottingham, London, Oxford, Philadelphia, San Francisco, Sussex, Warwick, Warsaw, and Washington, DC. Among attendees, chairs, and discussants, we would particularly like to thank Andrea Aldrich, Nick Aylott, Andreas Bågenholm, Daniel Bochsler, Niklas Bolin, Stefanie Bailer, Tim Bale, Monika Bauhr, Mark Bennister, Nicole Bolleyer, Endre Borbáth, Fernando Casal-Bértoa, Paul Chaisty, Mihal Chiru, Michael Coppedge, Kevin Deegan-Krause, Holger Döring, Alina Dolinska, Piret Ehin, Zsolt Enyedi, Simon Frantzmann, Chris Gerry, Cristina Gherasimov, Marcia Grimes, Olli Hellmann, Paul Heywood, Dan Hough, Jennifer Hudson, John Ishiyama, Richard Katz, Georgia Kernell, Herbert Kitschelt, Spyros Kosmidis, Petia Kostadinova, Alenka Krašovec, Krystyna Litton, Martin Mölder, Laura Morales, Tom Mustillo, Simeon Nichter, Vello Pettai, Monica Poletti, Grigore Pop-Eleches, Gideon Rahat, Nicolas Sauger, Paul Taggart, Lori Thorlakson, Mariano Torcal, Ingrid van Biezen, Marc van de Wardt, Cees van der Eijk, and Paul Webb. We are equally indebted to Eleanor Neuff Powell, Joshua Tucker, Scott Mainwaring, Carlos Gervasoni, Annabella España-Najera, and Margit Tavits for generously sharing their raw data.

Leslie Pitman and Eszter Tarsoly helped to guide us through the intricacies of data protection regulations and Hungarian names, respectively. Elizabeth Bailey, Morten Harmening, and Max Stafford helped us to collect further data on candidates and party leaders, while Felicia Riethmüller and Hiske Carstens proved invaluable in proofreading the book proposal and sample material as well as formatting the final manuscript. Allan's computer, which features prominently in our introduction, endured numerous modifications but never gave up (Philipp, however, eventually bought a new one).

This book would not have been possible without generous financial support from several projects and institutions. After our work was initially funded by the EU FP7 ANTICORRP Project (Grant No. 290529), we received further assistance from UCL SSEES, the CCCU Research and Impact Excellence Fund, and the Department of Political Science at Leibniz University Hannover.

The fact that our research now appears in print is not the least due to Titus Hjelm, Jan Kubik, and Alena Ledeneva who provided valuable feedback on our initial proposal. Dominic Byatt at Oxford University Press as well as Emilie van Haute, Ferdinand Müller-Rommel, Susan Scarrow, and Jonathan Slapin as past and present editors of the ECPR Comparative Politics series similarly offered excellent (and patient) guidance throughout the process. We would also like to thank Vicky Sunter, Gangaa Radjacoumar, Sam Augustin Durai Ebenazer, and the rest of the Oxford University Press production team for their excellent work in getting the book ready for publication.

Finally, we would like to thank our friends and families for their loving support throughout the last few years. This book is dedicated to them.

Allan Sikk and Philipp Köker
London and Hanover
March 2023

1
Introduction

Candidates and party evolution

How old is Allan's computer?[1] (It is a PC, but we hope you do not put down the book because you prefer Mac or Linux.) I bought the computer ten years ago, upgraded the memory nine years ago, installed a new hard drive seven years ago, replaced the keyboard six years ago and the printer four years ago; not to mention the power supply, fan, and other parts that I may have forgotten about. In addition to the hardware changes, I updated Windows five years ago and installed or upgraded countless other software. Is the computer on which I am typing this introduction exactly the one bought a decade ago or is it a new one? If new, when did it cease to be old? Perhaps it is neither new nor old but *changed*? Still, the humble black case looks the same as on the day of purchase; no change can be detected from the outside. It would look the same even if all the components inside were to be removed, rendering the computer useless.

Now, if I took all the components and put them inside a shiny red case, the computer would function identically; I could even edit this very text. Would the hollow black case be the same computer I initially bought? Would the shiny red one be completely new? Going even further, what would happen if Philipp took *some* of my components and used them to put together another PC? This computer would certainly be different from mine. Would it be part his, part mine, or a new computer altogether? This is of course only our modern and, admittedly, nerdy take on a classic puzzle: for over 2,000 years philosophers have argued and failed to agree on, whether the ship of Theseus whose planks, mast, and oars were gradually replaced (like Allan's computer) would remain essentially the same or become a new ship, not to mention a ship built from the old parts (see Wiggins 2001).

This book is not about computers or ships; it is neither about the animals nor plants that we will encounter a few pages on. This book is about political parties and their candidates; more broadly, it is a book about change or *evolution* among computers, ships, living things, and political parties alike. It is a

---

[1] Both authors contributed to this section, we use the first-person singular for stylistic purposes only.

Party People. Allan Sikk and Philipp Köker, Oxford University Press. © Allan Sikk and Philipp Köker (2023).
DOI: 10.1093/oso/9780198868125.003.0001

book about evolution that is sometimes difficult to spot from afar or from outside the evolving object. The evolution that, we argue, can be measured and tracked in political parties by looking at the turnover in electoral candidates.

1.1 Beyond old and new parties

Much of the literature on party system evolution and institutionalization implicitly assumes that political parties are either new or old. Electoral volatility—party vote share changes between elections—and levels of support for new parties are often used as simple measures of party system (in)stability. Others go beyond describing what parties there are and how well they do, and study changes in their interactions. We agree with the importance of putting systemness into the study of party systems (Casal Bértoa & Enyedi 2016; Mair 1997). However, to maximize understanding of interactions we need a fuller understanding of the parties that are interacting.

Many scholars have studied change within individual parties (e.g. Bale 2012)[2] Various aspects of this change—e.g. programme, leader, or organization—have been studied together or individually (including in some classic works such as Harmel & Janda 1994; Katz & Mair 1994). However, *party change* is seldom considered relevant for understanding *party system evolution*. The literature on party systems and electoral change generally brushes over the change within parties and focuses on their birth, death, mergers, and splits as well as their close cousins, the formation and breaking up of electoral coalitions (Barnea & Rahat 2011; Litton 2015 are notable exceptions). One of the aims of this book is to link internal party change to the empirical study of party systems, using party change to enhance our understanding of new and disappearing parties, electoral volatility, and party fission and fusion (see Chapters 5–7). More specifically, we propose a holistic approach that acknowledges different dimensions of party change and incorporates the—as we will see, very real!—the possibility of gradual and partial change into the study of party systems and political change.

We argue that this more nuanced approach is needed for a proper understanding of political change. Parties are obviously 'born' and they 'die', or *enter* and *exit*, to use less anthropomorphic language. They can also experience *fission* and *fusion*, splitting up and recombining in different ways (Mair 1990). However, limiting party change to only these events yields a monochrome

---

[2] Sometimes referred to as 'adaptation' or 'transformation' in the literature.

picture. Change within parties and complex connections between parties past and present need to be taken seriously for three reasons.

First, squeezing parties into containers labelled 'old' and 'new' often overlooks political realities. Many fairly stable parties in Western Europe—and some in Eastern Europe—have experienced gradual change over time. Christian Democrats across Europe adapted to the loss of their confessional base, transforming slowly into essentially secular parties (Kalyvas 1998). Similarly, many Social Democratic parties moderated in response to economic and social changes from the 1970s onwards, culminating in the Third Way politics two decades later (Huo 2009; Kitschelt 1994). Other parties have experienced even more dramatic transformations. Fidesz in Hungary in the 2020s is indisputably very different from the party that emerged in 1988 or led the first Viktor Orbán government in 1998–2002. Even though Orbán remains its leader, a liberal party of young anti-communists has morphed into an illiberal party of authoritarian conservatives. The German Green Party has evolved from an environmentalist protest movement to a comfortable coalition partner in centre-left and (in individual states) cross-spectrum governments. Major changes aside, no party is ever identical—or perfectly *congruent*—to any party in an earlier election. Party evolution can be slow and evolutionary or punctuated, alternating between periods of stability and rare bursts of change (Bale 2012: 3–8), but it always happens.

Second, new parties seldom appear out of nowhere—they commonly have weaker or stronger links to earlier parties. Put differently, they often fail the test of *genuine newness*, i.e. the absence of prominent organizational or personnel links to existing parties (Sikk 2005). For instance, Law and Justice (PiS) and the Civic Platform (PO) stormed the Polish political scene in 2001 but had clear roots in the weakened Solidarity Electoral Action (AWS). Team Stronach, a moderately successful party in the 2013 Austrian elections, drew some of its top brass from the Alliance for the Future of Austria (BZÖ), itself a one-time breakaway from the Austrian Freedom Party (FPÖ). Such ties are often obvious for major splinters. For instance, the Danish People's Party (DFP)—a high-flying early bird among radical right parties—broke off from the Progress Party (FP) in 1995. While a stump FP survived and DFP looked like a newcomer, it pinched a large slice of its members and FP's former leader (Sikk & Köker 2019). The British Social Democratic Party (SDP) split from Labour in 1981, spearheaded by four former and current MPs. It recruited most of its membership from outside, but 10% of Labour's MPs (and one Conservative) also defected to the new formation. Thus, 'the SDP was a young political party, but it was never a *new* political party' (Sykes 1988: 1; italics added). These parties were all new in many ways; however, they lacked genuine newness. Genuinely new parties have been much less common than such spinouts, especially in Western Europe, albeit with some notable exceptions, e.g. de Gaulle's Rally of the French People (established in 1947), Emmanuel Macron's En Marche! (2016), the Italian Five Star Movement (2009), and the Dutch List Pim Fortuyn (2002) (see Emanuele & Sikk 2021).[3]

Finally, parties that appear to 'die' do not always end up six feet under: while some may disappear for good, others leave chunks of themselves behind (Litton 2015: 712). The Italian Christian Democracy dissolved in 1994 but donated senior members to a range of parties, including the newly founded Forza Italia (Morlino 1996: 9–10). The French Rally for the Republic (RPR) disappeared in 2002, but only because of a merger into the Union for a Popular Movement (UMP, Haegel 2004). In Poland, the Democratic Union (UD) and Liberal-Democratic Congress (KLD) disappeared in 1994 by fusing into the new Freedom Union (UW). Other 'deaths' have been even less terminal. The Belgian Vlaams Blok (VB) was killed off by its leaders in 2004 after it was declared racist by the courts and lost access to state funding, only to be reborn as Vlaams Belang on the next day (Erk 2005). Similarly, the Lithuanian Labour Party (DP) was disbanded in 2013 to avoid penalties for fraudulent bookkeeping. It merged with the small Labourist Party and adopted a slightly different name Labour Party (Labourists) (Jastramskis & Ramonaitė 2015: 206). The continuity in VB and DP was obvious and the staged 'deaths' only fooled the Belgian and Lithuanian law; their self-termination was entirely strategic. The fact that party death is not necessarily a sign of weakness has been noted by others (Beyens et al. 2016; Bolleyer et al. 2019a; Bolleyer et al. 2019b). For these reasons, instead of 'death' we use the less grave and anthropomorphic term *party exit*.

Once we recognize that the black-and-white categories of old/new and exiting/continuing parties may neglect important continuities, a different image of parties and party systems transpires. In this picture, parties are fluid and transient. Sometimes it is almost impossible to pin down a party over time—a problem that is very familiar to students of Central and East European (CEE) politics, but that is not absent in Western Europe and other, ostensibly more stable party systems either, as demonstrated by the examples of the Danish People's Party (DFP) discussed above and that of Kadima, established before the 2006 parliamentary elections in Israel (Barnea & Rahat 2011; Sikk & Köker 2019).

---

[3] En Marche! is actually a case of a partially new party, see Chapter 5 of this book.

How should we conceptualize and measure party novelty and change? Building on classic works on (new) political parties (Harmel & Janda 1994; Harmel & Robertson 1985; Janda 1980; Key 1964), political scientists have argued before that party change is a multidimensional phenomenon (Bale 2012; Barnea & Rahat 2011; Beyens et al. 2017; Litton 2015; Sikk & Köker 2019). Change can affect party programmes, policies, ideological orientation, or coalition patterns. Parties can also change their internal organizational structure, e.g. the size and role of membership (Kölln 2015; Scarrow 2014; van Haute & Gauja 2015) or rules on candidate selection (Bille 2001; Gallagher & Marsh 1988; Hazan & Rahat 2010; Lundell 2004). Parties regularly change leaders, by gradually replacing the old guard with younger cohorts or by purging entire national executive committees (Sandri et al. 2015; see also contributions in Cross & Pilet 2015; Pilet & Cross 2014; and Chapter 8 of this book). To summarize, '[p]arties are like living organisms. They emerge, breathe, grow, change, go through ups and downs in their lives, and die, often leaving lasting legacies and pedigrees' (Litton 2015: 712).

We consider the multidimensional novelty to be a continuous rather than a dichotomous quality. However, most dimensions of change just mentioned are either difficult to measure or do not apply to all parties or countries. For example, party ideology touches the core of what parties are and has been studied extensively; yet, policies and programmatic profiles and, even more so, their change are notoriously difficult to measure across countries, parties, and over time (see Chapter 9 and Benoit & Laver 2007; Budge & Pennings 2007; Laver 2001). Governing coalition patterns and ministerial turnover are also important dimensions (Barnea & Rahat 2011), but ignore change among opposition parties. Turnover of ministers and MPs (Gherghina 2015) is also a problematic indicator if their numbers per party are small—impressions of change can fluctuate greatly if only one portfolio or seat is lost, gained, or retained.

Now, these three dimensions remain: (a) organization including name, (b) leadership, and (c) candidates (Sikk & Köker 2019); but candidate change is the most useful among them, as we will explain below. Not only are the three dimensions most widely applicable, but they also address what parties *are* (their substance) rather than what they *do* (their behaviour)—in contrast to other aspects mentioned above. The three are also *necessary ingredients* of any party—echoing most classic definitions of political parties. One can concoct a party without ministers or MPs, or even without a programme or members but *not* without a name, a formal or informal leader, or candidates.

The selection and change of party leaders and their electoral effects have been studied extensively across a wide range of countries (Aarts et al. 2011; Bynander & 't Hart 2008; Cross & Pilet 2015; Marsh 1993; Pilet & Cross 2014; Quinn 2012). Change in party organizations has likewise been widely researched (Allern & Pedersen 2007; Katz & Mair 1994; Samuels & Shugart 2010; Tavits 2013; van Biezen 2003). In contrast, *candidate change* has hitherto received hardly any attention, as scholars largely focused on the personal qualities of candidates (Campbell & van Heerde-Hudson 2018; Dubrow & Palaguta 2016; Karlsen & Skogerbø 2015; Lloren & Rosset 2017; Lutz et al. 2018; Popescu & Hannavy 2001; Zittel 2015; for notable exceptions see Kreuzer & Pettai 2003; Shabad & Slomczynski 2004). We propose that candidate change is intrinsically linked to other aspects of party change: a claim that we test in Chapters 7-9 of this book. We discover that greater levels of overall party change are accompanied by high degrees of candidate turnover and party stability is associated with a relatively stable pool of candidates. Candidate change is a promising indicator of party change, at least as a broad proxy, because compared to other aspects of party change it is considerably easier to conceptualize, operationalize, and measure, especially on a continuous scale.

This book is mostly about people in parties, specifically about change among electoral candidates—their entry, exit, and movement between parties—and its relationship to other aspects of party change (fission and fusion, leadership change, programmatic change). In every election, candidates either reappear on the ballot paper or drop out of electoral politics; new candidates appear while old ones move up and down party lists as well as between parties. Candidate change happens at variable rates: a party can recycle their list of candidates or change them all, although in practice it nearly always settles between the two extremes. We argue and show that rates of candidate turnover—and candidate movement between parties—allow for a reasonably standardized, valid, and reliable measurement of party change and novelty and the establishment of connections between parties between elections—or 'slates' to use our common term for parties, electoral coalitions, etc. in a particular election. The remaining sections of this chapter explain our motivation for studying electoral candidates and candidate change in more detail. We propose a 'genetic' approach to the analysis of party politics, explain how we put it into action using 'big but thin data' on candidate slates, and conclude by summarizing the main contributions of the book.

1.2 Party people: candidates as party genes

Politics and political parties are nothing without the *people* involved. People occupy political offices, formulate policies, and fight over them, and mobilize electoral support. Parties likewise involve various kinds of people: from the rank-and-file members through branch organizers and elected representatives to party leaders and high office holders. What parties stand for ultimately stems from the people who inhabit them, and without these people, a party would cease to be. If anything, people are becoming increasingly important for political parties (Rahat & Kenig 2018).

Parties are largely vehicles serving the people that create them and only derive meaning from human motivations. Parties can be facelifted if they flounder or can even be scrapped once no longer useful for the people involved.[4] The notion of 'parties as vehicles' best fits business–firm parties, such as Silvio Berlusconi's Forza Italia or the ANO 2011 party of Czech tycoon-turned-politician Andrej Babiš (see Hopkin & Paolucci 1999; Kopeček 2016). It is also apt for other unorthodox parties such as 'memberless parties'—for example, the Dutch Party for Freedom of Geert Wilders (Mazzoleni & Voerman 2017)—that clearly serve their leader first and foremost. However, even the more traditional varieties of parties serve the people involved in them, i.e. the leader, elected representatives, and other party elites and candidates. Among them, electoral candidates are the biggest visible and well-defined slice of people that constitute political parties.

People in parties change. We propose a 'genetic' approach to party politics measuring party evolution by candidate novelty and dropout within parties and tracking candidate movement between them. The rate of candidate change varies ranging from a slow replacement of the old by the young to seismic takeovers by newcomers or purges of the old guard. This is not dissimilar to genetic transformations in species over generations, where a constant ticking of the evolutionary clock is interrupted by occasional faster mutations (Kumar 2005). Just as differences in genetic sequencing allow biologists to measure evolutionary distances between species, we suggest that 'candidate sequencing' can capture similarities between parties past and present and can measure the speed of change in parties. In comparative genomics, the constant ticking of molecular clocks is used to measure the time when two contemporary

---

[4] For example, the Estonian Coalition Party and Latvian People's Party disbanded in 2002 and 2011, respectively, after long spells at the helm of the government.

species diverged from each other, i.e. went separate ways in the evolutionary tree (Kumar 2005). We use candidate overlap or *congruence* between parties in successive elections to uncover linkages between parties over time.

We study congruence by looking at electoral slates: a political party or electoral coalition (or any other formation) in a single election. The term brings to focus the electoral face of parties and avoids the often unnecessary distinction between parties and coalitions.[5] It also alludes to classic party definitions such as 'any organization which nominates candidates for election to a legislature' (Riggs 1968: 51). Thus, we use 'slate' to refer to 'parties and electoral coalition' or 'electoral units', reserving 'party' mostly to 'party as an organization'. Only occasionally do we use 'party' as a synonym for 'slate' for stylistic purposes where the context is clear.

To return to the genetic analogy, parties can also experience 'cross-breeding' of candidates over time, combining genetic material from several sources, resulting in hybrids such as mergers or electoral coalitions. Like species, parties can become extinct; as we will see later, candidates—or the 'political genes'—can easily survive in new parties, just as the genetic material of extinct species survives in related species. The genetic analogy does not fit some common events among parties that have no obvious parallels in the natural world; for example, the rise of genuinely new parties based on political novices (new political genetic material) can at best be likened to genes arriving from outer space. Nevertheless, the idea of candidates as political genes is justified by the fact that the analogy does work in surprisingly many ways, as discussed above and later in this chapter.

Appearances can be deceptive, be it in animals or political parties. In the olden days, appearances were often the biologists' only clue to distinguishing between different species (unless they cut them open, of course). For example, some species of albatrosses are very similar to each other (Figure 1.1); albatrosses look similar to seagulls to whom they are only distantly related; they are much closer to penguins and storks. Storks, in turn, are visually similar to cranes but more closely related to both penguins and albatrosses (Prum et al. 2015). Breeds and varieties of ducks and hens, but especially of dogs and cabbages are so diverse that an amateur could easily take them for different species. As we know, they are not. Nowadays differences and relationships

---

[5] It is often difficult to tell parties and coalitions apart. Electoral results do not always distinguish between them and coalitions can transform into parties. Furthermore, party lists can include members of other parties without a formal coalition, or 'dummy parties' can mix candidates without a formal merger when electoral rules are unfavourable to electoral coalitions. Finally, some electoral coalitions are fleeting while others are remarkably stable, e.g. the long-standing CDU–CSU alliance in Germany or the Union of Greens and Farmers in Latvia.

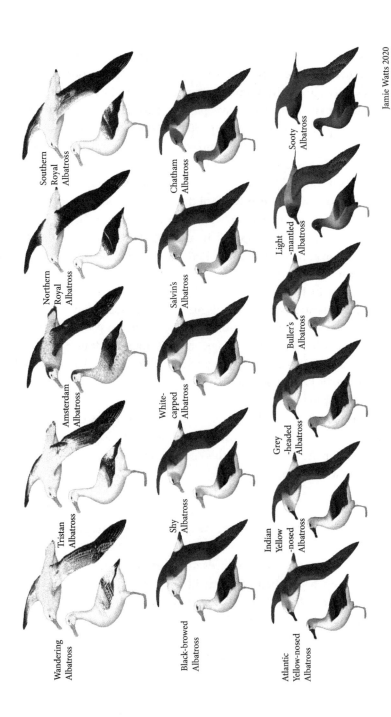

Figure 1.1 Albatrosses of Southern African waters, Gough Island, and the Prince Edward Islands

Source: Jamie Watts, www.jamiewatts.co.uk/

between species are generally established based on genetic evidence rather than visual observations.

Appearances of political parties can just be as deceptive. If we only used party logos (or names) to establish relationships and continuities between political parties, strange families would emerge. A torch has been used as a symbol by both main British political parties. Labour ditched the torch around 1980 (Manuel 2015), only to be picked by the Conservatives a couple of years later (https://logos.fandom.com/wiki/Conservative_Party); obviously, this does not imply any relationship between the two. Similarly, the Conservative Party has since 2006 flaunted a tree that suggests a false similarity to the logo of the short-lived Green Party of the German Democratic Republic (in 1990, https://en.wikipedia.org/wiki/East_German_Green_Party) or the Spanish Partido Ecológico Español in the late 1970s and early 1980s (https://logos.fandom.com/wiki/Partido_Ecológico_Español). While the latter two come from the same party family and then-Conservative leader David Cameron did flirt with environmentalism, a classification based on such superficial similarities would be misguided. Conversely, the two logos of the Polish Law and Justice (PiS)—one with a Viking ship or Noah's ark and the other one with a crowned eagle https://logos.fandom.com/wiki/Prawo_i_Sprawiedliwość)—fail to suggest a relationship, although it remained exactly the same party. Of course, no sane political scientist would base party relationships on party logos. Nevertheless, the differentiation between old and new parties and identification of successor parties often relies on criteria—such as names—that can be almost as superficial; to return to the example of Allan's computer from the beginning of this chapter, a tired black case can hide more novelty than a shiny new red one.

1.3 A candidate-based view of party evolution

Our brief excursion into the realm of birds and party logos underscores that evolution should not be studied offhandedly. In particular, we need to go beyond appearances and look at 'party genes' to distinguish between different parties and find similarities over time. We are not the first to use biological or genetic metaphors for the development of political parties. The idea of 'evolution' in individual parties and party systems has been mooted for decades (Coppedge 1997; Laver & Benoit 2003; Machin 1989; Tavits 2008b). Despite some similarity at first glance, Panebianco's (1988) 'genetic model' refers to something quite different: he argues that circumstances at the time of party *genesis* shape its nature in the long run (see also Krouwel 2012; Passarelli 2015), in contrast to our interest in how party *genes* change over time.

We use the analogy of biological evolution and refer to candidates as party genes in more than a merely metaphorical sense. There are important differences between molecular and political genes, highlighted by the 'alien invasion' analogy of genuinely new parties mentioned above, and the very different pace and causes of change in political parties and living species. Yet, the analogy allows us to borrow from ideas in evolutionary biology and make a distinction between political parties (as species) and drivers of change (candidates as genes).

At this point, some of our readers may complain: unlike people, genes have no agency! We agree, yet propose a shift of perspective similar to that heralded by Richard Dawkins's work *The Selfish Gene* (1976) in evolutionary biology. (We solely refer to Dawkins's work in biology. His controversial views on religion and gender are irrelevant to our argument in this book.) According to Dawkins, evolutionary biology long put the focus of analysis on entire species and their survival (see also Dawkins 1982). However, it is not species or organisms that drive evolution in the long run, but their genes. Groups of genes collaborate to ensure their collective survival, yet in the end, they are all 'selfish'.[6] They seek to be passed on to the next generation, even if they are not beneficial for the organism as a whole or have no particular effect at all genes (Yanai & Lercher 2016).

Organisms are thus 'survival machines'—collections of genes that cooperate to ensure their own survival (Dawkins 1976: 19)—that are cast aside if they no longer fulfil their purpose (35). In the gene-centred view 'evolution . . . occurs step-by-step, through the differential survival of genes in the gene pool' (60). Dawkins argues that instead of merely acknowledging that smaller units make up organisms, we should analyse evolution through the lens of genes and genetic change.

Political scientists have long seen parties as the principal unit of analysis for understanding party system evolution, even when recognizing that these 'political organisms' consist of smaller units (organizations, programmes, leaders, rank-and-file members, and candidates). We argue that the focus of our analysis should be reoriented towards these smaller units, of which candidates are the best defined, most visible, and most conveniently measured.

There are obvious limitations to the analogy between genes and candidates. Electoral candidates do not necessarily organize themselves in parties; unlike

---

[6] Dawkins uses the term 'selfish' figuratively and does not imply that genes have free will.

genes, candidates can consciously pick and abandon their 'survival machines'. Still, the idea of candidates as party genes is more than just a metaphor. The analogy of genes leads to a better understanding of parties and party systems when we think about candidates—and other party people—as the driver of their evolution.

Candidates are not the only conceivable 'genetic marker' within parties. However, in contrast to alternative markers of party change—programmatic profile, membership, voters, etc.—candidates are physical and visible, hence much more easily trackable. In common with key concepts in molecular biology and in contrast to most concepts in political science, researchers hardly ever fight over the definition of a 'candidate'. This makes it easier to use it for operationalization and standardized analysis compared to alternatives (e.g. leadership or organizational change) which often require extensive expertise on individual parties. Such in-depth information is not just difficult to obtain but plainly unavailable even for a fraction of the nearly 1,500 electoral slates considered in this book. Importantly, we find that candidates as genetic markers are remarkably valid. In Chapter 6 we map out party evolutionary trees automatically produced based on 'candidate sequencing' that paints a remarkably accurate picture of party system developments.[7]

Our argument about parties as 'survival machines' challenges one of the fundamental principles of accountability in representative, party-based democracy, i.e. the (sometimes implicit) assumption that political parties must care about their re-election and aim to maximize future gains (Katz & Mair 1995; Strøm 1990; Strøm & Müller 1999). We believe it is much more appropriate to ascribe such a rational survival instinct to party people (e.g. candidates) than organizations that, sans people, lack agency. All the while, the objective of re-election can be challenged even from the perspective of individual politicians. Some politicians may find intrinsic value in keeping political office, but this is not always best served by preserving their parties. It is also perfectly possible to satisfy one's political desires during a single term and happily leave politics. Even those who are determined to pursue a political career may move on to other offices and become presidents, senior civil servants (the line between whom and politicians is often fuzzy, see Kopecký 2006; Sikk 2006b), members of the European Parliament (Sikk & Cianetti 2015), or officials in international organizations.

---

[7] Evolutionary trees of life have been also constructed automatically based on genetic data (see Ciccarelli et al. 2006).

Many political opportunities exist outside of parliaments. By the same token, the people who enter politics may have desires that can be fulfilled outside of politics: in business, arts, media, etc. Hence, if candidates and MPs are rational, self-seeking actors concerned about their physical survival and personal fulfilment, their utility may not best be served by holding on to support in the electorate or the selectorate within a party. Even for those who maintain political ambitions, parties may become disposable 'survival vehicles' if their careers are better pursued elsewhere, or if their parties happen to turn from Ferraris into Trabants. While disposable parties may not be very common, parties can be transient in the sense that they can form electoral alliances or merge with other parties, sacrificing organizational continuity for the advancement of the political careers of the people within.

To summarize, there are important reasons to consider moving the focus of analysis from political parties to the people within them. People, especially electoral candidates, are essential to political parties and for performing their fundamental functions. Parties only gain substance and meaning in the context of the motivations, desires, and incentives of the people who constitute them. Therefore, change among these individuals reveals new patterns of party evolution and allows for a deeper understanding of party politics. This does not mean that candidates are all that matters—parties can change in other regards;[8] we address the empirical question of how different dimensions of party change are linked to each other in Chapters 7–9 of the book.

1.4 Resolving complexity with 'big but thin' data

For us, big electoral data is for party evolution what big genetic data is for trees of life—a means to understand evolution. This book covers only limited 'political trees of life' as we focus on party politics in nine CEE countries: Bulgaria, Czechia, Hungary, Latvia, Lithuania, Poland, Slovakia, and Slovenia. Still, we hope it will be read by people who are not experts on the region, and we try to explain the examples that may otherwise only be familiar to specialist readers. Despite the regional focus, our thinking extends beyond regional borders, and we believe that new approaches to the study of political parties can and should be developed based on lesser-known (or less-'developed') corners of the world.

---

[8] We also do not mean to imply that studies treating parties as organisms, rather than as a collection of party genes, are 'wrong'. Similar to Dawkins (1982: 1), we merely seek to show the other side of the Necker cube: a different perspective on political parties and party change.

Ever since the fall of communism, instability and change have been defining features of politics in most of CEE. Successful new parties and novel electoral coalitions have emerged in abundance (Hanley & Sikk 2016; Ibenskas 2014; Pop-Eleches 2010; Sikk 2012; Tavits 2008b), complemented by high levels of electoral volatility and instability of alliances (Bakke & Sitter 2005; Casal Bértoa 2014; Haughton & Deegan-Krause 2015; Powell & Tucker 2014; Robbins & Hunter 2012; Rovny & Edwards 2012; Sikk 2005; Tavits 2005, 2008a). Moreover, compared to older democracies, party government in CEE is less stable (Baylis 2007; Keman & Müller-Rommel 2012: 4; Nikolenyi 2014: 6) and voter ties to political parties are weaker (Innes 2002; Klingemann et al. 2006; Millard 2004; Rohrschneider & Whitefield 2012; Tavits 2005; van Biezen 2003). Therefore, CEE is particularly suited for demonstrating how a candidate-based perspective can help to make sense of—sometimes overwhelming levels of—change and complexity.

Despite our regional focus, this is not a book specifically about the region. Most of our arguments apply to democratic electoral and party politics anywhere; even to single-party, dominant party, and hegemonic party systems, although the exact meaning of change may vary by region and political regime. We certainly argue that approaches developed in and tested on newer democracies are increasingly relevant for older democracies given the increasing levels of electoral instability in Western Europe and beyond (Chiaramonte & Emanuele 2017; Emanuele & Chiaramonte 2018; Emanuele & Sikk 2021; Hernández & Kriesi 2016; Lisi 2019; Mair et al. 2004). We agree with those who have argued that party politics à la CEE might herald the 'new normal' that also applies in old democracies (Hanley 2001; Haughton & Deegan-Krause 2015, 2020; Rohrschneider & Whitefield 2012; van Biezen 2005). If true, the region would make for an excellent source of raw materials for the industry of developing political science models to be exploited elsewhere. Our approach—like others sprouting from the study of the post-communist world—is even more likely to be useful for the study of Latin America and other complicated party systems. One particular feature in many of these systems is that party labels are more transient than they have historically been in Western democracies and a candidate-based approach to party development could help to make sense of such systems.

This book is based on an original data set 'Electoral Candidates in Central and Eastern Europe' (ECCEE). ECCEE includes 200,000 electoral candidates, covering over sixty elections in nine CEE democracies since 1990 and is to date the largest single cross-country data set on electoral candidates. Our candidate data shares several features of 'Big Data' (Kitchin 2013: 68): it is substantial in volume (given that many more candidates run for parliament than there are seats, electoral lists quickly grow into large data sets), exhaustive in scope (all candidates of all parties are included), relational (allowing for linking with other data sets), and scalable (can be expanded relatively easily).

Still, candidate data is 'big but thin', meaning that the number of indicators for candidates is often limited (i.e. candidate name, party, district, list placement, and result). To extract information from the data, we developed an algorithm and code in R that tracks candidate movements—in and out of politics and between parties—over consecutive elections and makes the best use of the limited information available. The limited depth in the data may appear to be a weakness of the data set and the approach at first glance. However, it can also be seen as an advantage—extending the approach to other countries, time periods, and other types of elections is easy and inexpensive. At the very least it is effortless compared to approaches that would require more detail on individuals—which is often simply not available.

Our approach standardizes and, to a degree, automatizes the analysis of party change. However, we also take advantage of numerous in-depth and insightful studies on party politics in CEE. Throughout this book, we use this wealth of knowledge to complement our quantitative analysis with discussions on important or anomalous cases and to validate and fine-tune our approach. Even dealing with seemingly simple data such as candidate names requires regional and linguistic expertise. For instance, 'Kovács Lászlóné' (the name of a 1994 Hungarian Social Democratic Party candidate) may look like a misspelling of 'Kovács László', a common name among Hungarian candidates. However, Kovács Lászlóné was in fact the wife of some Kovács László: the suffix '-né' is just one of several ways in which Hungarian women can change their name after marriage. A thorough understanding of such regional intricacies was essential for our analysis, e.g. devising the algorithms for tracking candidates and party change over time that are discussed in detail in Chapter 3.

Finally, despite our focus on individual candidates as drivers of party change, we do not seek to explain the behaviour of individuals. This is an important topic—individual motivations and incentives underlie much of candidate turnover—and we outline some theoretical expectations in Chapter 2 to be tested from an aggregate perspective in the analysis of basic determinants of candidate turnover in Chapter 4. However, our principal aim here is to analyse parties and party systems by taking a bird's-eye view of electoral candidates and party evolution.

1.5 The contributions of the book

There are very few comparative studies on electoral candidates. We acknowledge the recent efforts of the Comparative Candidates Survey (www.comparativecandidates.org) and UK Candidates Project (Campbell & van Heerde-Hudson 2018) that yield insights into candidates, their background, motivations, and campaign strategies. This book is complementary to these efforts—our insights on individual candidates may be more limited but we cover more elections in a range of countries and all candidates from all parties that would be possible in a candidate survey or a data set with detailed information about individual candidates.

In this chapter, we have outlined our thinking about electoral candidates and their potential to enhance our understanding of party and party system change. The following chapter elaborates a more fine-grained theoretical framework of candidate turnover and its relationship to other aspects of party change. In Chapter 3, we present our data set in more detail and introduce several essential concepts and measures for analysing candidate change in individual electoral slates. The general determinants of candidate turnover are analysed in Chapter 4, building on those suggested in the literature on party change and proposing others specifically relevant to candidate change. We show that party size and vote change as well as increasing perceptions of corruption serve as important predictors of candidate turnover.

Chapters 5 and 6 are concerned with party system change and candidate turnover—we look at party continuity and discontinuity (party entry and exit) and electoral volatility. Our analysis suggests that parties are seldom fully 'new' or 'old'—while there are some examples of successful genuinely new parties, few parties ever truly exit the electoral scene, as even the candidates of disappearing formations tend to continue in other formations (Chapter 5). Similarly, our proposed candidate-based electoral volatility index, which takes into account multiple predecessors and successors, and clearly distinguishes genuinely novel parties from others. We show that economic developments affect electoral volatility operationalized in this way—an effect that has been reported for other regions but has eluded analysts in CEE (see Chapter 6).

One of the main aims of this book is to propose candidate turnover as an indicator of party change, and to study its relationship to party (dis)continuity and other forms of party change. We turn to the latter in Chapters 7–9, considering fission and fusion, leadership change, and programmatic change. Candidate change is significantly related to each of these dimensions of party change, confirming the construct validity of candidate change as an indicator of the more general phenomenon of party change. Our measure of candidate change may not fully capture all important aspects of party change, but it provides a simple, easily standardizable, and extendable way of moving beyond the simple dichotomy of party continuity and discontinuity.

Throughout the book, we discuss in detail interesting or anomalous cases that emerge from our quantitative analysis. This helps us to test the validity of our approach and makes the text more accessible by complementing data analysis with illuminating examples from CEE and beyond. We believe that adding a qualitative angle is crucial both because regional context matters and because systematic knowledge of the determinants of party change is limited. The robustness of our quantitative findings is also difficult to assess solely on the basis of regression models as these tell us little about the quality and validity of our approach. As not all readers will be fully familiar with the intricacies of CEE party politics, we keep our examples accessible by providing additional context where necessary.

The focus of this book is a 'genetic' analysis of party evolution. Yet, the basic idea that the evolution of the 'big' can be best understood by disaggregating— following the 'small'—can be extended to any organizations such as parliaments, cabinets, local or regional assemblies, governmental, business, or voluntary organizations and even towns, cities, etc. where population data is available. It could even be extended beyond people; for example, we could study the evolution of investment funds by tracking the movement of stocks. The possibilities of using our main idea to track the 'micro' to understand the 'macro' do not stop here.

We also believe that the complementary data set to the book (see https://osf.io/nm5ek/) will be a useful tool for a range of studies. It could be especially valuable when linked to other data, for example on government composition. As the first step, we have linked our data to widely used data sets on political parties and party system development on the book website.

Our ideas and methods have a wide range of uses, but this volume has a narrower ambition: to boost our understanding of party change, new parties, and party system evolution. Powell and Tucker (2017) argue that so far little is known about the correlates of electoral volatility and party system instability. This, in turn, implies a limited understanding of their impact on important issues such as the quality of democracy, economic and social development. We believe that our candidate-based approach to party change and party system evolution will help to extend these horizons.

2
A conceptual model of candidate and party change

Modern electoral organizations are 'survival machines' serving the interests of people who want to run as candidates and enter, or remain, in public office. Most political scientists would agree with this statement—after all, the nomination of candidates has long been central to definitions of political parties (Janda 1983; Lasswell & Kaplan 1950; Mershon & Shvetsova 2013: 4; Riggs 1968; Sartori 1994). However, the existence and persistence of political organizations are often seen in isolation from the political survival of the people who populate them and the change among people is often deemed only tangentially relevant to the continuity of the organization. We believe that people and organizations are intrinsically linked. Even more importantly, we propose that electoral organizations are not immutable but ever-changing organisms '[that] breathe, grow, change' (Litton 2015: 712), evolving alongside and because of the change among their people.

While the term 'party change' is commonly used in studies on parties and party systems, there have been few attempts to conceptualize the term. Although several scholars have acknowledged and recognized change within parties, much of party research broadly follows an 'organizational paradigm'.[1] In this paradigm, parties are seen primarily as organizations of a particular nature and legal status rather than in terms of their core function of presenting candidates for elections. Parties appear when registration documents are lodged with the authorities and vanish when they lose their legal status. While parties so defined can experience changes in their leadership or programme, or could even see their entire membership replaced, this does not undermine their 'essence' or organizational integrity. The relationship between parties and turnover among their people resembles that of buses and their passengers: commuters embark and disembark at regular stops; drivers exchange after their shifts; a bus could even drive different routes. Yet a bus does not

---

[1] This umbrella term does not refer to any specific approach but to a set of commonalities shared by a broad body of scholarship.

Party People. Allan Sikk and Philipp Köker, Oxford University Press. © Allan Sikk and Philipp Köker (2023).
DOI: 10.1093/oso/9780198868125.003.0002

fundamentally change, carrying its registration plate duly from entering the service until retiring to the scrapyard.

While the focus on organizational continuity has led to advances in the study of party membership, elected representatives, leadership, and programmes, it poses constraints on the understanding and measurement of party change. By viewing parties primarily as legal organizations, the organizational paradigm imposes a strict dichotomy between 'old' and 'new' parties even though, in reality, parties frequently fall somewhere in between. Furthermore, the organizational paradigm emphasizes certain aspects of party life more than others. Contemporary parties often transform substantially throughout their existence but can still classify as old by organizational standards; some may be treated as newcomers despite strong personnel and organizational links to previously existing parties, and others 'die' in the eyes of party law only to flourish under a different name. Hence, to understand substantive party change in all its aspects and analyse parties as political (rather than legal) actors, a new approach is needed. To use the metaphor of buses, we therefore choose to focus on the passengers or bus routes rather than the actual vehicles.

This chapter outlines our 'evolutionary' or 'electoral' paradigm as an alternative analytical basis and discusses its consequences for studying party change. Following classic definitions of political parties, we focus on candidates as the cornerstone of electoral politics. In our view, candidates band together, forming or sustaining political vehicles to ensure their political survival. As candidate slates change—which they naturally do to a lesser or greater extent—so do political parties. Vice versa, substantive changes in other aspects are likely to be connected to candidate change. Our argument draws on ideas from an influential paradigm in evolutionary biology first outlined in Richard Dawkins's work *The Selfish Gene* (1976). According to Dawkins, it is not organisms or species that drive evolution but, instead, organisms are inhabited and—evolutionary speaking—guided by their genes. In a similar vein, we argue that parties are inhabited and guided by their people. Among these people, electoral candidates form a prominent yet also broad enough stratum. Just as the genetic make-up shapes the characteristics of an organism and can be seen as the driving force behind adaption, so do changing sets of candidates mould and transform various aspects of their survival machines.

While our approach is inspired by evolutionary biology and uses the gene-centred view of evolution as an analogy rather than a mere metaphor, we are not adopting any ideas uncritically and—to make it very clear—do not advocate biological or genetic determinism of, say, political behaviour.

(Neither do we wish to endorse Dawkins's controversial views on religion or gender.) Indeed, we are not concerned with the actual DNA of candidates at all! Also, we acknowledge that the view of 'genes as agents' is not unproblematic in evolutionary biology. This is partly because the idea of even the most gigantic molecules possessing an 'agency' challenges some (though not all) of the fundamental features of what we mean by 'agency' (Okasha 2020: 44–6). However, our key idea that party people possess agency should be completely uncontroversial—indeed, less controversial than subscribing agency to political parties, expecting non-human legal entities or formal institutions to guide their own evolution or that of party systems.

Section 2.1 of this chapter outlines our view of party change as a multi-dimensional phenomenon where party people hold a pivotal position. We discuss links between candidate turnover and other major dimensions of party change (programmatic, leadership, and organizational change), situate our approach in the literature and consider potential causes and consequences of change. Section 2.2 introduces 'slate' as an umbrella term for electoral formations (parties, coalitions, alliances, lists, etc.) at the time of an election which we use as the main unit of analysis throughout the book. We outline a model of candidate list formation as an interactive process between candidates and (proto-)slates that highlights the demand and supply side mechanisms of candidate turnover between elections and explains our notions of candidate entry, exit, and return. In section 2.3, we deduce a simple baseline model of the natural rate of candidate turnover—the expected pace of change in the absence of any accelerating events. This baseline will be considered when interpreting empirical levels of candidate turnover in later chapters.

This study overlaps with various streams of literature on political parties and electoral politics such as research on party system stability, party organization, party (system) institutionalization and consolidation, candidate selection and recruitment, legislative turnover, and party switching. We discuss their rich traditions although they are often concerned with politics in countries where parties are quite different beasts compared to Central and Eastern Europe (CEE), such as the United States or Latin America. Our main concern in this book is to analyse party (system) change through the lens of candidates rather than explain variation in levels of turnover or the actions of individual candidates. Therefore, we cannot claim to provide a complete and balanced review of all related publications: we aim to highlight links between this study and the literature, even if in many cases we are just scraping the surface of rich traditions in extant scholarship; we will provide additional detail on other dimensions of party change in Chapters 7–9.

2.1 The many faces of party change

'Party change' has been evoked in various ways in existing literature but tends to be conceptualized rather casually. It is sometimes referred to broadly as 'adaptation' or 'transformation' (Bardi et al. 2014; van Biezen 2005) which, in our view, are subcategories of party change. 'Adaptation' emphasizes external causes—parties adapting to something—and a singular agency, a party as a monolithic organization doing the adaptation. 'Transformation' suggests metamorphic change, i.e. transformation from something into something rather different. 'Party change' as an overarching term incorporates 'adaptation' and 'transformation' but also smaller and bigger changes that do not neatly fit either of the terms. Furthermore, 'adaptation' and 'transformation' suggest discrete or intermittent events; hence, a focus on these subtypes of party change can overlook the continual alteration of parties. Our aim here is to provide a standardized conceptualization and operationalization of *party change as a perpetual process* that varies in terms of pace (slow changes versus sudden eruptions) and extent (piecemeal versus transformative change) but always happens, yet never reaches an equilibrium state of 'completion'.

In the literature 'party change' sometimes refers to the changing nature of individual parties or even of party politics in general (Krouwel 2012). Rahat & Kenig (2018) in their study of party change and political personalization examine the overall levels of party membership, electoral volatility, electoral turnout, the background of ministers and MPs, and party-interest group linkages across countries. Others focus on changes in the (dominant) form of party organization (Katz & Mair 1995; Krouwel 2006; van Biezen 2005). While we consider these changes at the level of political systems highly significant, they concern a very different aspect of politics and usually happen at a more glacial pace.

Our holistic approach builds on a multidimensional notion that regards different facets of party change as parts of an interconnected whole. The idea of multidimensional party change has been suggested by several scholars. Early accounts, such as those by V. O. Key (1964), describe parties as 'tripartite systems of interaction' involving the party-in-the-electorate, the party-as-organization, and the party-in-government. Similarly, Harmel and Janda distinguish between three major faces of party change: 'alteration or modification in how parties are organized, what human and material resources they can draw upon, what they stand for and what they do' (1994: 275). More recently, explicit and more clearly operationalized multidimensional concepts of party change have been suggested. For instance, Bosco and Morlino establish a comparative analytical framework based on four dimensions of party change: 'values and programme, the organization, competitive strategy and campaign politics' (2007: 2). Barnea and Rahat (2011) operationalize the three dimensions formulated by V. O. Key using a set of eight indicators centred on (a) label, ideology, and voters (party-in-the-electorate), (b) formal status, institutions, and activists (party-as-organization), and (c) representatives and policies (party-in-government). While Barnea and Rahat do not discuss the system of interaction between these dimensions, Litton (2015) goes further. She argues that 'in a given electoral cycle, any party is new to some degree' (712) and presents a model of party change on the two interconnected dimensions of party attribute change (programme, leader, name) and change of structural affiliation (splits, mergers, changing alliances). In a similar vein, in his study of the British Conservative Party, Bale suggests that party change varies in pace as it may come in the form of rare, punctuated instances of change among overall stability and suggests that change in leaders or policies could be symptoms of party change in other dimensions (2012: 7). The existing literature has provided useful insights on explaining particular facets of party change—for example, by distinguishing between external and internal factors (Bosco 2000; Bosco & Morlino 2007; Harmel & Janda 1994; Lisi 2015). However, for more insightful cross-national analysis, we need a clearer conceptualization and measurement of party change that acknowledges both its multidimensionality (including the interconnectedness of various aspects of change) and its perpetual, non-discrete nature.

Parties can change in various aspects and change in one aspect always creates at least a potential for change in the rest of the party (Figure 2.1). Most parties aim to present themselves as stable and monolithic actors—emphasizing steadfastness and harmony between all facets like leaders, manifestos, members, candidates, levels of organizations, voters, etc.—but they are complex creatures. Even parties that look unified and stable from afar can, on closer inspection, reveal incongruities between different facets or change over time. One of the most famous examples—if contested in detail—of internal diversity is May's law of curvilinear disparity arguing that political orientations of people at different levels can vary within parties (May 1973).[2] Such discrepancies self-reproduce as change across dimensions never perfectly syncs: some aspects change fast and frequently, while others take more time; changes can

---

[2] Perhaps it is more appropriately called a conjecture as the claim of curvilinearity has received mixed empirical support (Kennedy et al. 2006; Norris 1995; van Holsteyn et al. 2017; cf. Bäckersten 2022). However, it is hard to argue with the basic idea that the political positions of members and elites *may* diverge (cf. Kölln & Polk 2016).

necessitate further modifications or have unintended consequences. Hence, party change can rise naturally from internal dynamics as well as external factors (the right side in Figure 2.1). As parties are always somewhat diverse internally and incongruent between dimensions, the potential for change is always there.

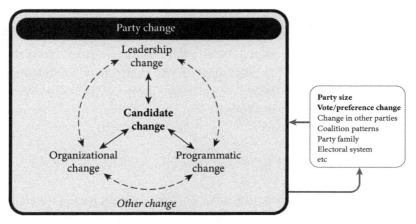

Figure 2.1 Multidimensional party change

This book focuses on four interconnected dimensions of party change: candidates, leadership, programme, and organization. These are not only the most widely applicable dimensions but are also necessary ingredients of political parties.[3] While we place candidate change at the centre, this does not mean that it trumps other dimensions in importance. Rather, we hypothesize that candidate change is a useful proxy for overall party change as other changes are likely to be reflected in a changed candidate line-up. In addition to these four aspects, parties are subject to various other changes, including changes in their support base, party statutes, organizational structure, cooperation patterns with other parties, or the numbers, nature, and activism of their members. Without dismissing the importance of such (mostly discrete and more occasional) changes, we believe that the four aspects—candidates, leadership, organization, and programme—are the most visible and can be measured most easily in a standardized fashion, as demonstrated in the later chapters of this book. Finally, we do not only expect different aspects of party change to be related to each other but party change is also related to *party system* change. First,

---

[3] While a programme is not strictly necessary to present candidates at elections, virtually all parties release some kind of manifesto or statement of priorities; at the absolute minimum, they must stand for *something*—a party that *always* refuses to take positions on political matters is inconceivable.

changes in parties are likely to affect their electoral fortunes and coalition patterns. Second, such changes can, in turn, create discontent within parties—leading, in extreme but not rare cases, to defections or splits—or between parties and their electoral/executive coalition partners (breaking up of governing coalitions and electoral alliances). Alternatively, they may heal intra-party rifts, bring parties together with others and ease government cooperation, in electoral alliances or even mergers.

In the following, we discuss each of the four dimensions in turn and highlight linkages to existing research. We also formulate some expectations about the relationship between candidate turnover and change in other dimensions, to which we return in Chapters 7–9 which also provide a fuller discussion of the respective aspects of party change.

2.1.1 Candidate change

The change in candidates is pivotal to our understanding of party change. Together with a name and some arrangement of leadership, candidates are a prerequisite of any formation seeking to contest elections, be it as a formally registered party or not. Candidates' desire to be elected or at least partake in the election is the principal reason that electoral survival machines—i.e. parties and other organizations contesting elections—are formed and set off in the first place (we will discuss their desires and motivations in more detail below). Candidates shape these machines to suit their goals and, in a very literal sense, determine their appearance. Change in candidates is thus inevitably linked to change in other dimensions of the party.

Research on candidates has hitherto largely focused on their personal qualities (e.g. Campbell & van Heerde-Hudson 2018; Dubrow & Palaguta 2016; Karlsen & Skogerbø 2013; Lloren & Rosset 2017; Lutz et al. 2018; Popescu & Hannavy 2001; Zittel 2015) and has only rarely considered candidate change as a phenomenon of interest (for notable exceptions see: Kreuzer & Pettai 2003; Shabad & Slomczynski 2004). Our analysis of candidate change is most closely related to research on various forms of diversity and change among members of parliament. Addressing topics such as legislative turnover (Golosov 2017; Ilonszki and Edinger 2007; Matland and Studlar 2004; Norris 1997; Salvati & Vercesi 2018), re-election and career paths (Altman & Chasquetti 2011; Semenova, Edinger, & Best 2014), and legislative switching (Klein 2021; Kreuzer & Pettai 2003; McMenamin & Gwiazda 2011; Mershon & Shvetsova 2013; O'Brien & Shomer 2013) scholars have interpreted change among party personnel as indicative of stability and change in institutions. Some have also linked MP turnover with party and party system instability (Gherghina 2014; Hino 2013; Shabad & Slomczynski 2004). Barnea and Rahat (2011) were, to our knowledge, the first to include candidates among their dimensions of party change. Although these works provide important insights into the dynamics of elite change, studies on legislative switching in particular often focus more on individual motivations rather than what these changes mean for parties. Furthermore, given their quest for individual-level explanations, studies on MP turnover tend to be limited in scope and only focus on MPs, the tip of the party personnel iceberg.

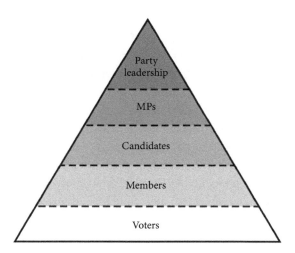

Figure 2.2 The levels of party people

Note: Lines are dashed as all are permeable and lower levels, as a rule, incorporate upper levels.

Candidate change, like change among legislators or party members, is a form of elite change or personnel change that occupies in many ways a sweet spot for analysis (Figure 2.2). The top-ranking candidates in national-level legislative elections are—with some very limited exceptions (e.g. MEPs, presidential candidates, or leaders of subnational governments)—the pinnacle of political elites; they are usually leading party figures and, if elected, MPs. Electoral candidates present a superset of MPs and party elites, and a subset of all 'party people' down to local organizers and the rank-and-file, perhaps even including the voters. While MPs and some other top-ranking candidates are certainly more important than low-ranking candidates, looking only at MPs one cannot distinguish between: (a) more and less important candidates (see Chapter 3 for more detail on weighting candidate importance), (b) unsuccessful candidates and those no longer running, and (c) new candidates and newly elected candidates. Data on MPs also excludes significant parties without or interrupted parliamentary representation (e.g. the German Free Democrats, 2013–17, the Polish Democratic Left Alliance 2015–19, the Austrian Greens 2017–19). For smaller parties, MP turnover is also sensitive to trivial changes. For example, in the 2015 UK general election, one out of three Plaid Cymru (PC) MPs changed. This smallest possible change amounted to a substantial 33% turnover. For the Conservative Party, an equivalent rate would have required the change of more than 100 MPs. Just one additional new PC MP would have increased turnover to 67% while only one fewer would have brought it down to zero. The analysis of changes in a larger group of all electoral candidates allows for a more comprehensive and nuanced picture of party change that can be linked to other substantive party transformations.

The indicator of candidate change also carries methodological advantages. Candidate turnover is easy to observe and quantify as electoral lists are generally public and easily accessible; candidate change is also fairly straightforward to operationalize on a continuous scale (see Chapter 3). In comparison, changes in leadership or party programmes are often less clear-cut and momentous changes—e.g. the selection of an outsider as a leader or wholesale ideological shifts—are infrequent. We are proposing (semi-)quantitative scales for a nuanced measurement of leadership and programmatic change in Chapters 8 and 9. Yet, both of them can usually be analysed only when parties continue in an unchanged form rather than splitting up, merging, or making and breaking electoral coalitions. In the fundamentally unstable party systems of CEE, parties (the key units of analysis in the organizational paradigm) often cannot be unambiguously pinned down in consecutive elections; focusing on candidates allows us to develop approaches and means to navigate fluid party landscapes.

To sum up, candidates can enter and exit the electoral scene; they can return to their old survival machine but may also move on to another one. Naturally, particular candidates (and other party people) are always more attracted by some features of their parties than others. Yet every time a party changes in one aspect, it can provide an impetus for change in another dimension. Candidates weigh their options: some will choose to part ways, while others join up and provide a catalyst for further change. Thus, candidate change can be the cause but also the consequence of party change in other dimensions, including the ultimate rupture—the creation of new parties based on splits, mergers, or from scratch.

2.1.2 Organizational change

Organizational change—party entry, exit, splits, and mergers—presents perhaps the most fundamental and challenging dimension of party change. More than any of the other dimensions, it highlights the contrast between the organizational paradigm that emphasizes stability and discrete events and our evolutionary understanding of party change that focuses on continuous and complex change.

In the organizational paradigm, the registration and deregistration of political parties are the pivotal events in the life of a party. Hence, many scholars have researched the emergence and disappearance of parties, often labelling them party 'birth' and 'death' (see Beyens et al. 2016; Bolleyer et al. 2019a, 2019b; Haughton & Deegan-Krause 2020). However, these anthropomorphic terms or the treatment of parties as 'dead' once they cease to participate in elections, neglects the fact that a multitude of links—some weaker, some stronger—often connect parties past and present. Supposedly newborn parties frequently draw on (formal or informal) organizational structures, programmes, and people of political experience from previously existing parties. Sometimes parties merely feign death in the eyes of the law and re-emerge virtually unchanged—while such parties may present new legal entities, they fail the test of genuine newness (Sikk 2005). Nevertheless, our electoral paradigm also recognizes that such changes are major events that often coincide with other dimensions of party change. However, as our understanding stresses the political continuity of parties beyond legal continuity, we prefer to use the terms party 'entry' and 'exit' instead of any anthropomorphic terms—not all entrants are fresh-faced political babies and exiting may not toll a bell to a political project and even less to the people involved.

Significant organizational change in parties also happens in the form of splits and mergers or the creation or break-up of electoral coalitions. Examples of such *fission* and *fusion* abound, especially in CEE (Ibenskas 2016b, 2020; Ibenskas & Sikk 2017) but have also accumulated in West European party systems over decades (Bartolini & Mair 1990; Ceron 2015; Giannetti & Laver 2001; Marinova 2015). While fission and fusion clearly involve continuity despite changes to the parties' legal status, many (most prominently students of electoral volatility, see Casal Bértoa, Deegan-Krause, & Haughton 2017) consider merged parties and new electoral alliances either as continuations of just one of the parties or entirely new formations. Likewise, only one party is often treated as the successor following a split.

In Chapter 7, we show how to identify and classify fission and fusion based on candidate movements. Fission and fusion are instances of candidate survival machines' disassembly and reconstruction. When parties fuse to form an electoral coalition or a new party, they need to present joint lists that integrate candidates from several parties. Fusion may lead to candidate flight because the new formation may not be palatable to some and plum spots on the list are more limited, although presumably compensated by enhanced electoral prospects. Meanwhile, increased electoral attractiveness may attract new candidates or even defections from parties not involved in the fusion. Following fission, candidates may find it easier to continue in successor parties as they can benefit from enhanced list positions; yet, the electoral prospects may not improve for all successors which can lead to candidate exit or defection to other parties. Furthermore, ideologically clearer or more cohesive parties can be attractive to new candidates despite uncertain electoral prospects.

Parties can also undergo more superficial organizational changes that can leave only an impression of entry or exit. Data on candidate continuity can flag up such cases where parties seem to come and go but, in fact, remain fairly intact. The most obvious example is the common phenomenon of name change (Kim & Solt 2015: 439–40): many parties with new names are indeed new, while others amount to a mere repackaging of an ailing project serving its people poorly. While any name change is likely to increase the potential for candidate change—for the reasons that precipitated the name change alone—we expect more fundamental transformations to be accompanied by higher levels of candidate change. Sometimes parties change their names and experience limited change otherwise—consider, for example, some of the name changes of the French 'Gaullist' centre-right—yet at other times a new name signals a more substantive change. For example, when the Estonian Moderates (MD) readopted the name of Social Democrats (SDE) in 2004, it was accompanied by a modest but distinct and permanent move to the left. Thus, candidate turnover can reveal continuity or help to gauge the significance of name changes. It can also be used to identify the main successor in splits, which may not necessarily be the one inheriting the name (see Chapter 7).

Even when parties eschew major formal organizational changes, candidate turnover can indicate important sub-surface changes. One such phenomenon is collective switching, where a group of politicians moves from one party to another, that only sometimes involves a formal split depending on whether any interim organization was set up or not (see Close & Gherghina 2019 for one of the few systematic analyses of the phenomenon). As our electoral approach does not strictly distinguish between continuing and discontinued parties but instead allows for links between several parties in consecutive elections, it can detect such instances of party change not captured by the organizational paradigm. This can include cases of de facto fission and fusion where no evidence exists of a formal split, merger, or coalition agreement. Finally, our approach distinguishes between equal and unequal instances of fission and fusion, separating the mergers of mice and elephants from the alliances between two foxes.

2.1.3 Leadership change

Leadership change is both a highly visible form of party change and can alter the essence of a party.[4] The change at the helm can be dramatic or more routine; consider, for instance, the leftist Jeremy Corbyn replacing the moderate Ed Miliband as the leader of the British Labour Party in 2015, or Mirek Topolánek replacing Václav Klaus as leader of the Czech Civic Democratic Party (ODS) in 2006,[5] compared to numerous instances of a next-in-line or previous leader's protégé taking over the reins. Nearly all long-standing parties have inevitably experienced leadership changes. However, this is typically an infrequent event as few party leaders want to leave voluntarily and, by the virtue of holding office, leaders possess the means to help them stay there. While leadership does have a strong resistance to change (Bolleyer 2013), 'punctuated' leadership change (Bale 2012)—general stability interspersed by bouts of significant change—can occur in response to electoral backlashes or other events.

Existing comparative literature on party leadership has focused on the rules of leadership selection and their impact on intra-party competition (e.g. Cross & Pilet 2015; Marino 2021; Pilet & Cross 2014; Sandri et al. 2016). Other studies have analysed the transformative potential of leadership. Whereas findings on the electoral impact of party leader characteristics have been mixed (e.g. Aarts et al. 2011; Garzia 2012), a range of studies have suggested that leadership change has a tangible impact on other aspects of political parties. Harmel et al. (1995: 25) find that leadership change is even more likely than poor electoral performance to trigger other (organizational and

---

[4] Leadership change can be also studied as the change in leaders' characteristics or traits—that can even change during their tenure and impact parties' electoral performance and organization (see Gherghina 2020). Nevertheless, such changes are virtually impossible to measure in a standardized fashion for many parties in multiple countries over several elections.

[5] Although perhaps a lesser-known example, it presents one of the most dramatic leadership changes among CEE parties. Topolánek was a relative outsider and Klaus openly criticized him before the selection.

programmatic) changes in parties. Party change is also affected by the nature of party leadership: dominant leaders influence the institutional, policy, and electoral 'faces' of parties, at a cost of instability when they leave office (Alexiadou & O'Malley 2022); Schumacher and Giger find that dominant party leadership is associated with fluid party platforms (2018).

Leadership change could also be expected to be linked to candidate turnover. Leaders can attract and repel candidates through their personal qualities (Barnfield & Bale 2022) but also serve as important information shortcuts on parties' programmatic positions (Bridgewater 2021; Fernandez-Vazquez & Somer-Topcu 2019; Somer-Topcu 2016). Gouglas et al (2020), examining eight West European democracies, find that leadership change increases MP turnover. Irrespective of whether candidates run because of loyalty to the party leader or its programme, replacing the leader will increase the potential for change among party people. Leaders and their allies can also take an active role in introducing and promoting some candidates while demoting or even purging others.

We believe that not only the fact of leadership change but also its scale should covary with candidate change. Whereas the election of heirs apparent and uncontested successors should merely ripple the surface of the candidate pool, we expect a selection of an outsider as a leader to trigger more significant changes in the direction of the party. For this reason, we are introducing a quasi-quantitative scale of leadership newness in Chapter 8.

2.1.4 Programmatic change

Ideological stance and programmatic orientation are essential facets of party identity. Party platforms and election manifestos are drafted by people, in particular leading party figures (including leading candidates) and later debated, amended, and adopted by people at party congresses. As the general appearance of a living organism is an expression of its genetic traits, from the perspective of our genetic paradigm party programmes reflect views held by the party people involved in compiling them.

The programmatic positions of parties are not set in stone and change over time. Changes can range from small adjustments regarding individual policies to major shifts in ideological orientation; parties can move right or left on the political spectrum, become more environmentalist, xenophobic, or minority-friendly, i.e. emphasizing or de-emphasizing valence issues. While such changes are not mechanically linked to changes among party people, we can expect connections. Policy changes must be triggered by something and change in party elites or membership is at least one conceivable reason (Matland & Studlar 2004: 88). In fact, it is hard to imagine major policy changes without some changeover in people—both at the top and the bottom of the party people pyramid (Figure 2.2).[6] Candidates play a particularly important role—even if they are not involved in (re)writing manifestos and policy proposals directly, they are a key factor for the authors to consider. Significant policy changes may draw in new aspirants or raise the profile and improve list placements of candidates who fit better the new programmatic priorities. At the same time, long-standing candidates may be demoted or singled out for retirement as part of such changes; those alienated by policy changes may end up in another survival machine or exit electoral politics altogether.[7]

Several projects have grasped the challenge of measuring party positions across countries over time—most prominently the Manifesto Project (MARPOR, Volkens et al. 2020) and the Chapel Hill Expert Survey (CHES, Jolly et al. 2022; Polk et al. 2017). Yet, scholars have consistently noted the difficulty of measuring the change in party positions (see, e.g. Adams et al. 2019; Franzmann 2013), particularly in CEE (Mölder 2016; Tavits & Letki 2013). Most often, party positions are used as static measurements, for example, as explanatory variables (e.g. Krauss & Kluever 2022; Mölder 2017). Programmatic change, on the other hand, is frequently considered only in relation to shifts in patterns of party competition or other external stimuli (see, e.g. Abou-Chadi 2016; Borbáth & Borbáth 2020; Han 2015; Ibenskas & Polk 2022; Koedam 2021; Krause & Giebler 2020; Pytlas 2015), rather than a change in individual parties. Nonetheless, some studies have examined links between party programmes and party people. For instance, Kölln and Polk (2016) show that ideological incongruence of party members with their parties weakens party loyalty and increases the likelihood of exit; in the United States, the increasing ideological polarization has had the effect of repelling moderate candidates (Thomsen 2017). Similarly, Barnfield and Bale (2022) argue that the exit of party members is primarily driven by their perceived ideological difference from their party.

We expect the change in policy positions to be associated with candidate turnover, whereby a significant change in either dimension is likely to trigger

---

[6] The Hungarian Fidesz, discussed in more detail in Chapter 9 provides an important but rare exception.
[7] Additionally, candidate outflux—for whatever reasons—disrupts equilibria within parties and candidate change may also cause leadership or programmatic changes. Determining the directionality of the relationship is beyond the scope of this book; for the sake of simplicity, we either use candidate change as a dependent variable or make no specific assumption about directionality.

a change in the other. Nevertheless, we are aware of parties that have changed programmatically without experiencing much change otherwise—witness the transformation of Fidesz in Hungary from a liberal into a conservative-nationalist party under the leadership of Viktor Orbán which, as we will see later, experienced limited candidate turnover. In Chapter 9, we propose a measure of policy change that does not assume any particular dimensionality in political positions (i.e. the traditional left–right dimension that, as we will see, is in many ways problematic) and analyse the strength of the link between programmatic shifts and candidate turnover. Even though Fidesz does prove to be a prominent exception to prove the rule, it still underscores our general argument that parties can change significantly while remaining stable from a legal–organizational standpoint.

2.1.5 Party change and changing parties

Our electoral paradigm highlights the interconnectedness of different dimensions of party life and the constant potential for change stemming from inside the party. This is the focus of this book, but we are far from arguing that change happens in isolation from the outside world. Changes within parties are often triggered by external factors and have consequences outside an individual party. Particular features of parties can make them more or less susceptible to transformations (the box on the right in Figure 2.1). Considering the focus of the book on understanding changes within parties and reconceptualizing the notions of a party for the study of party system dynamics, we are only looking at a small range of core influences: party size, change in party size (i.e. electoral fortunes) and, as an example, the impact of corruption perception on candidate turnover. We propose a simple logical model on the relationship between party size and expected candidate turnover towards the end of this chapter and refine it further in Chapter 4, adding discussion on the impact of the change in party popularity and corruption, and providing an empirical test of relationships.

Our key message is that parties are constantly adapting in reaction to internal and external forces. CEE provides a fertile ground for studying party change and adjustment due to the more volatile nature of political parties that has been attributed to weaker party organizations, shallower voter attachments and greater ideological manoeuvrability (Bustikova & Zechmeister 2017; Gherghina 2014; Grzymała-Busse 2002; Ishiyama & Bozóki 2010; Scarrow & Webb 2017: 2). Yet, the ever-changing party landscape of the region also poses significant challenges to studying party and party system evolution. Explaining party change requires matching parties between pairs of elections but these are often impossible to pin down without making crucial yet debatable coding decisions. When discussing leadership and programmatic change, this book considers continuing parties, partly based on candidate continuity. While our new data provides a useful tool for detecting continuing parties, we are also aware of a certain selection bias here as continuing parties stem from the more stable end of the spectrum of party change by definition. Hence, in most of the book, rather than explaining the *change in parties*, our focus is on *changing parties*.[8]

2.2 How electoral slates form: candidate entry, exit, and return

Candidate change is ultimately grounded in decisions made by individuals—the candidates and other party people with a say over the make-up of electoral lists. This section explains three outcomes (candidate entry, exit, and return) from the perspective of individuals, considering actors' micro-level interactions and their macro-level observable implications to develop a model of aggregate candidate change in the following section. Even though this book is empirically not concerned with individual behaviour, we will augment our macro-level analyses with discussions on individual-level choices.

Electoral lists are always a mix of returning and new candidates, with rare anomalous exceptions such as repeat elections or individual candidates returning to run on their own. Until now, we have used the term 'political party' for organizations presenting candidates for elections. Yet, parties are only one specific type of such organizations. Candidates may also be nominated by citizen action committees, trade unions or social movements or by electoral coalitions that combine several parties and other organizations with varying degrees of formality and permanence. For these reasons, we use the term slate to refer to *any formal or informal organization that presents candidates in a single election*. In our analysis we focus on change and continuity between slates, as a formal change such as the formation of a political party based on an electoral coalition may involve only minimal programmatic or leadership changes and, conversely, the legal–organizational continuation of a party may conceal substantive changes.

---

[8] While some of the linkages between different aspects of party change could be better tested in historically more stable West European countries, they could present other challenges because of often glacial party change.

From the perspective of our electoral paradigm, there are, as such, no continuing parties that contest consecutive elections. Instead, elections are contested by ever-changing sets of slates, each of which exists for one election only. Some slates are dominated by new candidates (who did not stand in the previous election) while others are dominated by returning candidates. Even when candidates return with their parties—as is often the case—they never return to the 'same' slates; this is not only because slates are by definition transitory, but also because they are virtually never identical to previous slates. Rather than analysing whether candidates stay in the same party or other formal organization, we focus on whether candidates return with a similar or a different group of people.

Throughout the book we occasionally use terms like 'switching' or 'defections' in a casual sense, referring to candidates who part ways with their former comrades. Strictly speaking, however, one cannot 'switch' between slates. Pairs of slates in successive elections may be more or less *congruent* (i.e. overlapping, the measure is fully introduced in Chapter 3) in terms of their candidate lists. Where congruence is high, we can casually talk about a continuing party. Negligible congruence with any previous slate suggests an entry of a genuinely new party. A slate with very little congruence with any future slates is a 'genuine exit'; significant congruence with several previous slates suggests a merger; congruence of several slates with a single previous slate suggests a split. (We analyse fusion and fission through the lens of candidate congruence in Chapter 7.) Elections in stable party systems have been dominated by clear, one-to-one congruences—i.e. by parties that return with a broadly similar set of candidates and experience limited attrition or movement of candidates. Unstable party systems are characterized by the profusion of slates with either limited congruences (entry and exit) or slates that are congruent to several others in the preceding or successive election (mergers and splits).

We conceptualize candidate list formation or 'slate-making' as an interactive process that emphasizes the agency of all individuals involved—the people hoping or declining to become candidates and others who are often but not always coalesced into parties or other formal organizations. The literature on 'candidate selection' (Gallagher & Marsh 1988; Hazan 2014; Hazan & Rahat 2010; Krook 2009; Lundell 2004) or 'candidate recruitment' (Cross & Young 2013; Ishiyama 2000; Kazee & Thornberry 1990; Samuels 2008) sometimes treats candidates as passive agents willing to stand for the office almost on any terms dictated by their political parties. Our approach resonates more with the argument that it is 'seldom possible to determine where recruitment ends and selection begins' (Siavelis & Morgenstern 2012: 8) and Norris &

Lovenduski's (1995) demand and supply model of candidate selection that puts greater focus on the individual agency (see also Lovenduski 2016). A focus on the agency of candidates recognizes that in modern democracies the pools of electoral aspirants have become more vaguely defined as recruitment is not necessarily or fully party based. Party members may not always aspire to run, and non-members can be keen on running and may be courted by parties.[9] This is particularly true for CEE where party affiliations and loyalties have always been more fluid (Bustikova & Zechmeister 2017; Enyedi and Deegan-Krause 2017). Our model also explicitly allows for exit from electoral politics as a result of interactions between potential candidates and prospective slates. While several studies have analysed 'exit' among MPs, this has often been limited to individual or collective legislative switching or splits (Close & Gherghina 2019).

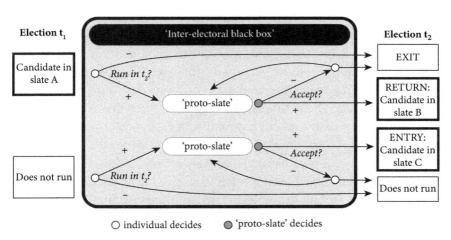

Figure 2.3 A conceptual model of candidate entry, exit, and return

Candidate slates are never identical from one election to the next. Figure 2.3 presents a stylized picture of possible sequences of events that can ensue between elections in t_1 and t_2. After an election in t_1, every eligible person faces a simple question: to run or not to run? Let us assume István Kovács (the most common name in our database) ran as a candidate for slate A in t_1. While many candidates run again in the following election, the simplest path for Kovács is to abandon the electoral game. Indeed, he may need to withdraw—he might

---

[9] Only limited literature has discussed the choice of parties by candidates (Aldrich & Bianco 1992; Desposato 2006) that our model considers explicitly.

die, be disqualified by accepting an incompatible office, serving a prison sentence, become unelectable due to scandals,[10] etc.—but he may also want to withdraw. This is the direct route to candidate exit.[11] However, even a voluntary political 'death' may not be the end of the world. Most candidates are rational self-seeking actors and sensible human beings concerned with their survival and thriving in a physical sense. Their overall utility may not be best served by running for office again or maintaining support in the electorate and selectorate in parties. Electoral exit is not necessarily a 'failure': candidates may decide to stay in politics only for a certain period to accumulate contacts and experience, return (after a 'trial') to what they did before or move on to lucrative careers in the private sector (Egerod 2021; Herrick & Nixon 1996; Kiewiet & Zeng 1993; Leoni et al. 2004). Therefore, under certain conditions, candidates and MPs may be indifferent to their *political* survival and the continued functioning of their 'survival machines'; the survival instinct applies to staying alive, not to staying in politics, let alone remaining a rank-and-file MP or a candidate with uncertain career prospects.

Nevertheless, many candidates prefer to run again and this is the default position for most professional politicians. However, this does not automatically lead to a candidate's return and does not always determine the slate they find themselves on. Contesting elections in party-based democracies is usually a collective endeavour, and how and where candidates return depends on the response of their potential running mates. More generally, it depends on those in charge of nominations, nearly always one subset of party people or another.[12] Often, little contemplation is involved if István Kovács decides to run again. In fact, most parties return with broadly familiar slates and most candidates return with their parties. However, party systems in CEE and beyond can be much less stable compared to the more consolidated West European party systems that have themselves experienced increasing instability in recent decades. Hence, a meaningful model of candidate list formation must not assume returning with the same party or running mates and must explicitly allow for more complexity.

---

[10] Bågenholm and Charron (2020) find that Romanian mayors implicated in corruption are less likely to seek re-election than those who are not. Praino et al. (2013) acknowledge that scandals can lead to both electoral defeats and retirements of candidates.

[11] Note that our notions of 'entry' and 'exit' do not map directly to the definitions of entry and voluntary/involuntary exits of MPs. A new MP may (or may not) be a new candidate. An electoral defeat is classified as an involuntary exit of an MP but constitutes a return of a candidate.

[12] Open and 'blanket' primaries (Hazan & Rahat 2010: 39–40) are a rare exception and even there, party members and supporters—who can be also considered as the least involved segment of party people—dominate.

Once István Kovács decides to run for office again, this must be accepted by what we call a *proto-slate*—a party or a looser set of potential running mates (Figure 2.3). In highly consolidated party systems with strong parties, the set of running mates is normally almost a given. However, the proto-slate may reject the bid for several reasons: for instance, Kovács might be seen as disloyal (e.g. because he supported the losing candidate in a leadership race) or an electoral liability.[13] Kovács's political positions may have become incommensurate with those of the party—either because his views have changed, or the party has experienced programmatic change. Importantly, the proto-slate that Kovács approaches will oftentimes not correspond perfectly to the party he was running for in t_1. Similarly, the fusion of Kovács's slate with others may mean that winnable seats become scarcer, and the aggregate demands of aspiring candidates may outweigh what the proto-slate can reasonably promise them.

Even if a proto-slate welcomes Kovács into its fold in principle, it may not be ready to meet his demands for safe list placement (especially if the electoral prospects of a party have deteriorated), promises of high political office, or prioritize issues high on his agenda. Hence, if they fail to find common ground, Kovács faces another choice: accept that the game is up and exit or make another bid. Some such exits are clearly distinguishable from the 'direct exit' mentioned earlier. The fallout between a candidate and their party (or another proto-slate) can be highly visible and negotiations conducted in public. At other times, a failed bid cannot easily be distinguished from a direct exit. For example, Kovács may quote 'personal reasons' for not running again without mentioning whether the reasons would have mattered if the party had made a better offer or accepted his bid. However, if Kovács returns as a candidate with a slate in t_2 we do not necessarily know whether this followed his first or only a subsequent bid to join. Even though negotiations are presumably straightforward in many cases, we seldom have a full view of processes inside the proverbial 'inter-electoral black box'. Importantly, we may not even know whether the successful bid was with the same proto-slate as the first and any subsequent ones.

Now let us imagine that István Kovács successfully became an MP and has a significant personal following. Kovács then decides to leave his par-

---

[13] A potential candidate can be seen as an asset or liability in electoral terms but also for making a party more or less coalitionable. For example, parties may be attracted to candidates who share views with potential coalition partners, and avoid those with unpalatable views or recent defectors from potential governing partners who may harbour bad blood.

liamentary group. Assuming he is seen as a valuable electoral asset and is programmatically close to several other parties, he may well receive several offers. Sometimes these are made public, but it is generally in the interest of Kovács and the bidding parties to keep the early conversations private. To complicate things further, Kovács has the incentive to suggest both publicly and privately in dealings with proto-slates that he has received lucrative offers from several parties as bluffing can raise his political 'market value'. This, again, highlights how complex and covert these negotiations can be: the exit or return of a candidate can be the outcome of different chains of events that can be virtually impossible to study. Snippets of evidence may leak out from the black box, but these may not represent the full picture and may even be misleading due to bluffing.

Finally, István Kovács may have neither intended to run as a parliamentary candidate nor been courted by political parties. In this, he would be like almost all citizens in all democracies. However, some who did not run in t_1 may consider doing so in t_2 either on their own initiative or after being approached by a proto-slate, potentially motivated by improved electoral prospects, appealing programmatic shifts, or leadership change. A bidding game similar to that involving former candidates ensues. A special case—but a very significant one for the countries analysed in this book—is the setting up of a genuinely new party. The formation of such a slate can be seen as a coming together of people in a proto-slate who intend to contest an election. Most genuinely new parties are leader-centric and the founding leader often *is* the proto-slate that either approaches potential candidates (the second arrow from the bottom effectively reversed) or is approached themselves by aspiring candidates. This highlights that proto-slates can take very different forms, ranging from a single aspiring leader or a loose circle of individuals to an established party, including splinters, mergers, and electoral coalitions. Most importantly, legally registered parties are not the only groups attracting aspiring candidates—parties are important and often play a key role but limiting attention to parties as legal organizations would be misguided, considering the full gamut of contemporary slates and varieties of party or party system change.

The principal focus of this book is to understand the evolution of parties and party systems rather than disentangle the route from t_1 to t_2 by explaining candidate selection and recruitment. In that, we do not mean to dismiss any studies that try to do so. If anything, we want to emphasize that the paths to candidate return, exit, and entry are diverse and deserve more scholarly attention. We emphasize that candidate list creation is:

- complex: it often involves organizational changes—party entry, splits and mergers, creation of electoral coalitions—and hence cannot be reduced to the decisions of candidates or stable parties only;
- interactive: the negotiations between proto-slates and potential candidates can be iterative and involve different proto-slates at various stages; and
- obscure: it is impossible to study all significant aspects of the process empirically as important interactions may never become public and those that do may involve bluffing.[14]

The model in Figure 2.3 emphasizes what is easily observable—candidate lists in t_1 and t_2—and what we can deduce by tracing candidate turnover and movement from one slate to another, i.e. candidate entry, exit, and return. Furthermore, even without being able to see inside the inter-electoral black box, we can use these observable implications of the slate-formation game to model and assess the extent and effects of external political and internal party change. Some of these—such as changes in parties' electoral fortunes which, in turn, affect candidates' electoral prospects and incentives to run or not run—form the basis of our explanatory models in Chapter 4. There, we also consider other factors, such as the effect of perceived levels of corruption, followed by an analysis of linkages between candidate change and other aspects of party change in later chapters.

2.3 A baseline model of candidate change

Candidate change always happens and so does party change in general. Even if changes are minimal, no slate returns perfectly intact. Evolution, whether biological or political, is an everlasting process rather than a teleological journey towards stability and survival. Our evolutionary understanding of party change posits that the 'molecular clock' of parties—like the one that measures the time lapsed from the evolutionary divergence of species based on the rate of genetic mutations (Zuckerkandl & Pauling 1965)—is constantly ticking. It is accelerated or slowed down by internal and external factors, potentially changing directions and performing a random walk

---

[14] This complicates the study of involuntary versus voluntary departures from the parliament the line between which is blurred but for simplicity's sake, the issue is ignored (Kerby & Blidook 2011; Moore & Hibbing 1998). As our discussion shows, the real reasons for leaving are often hidden in a black box.

rather than a march towards or away from any 'institutionalized' equilibrium. Although some historical parties survive because of stability, this is not necessarily the optimal strategy from the perspective of candidates. Parties may need to adapt rapidly or give way to survival machines better equipped to ensure the survival of their people—just as genes do not always benefit from the stability of their host organisms or species in the face of changing environments.

How much natural change among candidates should we expect? In other words, what is its 'natural rate' in the absence of accelerating factors? Determining a baseline rate allows us to interpret empirical levels of candidate change and gauge the impact of external factors on candidate change and the strength of the association between candidate change and other dimensions of party change (organization, leadership, and programme). We do so by devising a simple theoretical model of candidate change that serves as the basis for further analyses in the subsequent chapters.

The ignorance-based logical modelling approach proposed by Taagepera (1999) allows us to arrive at a logically grounded (if rough) baseline that can be subjected to empirical testing and further enhancements. Our starting point is the expected rate of candidate replacement. At every election, some candidates do not return due to retirement or death and need to be replaced by others. Hence, the natural rate of candidate change depends—at the most basic level—on candidates' 'political life expectancy'. As a starting point, we can assume that the political life of party people starts at the earliest at 18 (the minimum age required to stand for election in almost all European nations) and ends at the age 70 (some years beyond a typical retirement age), giving us a political life span of 70–18 = 52 years. If we further account for a typical electoral term of four years, we can expect candidates to contest up to 52/4 = 13 elections in their political lifetime. Based on a simple linear function, the *minimum* replacement rate (R) would be 1/13 = 7.7%.

This is almost certainly an underestimate, as many citizens become candidates at a later age and others retire or leave politics much earlier. More importantly, even successful candidates may not strive for unlimited re-election and many unsuccessful candidates give up politics after one election. In the extreme event that all candidates only contest a single election, the replacement rate would be 100%. Both the minimum and maximum rates are certainly unlikely—we would expect candidate turnover to be complete before fifty-two years and some candidates always contest several consecutive elections. Rather, we should use the geometric mean[15] of the two extremes to deduce the expected average turnover rate over time. A general estimate that allows for adjusting for both term length and political life expectancy would hence be:

$$R = \sqrt{\frac{t}{l}} \qquad (2.1)$$

where R is the replacement ratio, l the electoral life expectancy and t the length of electoral term (in years or any other units). Assuming, once again, a term length of four years and a political life expectancy of 52 years, we would expect candidate turnover of about 27.7% following a parliamentary term. This ratio can be interpreted either as the expected aggregate level of replacement or the probability of an average candidate being replaced.

This simple baseline expectation applies to all parties: major political actors, as well as marginal also-runs. However, we would expect a lower replacement rate among larger and more successful parties—as more of their top candidates build up proper political careers—than for tiny extra-parliamentary parties whose candidates may see contesting elections as a mere pastime. We suggest that party size, represented by its vote share, is an important determinant of candidate turnover. To deduce candidate turnover rates for parties at different levels of electoral strength, we consider candidate feasibility. Feasibility refers to candidates' likelihood of being re-elected and is most straightforward to operationalize as their list placement in a district.[16]

Candidate lists consist of v feasible and $1-v$ non-feasible candidates. The overall expected candidate replacement rate can be calculated as the weighted average of replacement rates of feasible and non-feasible candidates. Assuming that the replacement rate of feasible candidates is equal to the theoretical minimum ($R_f = 7.7\%$; see above), and to the theoretical maximum for non-feasible candidates ($R_n = 100\%$), the expected replacement rate for party p (R_p) is:

$$\begin{aligned} R_p &= R_f v_p + R_n \left(1 - v_p\right) \\ &= 7.7\% v_p + 100\% \left(1 - v_p\right) \\ &= 100 - 92.3 v_p \end{aligned} \qquad (2.2)$$

---

[15] A geometric rather than arithmetic mean is a more appropriate measure of central tendency here, considering the vast difference in the two values (see Taagepera 1999).

[16] For the sake of simplicity, we assume stable party support and stable list placements—i.e. that exiting candidates are replaced by newcomers, but the positions of other candidates do not change and that all slates run full candidate lists (= district magnitude).

Hence, for parties with $v_p = 50\%$, $R_p = 54\%$; for $v_p = 10\%$, $R_p = 91\%$ and for $v_p = 1\%$, $R_p = 99\%$. More generally, incorporating formula 2.1, we get:

$$R_p = v_p\sqrt{\frac{t}{l}} + 100\% (1 - v_p) = 1 - v_p\left(1 - \sqrt{\frac{t}{l}}\right) \qquad (2.3)$$

Naturally, not all non-feasible candidates give up politics after just one election. In particular, this applies to those who only narrowly fail to get elected; likewise, low-ranking candidates of large parties may also expect a gradual promotion to feasible list positions, while small parties that decide to run again may not have enough active members to substitute the failed ones. Thus, we may want to set the lowest expected turnover among non-feasible candidates at 50% instead of 100%. The formula hence becomes:

$$R_p = v_p\sqrt{\frac{t}{l}} + 50\% (1 - v_p) = 0.5 - v_p\left(0.5 - \sqrt{\frac{t}{l}}\right) \qquad (2.4)$$

This predictive model is only a rough approximation of the 'natural rate' of candidate change in every election. However, it incorporates the most important ideas of our evolutionary paradigm: the constant nature of party change and the role of candidates as key agents of change. Furthermore, it provides a baseline expectation for levels of candidate change and, in turn, for gauging any additional effects of party-internal and external factors. As explained in the following chapter, our focus is on weighted candidate turnover where more prominent candidates closer to the top of the list matter more than those lower down the list. A further reason why candidate turnover—even the weighted turnover that essentially discounts non-feasible candidates—is expected to be linked to party size is that stronger electoral potential implies better resources, e.g. promising spots on the electoral list or jobs in government or party structures (Poguntke et al. 2020). Party people are more likely to stay along for the ride and would be more hesitant to spend resources to modify their survival machines. Likewise, the organizational structures of large parties may also be more resilient to change. In contrast, we expect higher candidate turnover in smaller parties as uncertain electoral prospects can make candidate exit from the electoral scene more likely.

2.4 Conclusion

The notion of 'party change' is ubiquitous in the literature on political parties and party systems yet is rarely conceptualized in detail. This chapter has outlined our multidimensional approach to party change and highlighted connections to the literature on related questions of legislative turnover and party switching, party leaders and manifestos. Most previous scholarship has been conducted within what we term the 'organizational paradigm' that prioritizes legal–organizational aspects of parties; yet, in our view, this hinders us from fully understanding the evolution of parties and party systems. Nevertheless, even though our approach goes in a different direction, the connections to extant research are manifold and we draw significant inspiration from the existing scholarship. Our alternative 'genetic' or 'electoral' paradigm builds partly on theories of biological evolution and puts candidates alongside other 'party people' at the centre of our understanding of party evolution and change. We argued that party change is a perpetual process that may vary in pace and extent, but always happens and cannot reach a perfect equilibrium as a change in one dimension always creates the potential for change in another. Turnover in candidates is centrally connected to change in other aspects—most prominently, organizational, leadership, and programmatic dimensions. Consequently, we advocate using candidate change as an overarching proxy indicator of party change.

The centrality of candidates is also reflected in our theoretical model of slate-making in the second section of this chapter. We contended that much of the slate-making takes place within a black box and the interactions between individuals and proto-slates (parties and other sets of potential running mates) are very difficult to study because of their covert nature and significant incentives for bluffing. While we do not dismiss attempts to do so, the focus in this book is on the observable implications of these processes, i.e. candidate entry and exit to and from the electoral game and candidate movements between slates in consecutive elections. The final section of the chapter outlined our quantitative baseline expectation of candidate turnover—i.e. the pace of party evolutionary change in the absence of accelerating factors—contingent on party size that will serve as a basis for the interpretation of statistical results in the following chapters.

The remainder of this book seeks to validate our arguments empirically and further explore the relationship between candidate turnover and different dimensions of party change. The next chapter introduces our dataset as well as weighted measures of candidate turnover and the measure of candidate congruence. Chapter 4 empirically tests the theoretical model of party size and candidate turnover developed here before turning to a broader range of determinants of weighted candidate turnover: change in electoral support, corruption perception, and socio-economic developments. We then turn our attention to potential applications of candidate turnover indices as a means for distinguishing between genuinely new parties and partially new parties from others (Chapter 5) and to how our data and proposed measures can be used for enhancing electoral volatility indices (Chapter 6). Chapters 7–9 examine the relationship between candidate change and other core aspects of party change briefly discussed in this chapter: organizational change in the form of fission and fusion, leadership change, and programmatic change. These empirical chapters provide strong support for our proposal to use candidate change as a more general indicator of party change. On the one hand, we find statistically significant associations between candidate change and party change on other dimensions. On the other hand, our qualitative in-depth examination of selected cases—such as examples of complicated splits and mergers—shows that the candidate-centred view of party (system) development yields new insights. The conclusion of the book (Chapter 10) summarizes our findings and returns to some of the issues touched upon here: the added value of the 'genetic' paradigm in understanding party system evolution and its implications for the study of party system institutionalization and consolidation.

3
Measures matter
New concepts, methods, and big data

Appearances can be deceptive. As mentioned in the introduction, political parties—just like seagulls and albatrosses—can look spuriously similar while belonging to separate species. Political scientists have acknowledged these problems and usually seek out extra information when classifying political parties and tracing their development over time. Nevertheless, relationships between parties in consecutive elections are often established based on names or other superficial criteria, particularly in larger comparative studies. Historical linkages between political parties are often limited to only one successor or predecessor, even where several clearly exist.

In the preceding chapters, we have argued that party evolution can be more fully understood by adopting a candidate-based approach and shifting the focus from parties as organizations to candidates (or people more generally) as parties' 'political DNA'. Yet to shift the perspective from the 'macro' to the 'micro' and focus on the 'genes' whose effects manifest themselves in parties' outward appearance, we need new concepts, new data, and new methods.

In this chapter, we introduce the conceptual and methodological innovations of our approach. First, we present our 'big but thin' data set and outline the methods we developed for its analysis. Second, we propose a measurement of candidate change for individual slates, to use our common term for parties and electoral coalitions in a given election. We introduce candidate novelty and dropout as essential indicators and a weighting mechanism based on candidate prominence and slates' electoral support. Third, we discuss candidate congruence, a measure of overlap for pairs of slates in consecutive elections and show how all the measures can be put into practice. This chapter is important for understanding our analyses in later chapters. Therefore, we complement formulas and discussions of techniques with accessible examples that also serve to introduce some key political parties to readers who might not be experts on Central and East European (CEE) party systems.

Party People. Allan Sikk and Philipp Köker, Oxford University Press. © Allan Sikk and Philipp Köker (2023).
DOI: 10.1093/oso/9780198868125.003.0003

3.1 The ECCEE data set: making the most of 'big but thin' data

Our original data set Electoral Candidates in Central and Eastern Europe (ECCEE) complements several existing data sets on electoral candidates. While our focus is on candidates in slates, others have mostly analysed candidates themselves: their socio-economic background (Campbell & van Heerde-Hudson 2018; Dubrow & Palaguta 2016; Popescu & Hannavy 2001), strategic party switching (Kreuzer & Pettai 2003; Pettai & Kreuzer 1999; Shabad & Slomczynski 2004) campaign strategies (Karlsen & Skogerbø 2013; Lutz et al. 2018; Zittel 2015), or political views (Lloren & Rosset 2017). In contrast, we are mostly interested in candidates as 'party genes'. Our main aim is to study the relationship between candidate change and party system evolution; hence, our perspective on candidates is expansive rather than deep.

Existing candidate data provides some very valuable insights, but it often covers only a few (or individual) countries, elections, or parliamentary parties. The ECCEE data set includes about 200,000 electoral candidates, some 1,400 slates, and covers sixty elections in nine CEE democracies: Bulgaria, the Czech Republic, Estonia, Hungary, Latvia, Lithuania, Poland, Slovakia, and Slovenia. It was compiled from a diverse range of online and print sources that varied greatly in format, structure, and coverage, thus requiring significant manual data entry and cleaning—especially for earlier elections in our series. For most countries, we tracked down data for all elections since the fall of communism until about 2016. For these elections, ECCEE is a complete inventory of all electoral candidates and slates, not limited to candidates that entered parliament or slates that reached some other (arbitrary) vote threshold.

The data set has characteristics of 'Big Data' (Kitchin 2013). In particular, it is expansive in volume—many more candidates run for parliament than there are seats—and exhaustive in scope as it includes all candidates from all parties. The data is also relational, allowing it to be linked to other data sets, a potential we exploit in later chapters. Finally, the candidate data in ECCEE is also flexible in that it can be extended relatively easily, at least compared to data sets that focus on collecting information on candidates' individual details. Nevertheless, ECCEE data is 'big but thin' (Strasser & Edwards 2017). The range of available variables is mostly limited to candidate names, party affiliation, district, list placement, and preference votes. In the interest of flexibility and extendibility, and given that it is often not possible (or practical) to collect more detailed information, we have not actively sought to add any further candidate-specific variables. Thus, the use of this data poses novel challenges—not only owing to its scale but also because of a structure that differs from existing candidate data sets. In other words, the thinness of the data requires the development of new methods for analysis that also ease the extension of our approach to other elections and countries.

For the analysis in this book, we developed a range of methods appropriate for the size of the data set. Most importantly, we devised an algorithm to track candidates between elections; that is, to identify new, exiting, and repeat candidates. This is done by an elaborate code in the R statistical package that exploits the limited number of variables to their full potential to find and match repeat candidates in pairs of consecutive elections.[1]

The first step is straightforward: we match candidates with unique names in a pair of elections. For example, if one Elizabeth Alexandra Mary Windsor ran in two consecutive elections in Slovakia, she would certainly be the same person. However, this also works for far less exotic Slovak names: more than 98% of names in each election were unique. For duplicate names, we first use the information on party continuity assuming that a candidate of the same party with the same name must be a continuing candidate.[2] For example, if several candidates named István Kovács ran in two consecutive elections but only one on both occasions for the Traditional Party, we would assume him to be the continuing candidate.[3]

Where duplicates remain, our R code uses information about candidate movement between parties, assuming that candidates are likely to follow others rather than go their own way. For example, a unique István Kovács runs for the Modern Party in one election, but no candidate of that name runs for the Modern Party at the next election; nevertheless, two candidates named István Kovács now run for other parties. In this case, we would match him with István Kovács of the Ultramodern Party—a destination for other former Modern Party candidates—rather than with István Kovács of the Orthodox Party.[4] We use a similar approach for candidates with unique names within

---

[1] Our algorithm bears some similarities to the approach developed by Enamorado et al. (2019).
[2] Party continuity is not a trivial issue in Central and Eastern Europe. We rely on the continuity in coding in MARPOR (Volkens et al. 2020) and ParlGov (Döring et al. 2022) data sets.
[3] To limit the number of duplicates, we first match candidates that ran for the same party in the same district. Hence, if there were namesakes running for the same party in two elections, we would first match the one with a repeated district, leaving no duplicates within the party.
[4] István Kovács is the most common name in our data set, and we need more advanced methods for tracking some of them. First, we consider slate congruences as explained below. We also identified some candidates who might have changed surnames (usually after marriage) and manually coded a small number of high-ranking candidates from major parties to improve the accuracy of candidate turnover figures.

electoral districts, assuming that the candidate with the same unique name running in the same district must be a continuing candidate.

After these initial rounds of matching, we attempt partial name matching for longer names. For example, Janez Janša, the former Prime Minister of Slovenia, ran as Janez (Ivan) Janša in 2014, incidentally while serving a prison sentence for corruption, later overturned by the Constitutional Court. Removing the middle name from the long version allows us to match it with the shorter version. Finally, we check for approximate or 'fuzzy' matches between names that allow for minor mistakes or variations in spelling. For example, Tamás Suchman, a cabinet minister for the Hungarian Socialist Party in 1995–8, appeared in the 1990 electoral list as Tamás Suchmann.

This matching algorithm provides robust results with very limited errors as suggested both by the candidate-based party evolutionary trees below and the reliability checks that we ran on smaller samples of candidates. These certainly remain below the typical levels of misreporting, data entry errors, and non-response bias in typical political science survey data. Also, we are interested in levels of candidate turnover and continuity in parties rather than individual political careers, and mismatching some candidates does little harm to our overall findings. Furthermore, a key advantage of our approach is that it can be applied to any election even when data on individual candidates is limited to names and political affiliation. Even as more detailed candidate data sets with biographical information are becoming available (e.g. for Poland, Hungary, Ukraine, and the United Kingdom, see Campbell & van Heerde-Hudson 2018; Dubrow & Palaguta 2016), these are difficult and expensive to extend beyond their original scope. In particular, records on historical or other less well-documented elections can be too patchy to ascertain continuing candidates using biographic records. In contrast, our data can be extended with comparatively little effort, especially for contemporary elections and many past elections in the developed world for which full candidate lists are usually available online.

Our matching method can be applied beyond national parliamentary elections, e.g. to local or regional elections or other contests where the collection of information on individuals is unfeasible. We also believe that our approach to 'big but thin' data and the matching algorithms could be of interest to social scientists beyond those interested in electoral politics. It can be useful wherever names are accompanied by limited supplementary variables and those who need to match names with little additional detail (e.g. public electoral rolls, telephone directories, business and court registers, historical life event records).

3.2 Measuring candidate change: novelty and dropout

Once we have matched candidates between pairs of elections, we can study the level of 'genetic change' in parties; however, we need to conceptualize change and stability first. Or—returning to the example of computers in the introduction of the book—we need to establish ways to measure how many parts were exchanged and how many were retained. Furthermore, how should we account for the higher importance of some components (a processor) compared to others (a new USB cable)?

At the most basic level, candidate change takes two forms: new candidates joining the electoral race and former candidates dropping out. Candidate novelty refers to the share of new candidates, i.e. those who did not contest the previous election, either in the same or a different party. In contrast, candidate dropout is the percentage of candidates leaving electoral politics, i.e. those that no longer run in the subsequent election.

Clearly, the overall level of novelty and dropout must be equal: new candidates must replace those who drop out and, vice versa, new candidates can only fill positions vacated by others, unless there are major changes in the electoral system. However, the reality is often more complicated as party list lengths can vary significantly between elections. Even more importantly, not all candidates are created equal—most obviously in list-based systems, used in all nine countries analysed in this book. Top-ranking candidates are more important than those lower down the list as they stand a better chance of getting elected and are more visible to the voters. Hence, candidates must be weighted according to their prominence.

3.2.1 Candidate prominence

A simple solution to account for candidate prominence is to analyse top-ranking candidates only, who are easy to identify in list-based systems such as those we are looking at here (our approach to additional single-mandate districts (SMDs), which is relevant for some of our cases, is discussed below). For example, we could focus our attention on the top 25% of candidates (see Sikk & Köker 2019). However, the importance of candidates in a particular list position varies between parties. Imagine two candidates from two slates—the Goliath Coalition and the David Party—each ranked 25th among 100 candidates and hence the least prominent among the top 25%. If the Goliath Coalition is on course to win thirty mandates and the David Party only four, only the candidate of the Goliath coalition has a real chance of winning a seat. She is obviously more significant than the latter who is doomed to end up as an also-run. Therefore, it makes sense to consider the slate's overall support.[5]

Both the Goliath Coalition (50% of votes) and the David Party (5%) field 100 candidates on a nationwide list for 100 parliamentary seats. The simplest option would be to consider only candidates up to a slate's electoral support: under a fully proportional system, the Goliaths would win fifty seats and the Davids would win five.[6] Hence, we would include the top fifty and top five candidates, respectively. However, that would give equal weight to candidates at the very top of the list and those who just manage to get elected, even though the top Goliath is obviously more important than Goliath number 50 and is more secure in winning a seat. Likewise, it would equate David number six with David number one hundred even though the former might be in contention until the early hours of counting while the latter may have missed the count altogether as the result was a foregone conclusion (in political reality, the biblical outcome of David defeating Goliath never comes true). Hence, strict cut-off points ignore the uncertainty over electoral results: if a slate overperforms, some candidates unexpectedly enter the parliament; if it flops, some candidates presumed safe will be left out.

Overall, it is preferable to give more weight to the candidates at the top and less to those at the bottom. As shown in the Appendix to this chapter, the candidates with higher list placement are more important for parties (and vice versa) as they are more likely to return. The easiest option would be a negative linear sequence of weights: e.g. {1, 0.75, 0.5, 0.25, 0} for a district with magnitude M = 5. However, this gives excessive weight to some hopeless candidates such as the third and fourth candidates of the David Party that would need to be lucky to win two seats with 5% of the vote here. A linear sequence of weights would also completely ignore a slate's electoral support. Hence, we need a middle way between the strict cut-offs and linear weights: smooth weights that allow for a mild decline in the weights at the top, a faster drop in candidate importance in the middle (around the party's vote share) and a smooth dying off at the end.

---

[5] Our weighting scheme bears similarities to the index of electoral vulnerability of legislators (André et al. 2015), but serves a different purpose and applies to all candidates rather than only legislators.

[6] We make a simplifying assumption of perfect proportionality—not unreasonable, given the proportional electoral systems in use in the elections studied—and actual vote shares reflecting expected vote shares.

Before outlining our chosen weights, we need to introduce the notion of the *relative list position* (r) of a candidate. The relative list position is the candidates' percentile of the list placement. We calculate it as follows:

$$r = \frac{rank - 1}{M - 1} \quad (3.1)$$

where *rank* is the list position of the candidate and M is the district magnitude, $r = 0$ for all top candidates and $r = 1$ for all candidates in the bottom list position ($rank = M$). For candidates in the middle positions, consider the third candidate on the list in a district with $M = 5$ for whom $r = (3-1)/(5-1) = 0.5$. This median candidate is right in the middle of the candidate list with 50% of candidates before and 50% behind her.[7]

Suitable smooth weights can be based on the well-known logistic (or sigmoid) function, familiar to many readers from logistic regression where it is used to transform a dummy (0/1) dependent variable:

$$f(x) = \frac{L}{1 + e^{-k(x-x_0)}} \quad (3.2)$$

where x_0 is the sigmoid's mid-point, L the maximum value and k the steepness of the curve. For candidate weights we modify the formula:

- we substitute x by r, the relative list position;
- we substitute x_0 by v_e, slate e's vote share: e.g. at 25% of votes $v_e = 25$;
- the values of formula (3.2) range from 0 to 1, but as the weights must run from 1 to 0, we subtract the formula from 1 and set L at 1;
- we set $k = -25$ for a curve with suitable steepness;

We end up with the formula for the raw weight for candidate i in slate e:

$$rw_{ei} = 1 - \frac{1}{1 + e^{+25(r-v_e)}} \quad (3.3)$$

For reasons that will become clearer later, we want the weights of all candidates of a slate to add up to one. We obtain these *standardized weights* by dividing

---

[7] In some countries, it is common for parties to list more candidates than there are available seats. Candidates on oversized lists who rank below M have zero weights and do not contribute to novelty and dropout indices. They are still included among the candidates in that election and not considered new in the following election (or dropped out vis-à-vis the previous one).

the raw weighted values for individual candidates by the sum of raw weights for all candidates of that slate:

$$w_i = \frac{rw_i}{\sum rw_i} \qquad (3.4)$$

Figure 3.1 illustrates the standardized weights of three hypothetical slates with $v = \{5\%, 20\%, 50\%\}$ under three different district sizes $M = \{5, 15, 150\}$. For very large slates ($v = 50\%$), many candidates have high weights as more of them can be certain of winning a seat. The smaller the slate, the higher the weight of the candidates at the top of the list as few others stand a realistic chance of winning a seat. We assume that when fielding candidates, slates have some information about their likely support, and we use the actual share of votes as a proxy for expected vote share (and for the expected number of candidates getting elected).

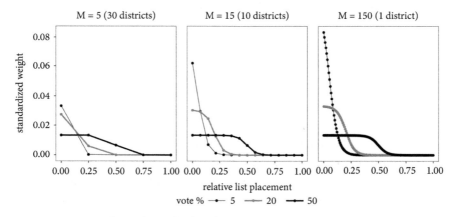

Figure 3.1 Hypothetical standardized weights

Notes: All are based on an assembly size of 150. Relative list placement $(rank-1)/(M-1)$ can be interpreted as the share of candidates at higher list positions.

Our discussion of candidate prominence and weights has so far referred to candidates' list positions. Determining list position is easy where party lists are closed; here, the rank simply refers to a candidate's placement on the respective list. With open party lists, voters can alter these positions by using preference votes. In these cases, rank refers to the final list placement, incorporating the preference votes cast.

Hungary and Lithuania employ mixed electoral systems that combine SMDs with multimember districts. A candidate who ranks low on the party list may be very prominent in SMDs and this needs to be reflected in their respective weight. However, in SMDs a 'list placement' is not defined—as a rule, parties only field one candidate—and candidate prominence requires a different approach.

We base candidate weights in SMDs on the ratio of their vote share to that of the strongest competitor. For the most popular candidate, the weight is based on the ratio of their votes to those of the runner-up (v_1/v_2). For all other candidates, it is based on the ratio of the i-th candidate to that of the winning candidate (v_i/v_1).

We calculate the raw weights for candidates in SMDs using the following formula:

$$rw_i = \frac{1}{1 + \left(\frac{v_I}{v_i}\right)^{2.5}} \qquad (3.5)$$

where v_i is the number of votes cast for candidate i and $I = 2$ for top candidates, $I = 1$ for all others.

Formula 3.5 gives more weight to candidates who win by a large margin than to those with smaller winning margins; it also gives more weight to runners-up only narrowly behind the winner than to those defeated by a larger margin. For example, in a two-way race with $v_1 = 0.7$ and $v_2 = 0.3$, the corresponding weights for the candidates are 0.84 and 0.16. If $v_1 = 0.55$ and $v_2 = 0.45$, the corresponding weights are 0.6 and 0.4.

One final quirk regards multi-district candidacies: in Latvia (until 2006), as well as in Bulgaria and Slovenia candidates can run in several districts at once. With such multi-district candidacies, we use the highest of the list placements and ignore the respective candidate in other districts, mirroring the practice in seat allocation. We use a similar approach with mixed systems and multi-tier list systems (Estonia, Hungary) where a candidate 'counts' in the tier with the highest weight.[8] For example, in the 2010 elections in Hungary, the president of the radical right Jobbik, Gábor Vona, was a candidate in all three tiers. He came only third in his SMD with 26% of votes versus 39% for the top candidate.[9] Hence, his raw SMD weight was 0.27. However, his raw weights as the top candidate for *Jobbik* in the county and national list were 0.98, trumping the low SMD weight.

---

[8] For example, in Estonia, a popular candidate may have a low placement in the national list if they are virtually guaranteed a district mandate. Vice versa, a party can place a candidate high up in the national closed list to insure them against poor district performance.

[9] We use vote shares in the first round so that all candidates could be assigned weights, including those who did not reach the second round.

3.2.2 Weighted candidate novelty and dropout

Having defined initial ('raw') weights for individual candidates under different electoral systems, we can now calculate the *weighted candidate novelty* (WCN) and *dropout* (WCD) for individual slates and determine how 'old' or 'new' a slate is based on its set of candidates. The overall WCN of slate *e*:

$$WCN_e = \Sigma_{i=1}^{n} NEW \cdot w_i \tag{3.6}$$

where *NEW* is a dummy for new candidates who did not contest the previous election, *w*, the standardized weight of a candidate and *n* the number of *e*'s candidates. For weighted candidate dropout (WCD$_e$) we replace *NEW* with a dummy for candidates that dropped out in the subsequent election. The aggregate WCN in an election can be calculated by adding together the scores, weighted by slates' vote shares (v_e):

$$WCN = \sum v_e WCN_e \tag{3.7}$$

Again, the formula for overall WCD is identical. v_e is still the vote share in the first (i.e. the reference) election—if it was the vote share in the subsequent election, WCD would not be defined for exiting parties, mergers or splits. Formulas 3.6 and 3.7 range from 0 to 1 where zero entails no new candidates (or no candidates dropping out) and one means that all candidates are new candidates (or all drop out).

The overall candidate novelty has been and remains consistently high in most CEE countries (Figure 3.2). For our set of elections, it was on average 0.42, with a very mild (statistically non-significant) decrease from 0.44 in the 1990s to 0.40 in the 2010s; only Estonia and Lithuania experienced a more pronounced, nearly constant downward trend since the early 1990s. Candidate novelty usually drops in snap elections (Bulgaria 2014, Czech Republic 1998, Latvia 2011, Poland 2007). When elections are held early, fewer candidates retire and there is less time to recruit new talent; also, fewer new parties are created. Extreme novelty is associated with extremely successful genuinely new parties. In Bulgaria, the National Movement Simeon II (NDSV, see also below) triumphed in 2001 and the Citizens for European Development of Bulgaria (GERB) in 2009; in Slovenia, two big breakthroughs came in succession: Positive Slovenia (PS) in 2011 and the Party of Miro Cerar (SMC) in 2014. Among continuing parties (see next chapter for a definition), candidate novelty has been lower after a drop until the early 2000s. The gap between the

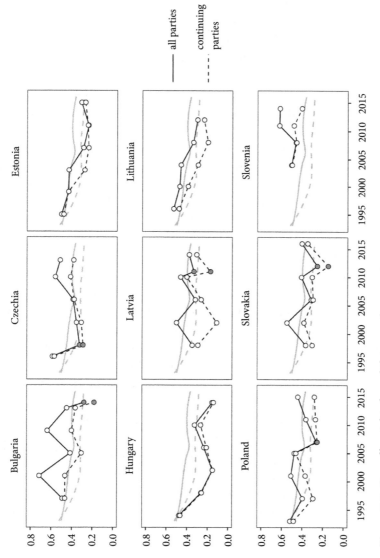

Figure 3.2 Overall weighted candidate novelty over time

Notes: Early elections are highlighted; grey lines show overall smoothed trends.

two lines in Figure 3.2 can be attributed to strong genuinely new parties. The trend in candidate dropout is similar, with at best mild decrease in turnover. Hence, in terms of candidates, party politics in CEE has overall become only very mildly more stable. However, the levels of candidate turnover vary greatly between countries and elections and, even more importantly, aggregate scores mask variation among individual slates.

Among established political parties, candidate novelty is generally lower. For example, the Slovak Direction–Social Democracy party (Smer–SD) ran a list with a very high number of returning candidates in the 2012 early election. Its weighted novelty was extremely low (WCN = 0.04) and the highest-ranking new candidate was found only in 52nd place among the 150 national list candidates. In contrast, candidate novelty can be very high in new parties. The most popular party with extremely high levels of novelty (WCN = 0.95) in our data set was the Bulgarian National Movement Simeon II (NDSV) in 2001. An archetypical genuinely new party set up shortly before the election, it relied heavily on political newcomers (Peeva 2001). Out of its 242 candidates, only seventeen had contested the previous election, and only two of the seasoned candidates topped one of the thirty-one district lists.

One of the lowest levels of dropout (0.03) was also recorded by Smer–SD between 2010 and the early election in 2012. Among major parties ($v \geq 10\%$), the highest candidate dropout (0.79) was recorded by the Czech Public Affairs (VV) as scandals consumed the new party after its very first election in 2010 (see Chapter 4). The aftermath of that election also saw the highest dropout among continuing parties, as the Civic Democratic Party (ODS) lost nearly two-thirds of its candidates (WCD = 0.60) after being mired in corruption scandals that led to the resignation of Prime Minister Petr Nečas and the loss of more than two-thirds of its seats. Massive electoral losses also accompanied high candidate dropout for the coalition of the Bulgarian Socialist Party (BSP) between 1994 and 1997 (WCD = 0.59), after its government stepped down amidst a major economic crisis, demonstrations, and strikes. This suggests a link between party breakdown, corruption scandals, and candidate turnover. We provide a systematic analysis of determinants of candidate turnover, including the role of corruption in the next chapter.

3.3 Candidate congruence

WCN and WCD provide a snapshot of change in individual parties. However, this does not tell us much about the relationship between slates over time. Candidate turnover is only a part of a larger evolutionary process in which slates emerge, change, merge, split, and disintegrate. To study these developments, we need to look at candidates' movement *between slates* and how they shape and reshape the political landscape. Party switching has been endemic in CEE: among continuing parties (i.e. those running in consecutive elections), about 18% of returning candidates had changed parties, decreasing only mildly to 13% for parties that won at least 20% of the vote.[10]

We propose the concept of *slate congruence* (C) to study candidate movements between parties. Congruence refers to the overall candidate overlap between pairs of slates or electoral districts that we used for candidate matching between elections. $C_{AB} = 1$ means that slate B presents a list of candidates identical to that of slate A in the previous election; $C_{AB} = 0$ means absence of common candidates between A and B.

A party—we use the term 'party' rather than 'slate' here because the latter refers to an electoral unit in one election only—that contests two consecutive elections while retaining most of its candidates is highly *self-congruent*. A party that loses a significant number of candidates (to competitors or as dropouts) has low self-congruence. Similarly, when a party splits and its candidates move on to several slates, several slates in t will be congruent with the parent slate in $t-1$. When slates merge or form an electoral coalition, it will be congruent with several slates in $t-1$. If only a few candidates defect to another party, it will be partially congruent with their original party. Finally, a pair of slates in consecutive elections is perfectly *incongruent* if they share none of the candidates.

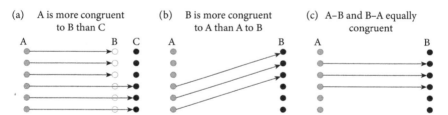

Figure 3.3 Congruence and list placement

For slate congruence, we must again consider candidate significance. Let us imagine that an Anthill Coalition (A) loses several top-ranking candidates to the Bumblebee Party (B) and *the same number* of low-ranking candidates to the Cockroach Movement (C, see Figure 3.3a). The congruence between

---

[10] This is roughly similar to levels of legislative party switching in the region (Klein 2021: 334; Semenova 2015: 281). However, our figures only consider returning parties and not the movement of candidates whose parties disintegrated. The figures may also overestimate defections as some of the candidates that nominally changed parties could have been running for essentially the same party where de facto continuity was obscured by complex splits, mergers, or electoral coalitions (see discussion on party fission and fusion in Chapter 7).

B and A should be higher than that between C and A as B's candidates are more important. To account for this, we use weights developed for candidate novelty and dropout above and calculate *weighted congruence* between two slates B and A in a pair of consecutive elections:

$$C_{AB} = \Sigma w_{AB} \qquad (3.8)$$

where w_{AB} stands for the weight of slate B's candidate who was previously running for slate A.

Congruence between slates can also depend on whether we adopt the perspective of the successor or the predecessor. If three low-ranking candidates from A occupy high list positions in B, B is more congruent to A than A to B because the candidates are more significant for B (see Figure 3.3b). In the unlikely scenario that the candidates assume the same list positions in B as in A, congruence is the same for both A and B (Figure 3.3c). The congruence of B from the perspective of A (hence the capital 'A') is:

$$C_{AB} = \Sigma w_{AB} \qquad (3.9)$$

And, vice versa, the congruence of A from the perspective of B is:

$$C_{aB} = \Sigma w_{aB} \qquad (3.10)$$

w_{Ab} and w_{aB} refer to candidate weights when running for A and B, respectively. As these congruences are seldom equal, we modify formula 3.8 to calculate aggregate congruence based on the average of congruences from formulas 3.9 and 3.10:

$$C_{AB} = (C_{Ab} + C_{aB})/2 \qquad (3.11)$$

The difference between the two perspectives on weighted congruence can be illustrated by looking at the electoral coalition between Fidesz and the Hungarian Democratic Forum (MDF) in 2002. Out of the 515 MDF candidates in 1998, fifty-three joined the new alliance. Only 13% moved up in the relative list placement, whereas 51% moved down. Figure 3.4 shows a high number of downward-sloping career lines and a small number of upward-sloping lines. This downward movement made MDF much less significant for the newly founded alliance than vice versa. The congruence of MDF to Fidesz–MDF was only medium-high as it lost several prominent candidates

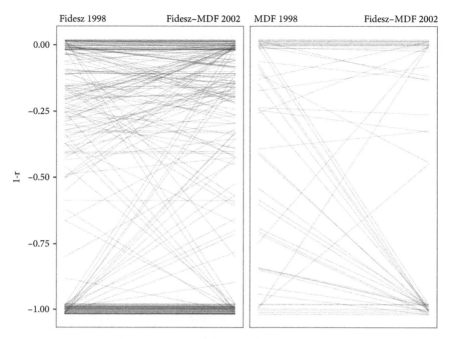

Figure 3.4 Fidesz and MDF 1998 candidates in Fidesz–MDF 2002

Note: Relative list placement deducted from r so that higher-ranking candidates appear higher up on the chart. 1–r is constrained at 0 for all candidates for whom *rank* > *M*. Jitter added to detail highly populated areas (top and bottom).

(including former Prime Minister Péter Boross who had lost his seat in 1998). The congruence of the new alliance to MDF was much lower as the top ranks of the coalition were clearly dominated by Fidesz while former prominent MDF candidates moved down, often from very high positions to very low ones (downward-sloping lines in Figure 3.4). For former Fidesz candidates, upwards movements were more common (30%) than downward movements (23%); 15% of all candidates remained in pole positions.

Table 3.1 shows that the weighted congruence of Fidesz—the alliance's main predecessor in 1998—to Fidesz–MDF was considerably higher (0.67) than the simple share of overlapping candidates (0.43) as returning candidates often landed in prominent positions. For MDF and other parties, the two measures were very similar. Columns (b) and (c) of Table 3.1 also list candidate novelty as it is a special form of congruence (to the 'party of candidates not running'). While 38% of Fidesz–MDF candidates were new, the overall weighted novelty was much lower (0.10), reflecting their usually modest positions.

60 PARTY PEOPLE

Table 3.1 The origin of Fidesz–MDF (2002) candidates

(a) Slate in 1998	(b) Absolute share of candidates	(c) Weighted congruence (Fidesz–MDF perspective)	(d) Weighted congruence (predecessor perspective)	(e) Overall congruence
Fidesz	0.43	0.67	0.83	0.75
MDF	0.11	0.12	0.50	0.31
Other	0.08	0.10		
Novelty	0.38	0.10		

Note: Excludes four joint candidates of MDF and Fidesz in SMDs in 1998 (176 SMDs overall).

Congruence can also be considered from the perspective of predecessors, e.g. Fidesz and MDF in 1998 (column d in Table 3.1). Fidesz was somewhat less important for the new coalition than the coalition was for Fidesz: an overwhelming majority of prominent Fidesz candidates ended up running for the coalition (one-way congruence 0.83). In contrast, the coalition was vastly more significant for MDF (congruence 0.50) than vice versa (0.12). This is because we are looking at a union of an elephant (Fidesz, $v = 28\%$ in 1998) and a mouse (MDF, $v = 3\%$). It is common for mergers and coalitions involving a larger and a smaller party to have asymmetric congruences as the union is usually vastly more important for the minor predecessor than the predecessor for the union. Finally, the overall congruence between a pair of slates (column e in Table 3.1) is the mean of the two perspectives (columns c and d).

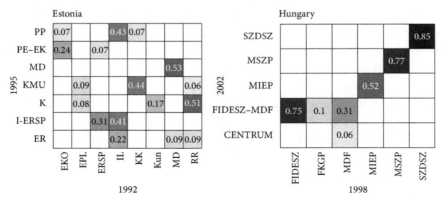

Figure 3.5 Pairwise slate congruences: Estonia 1992–5 and Hungary 1998–2002
Note: Slates with $v \geq 3\%$ and *congruence* > 0.05.

Some elections experience greater reconfiguration of slates than others (see Figure 3.5). Typically for emerging party systems in the early 1990s, most slates in the 1995 Estonian election were congruent to several 1992 slates. Some of the slates were partially new parties (Reform Party, ER), still drawing on the candidate pool of previously existing ones. Others were mergers (Pro Patria–National Independence Party, I–ERSP), splinters (the Right Wingers, PP), splinters merging with an existing party (Better Estonia–Estonian Citizen, PE–EK), electoral coalition reorganization (Coalition Party and Country People's Union, KMÜ) or parties benefiting from multiple defections (the Centre Party, K). In contrast, Hungary in 2002 shows considerable continuity apart from the very unequal merger of Fidesz and MDF; the latter also provided some candidate material to a new formation called Centrum. The two main opposition parties, and eventual winners of the 2002 election, SZDSZ (Alliance of Free Democrats) and MSZP (Hungarian Socialist Party) showed remarkable congruence with the 1998 election. The Hungarian Justice and Life Party (MIÉP), which entered parliament for the first (and only) time in 1998, underwent moderate change but showed no significant congruence with other parties.

We have now considered candidate turnover in individual slates and congruence between pairs of slates. This set of concepts and measures now allows us to analyse the wider developments of political parties and the evolution of party systems over time. For example, using candidate data, we can automatically draw evolutionary trees of party systems such as that for Poland in Figure 3.6. The thickness of lines between slates is proportional to their pairwise congruences. The colour of party labels indicates candidate novelty: darker hues stand for higher novelty. Although automatically drawn in R and based exclusively on the automatically matched candidate data, the evolutionary trees present a remarkably accurate picture of party system evolution in Poland. It highlights many of the main developments such as the creation of Solidarity Electoral Action (AWS) out of a wide range of parties in 1997 and its subsequent collapse that gave birth to Law and Justice (PiS), the League of Polish Families (LPR), and the Civic Platform (PO) that also absorbed part of the Freedom Union (UW). Likewise, we can see a remarkable self-congruence of the Polish Peasant Party (PSL) and the intermittent coalitions of the Democratic Left Alliance (SLD) with the Labour Union (UP) (Gwiazda 2015; see also Sikk & Köker 2019).

As we will show later, party congruence is useful for understanding party fission and fusion (Chapter 7) and can also aid the calculation of electoral volatility by considering nuances of party system development (see Chapter 5 and its Appendix of evolutionary trees for all nine countries). Figure 3.6 also

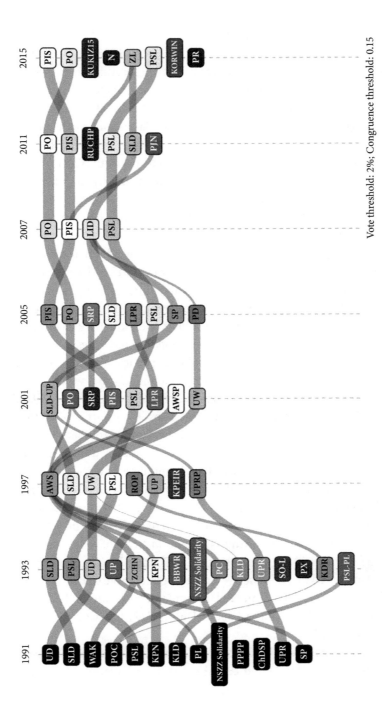

Figure 3.6 Tree of party evolution, Poland 1991–2015

Note: The thickness of lines between slates is proportional to their pairwise congruences. The shading behind party labels indicates candidate novelty: darker hues stand for higher novelty. The parties are ranked by their electoral results.

Vote threshold: 2%; Congruence threshold: 0.15

demonstrates that assigning only a single predecessor or successor for a slate can sometimes be highly problematic. Moreover, it highlights that party names are hardly a reliable means of identifying new or continuing parties: several slates that were significantly congruent to only one slate in the previous election changed their name in a way that would not necessarily suggest a continuation.

3.4 Conclusion

Political parties are nothing without the people involved—members, functionaries, leaders, and elected representatives all determine what parties are and what they stand for. The literature on party competition and party system change has mostly acknowledged this, yet generally still treats parties rather than sets of people as the main units of analysis. However, once we move away from analysing party change at the level of parties as 'political organisms' and focus on 'party genes' (people, specifically candidates) as an indicator and driver of these changes, we need to rethink established concepts and approaches. We introduced the theoretical considerations underpinning our 'genetic approach' in previous chapters, but shifting the perspective from the 'macro' to the 'micro' also requires new concepts, data, and methods.

In this chapter, we introduced our original ECCEE data set and explained how to make the most out of 'big but thin' data on electoral candidates. Second, we introduced two essential measures of candidate change in individual slates: candidate novelty, the share of new candidates who did not contest the previous election, and candidate dropout, the percentage of candidates who no longer run in the subsequent election. We also introduced a weighting scheme based on candidate prominence and slates' electoral support. Our brief analysis showed that overall, candidate turnover has not declined in Central and Eastern Europe since the early 1990s. However, we detected a decrease in turnover among continuing parties. This suggests that stability and instability go hand in hand: a 'subsystem' of persistent genuinely new party breakthroughs (Haughton & Deegan-Krause 2015) is balanced by increasing stability among the establishment. Finally, we introduced candidate congruence, a measure of overlap for pairs of slates in successive elections. In this chapter, we showed both how the new measures provide insights into the evolution of individual parties and how they can be used for an automated approach for drawing trees of party system evolution.

We hope that the discussions in this and the preceding chapter have not deterred the less technically inclined readers from following our argument. In the remainder of the book, we put these techniques into practice. We aim to keep our style as accessible as possible throughout, using relevant examples to illustrate the finer points of our analysis, and to keep it intelligible to those who may have skipped some of the formulas above. In the following chapters, we analyse the main determinants of candidate turnover (Chapter 4) and focus on candidate change and change at the level of party systems. We discuss how to use candidate novelty to distinguish between new, exiting, continuing, and partially new slates (Chapter 5), and how this can improve the measurement of electoral volatility (Chapter 6). The final three chapters of the book focus more on individual parties. We use measures of candidate turnover and slate congruence to study fission and fusion (Chapter 7) and examine the relationship between candidate turnover and changes in party leadership (Chapter 8), and policy orientation (Chapter 9).

3.5 Appendix: list placement, party size, and candidate novelty

If candidates in different list positions are different, we would also expect their novelty to vary. At the very basic level, we would expect the top candidates to be more 'important' to parties (and vice versa!) and we would hence expect them to stay put more often than lower-ranking candidates. Figure 3.7 suggests that this is very clearly the case in Estonia, chosen because of its fairly straightforward electoral system as well as the limited number of parties and complex cases. The lines for more established parties with low–medium candidate novelty slope upwards, i.e. candidate novelty increases as their list position deteriorates. We also see clear evidence of consolidation of established Estonian parties as the diagonal lines have been creeping gradually downwards over time. This pattern of increasing candidate novelty at lower ranks is also confirmed for the three partially novel parties in 1995 and even more clearly in 2015 (for discussion on partial novelty, see Chapter 5). The two genuinely new parties in 2003 and 2007 stand out as having an unusually high overall degree of candidate novelty.

To test the validity of our approach across the whole data set, we analyse the relationship between candidate novelty, their list placement, and slate size. First, we see that candidate novelty is overall lower among candidates with high relative list positions which indicates the percentage of candidates higher up on the list (left side of Figure 3.8a). Unsurprisingly, the average novelty depends on slate novelty. The lines of high and low novelty slates diverge for highly ranked candidates with low relative list placement on the left of

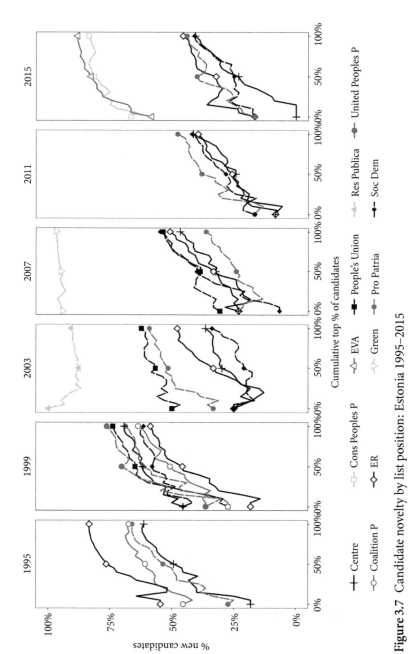

Figure 3.7 Candidate novelty by list position: Estonia 1995–2015

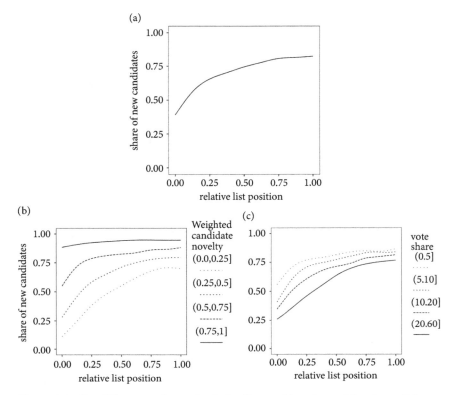

Figure 3.8 Candidate novelty and relative list position, by weighted candidate novelty and party size

Figure 3.8b: top candidates of high-novelty slates are considerably newer than those of medium- and low-novelty slates. The differences are less pronounced among low-ranking candidates.

Party size is negatively correlated with the share of new candidates (Figure 3.8c). Notably, the relative list position where the increase in novelty slows down depends on the slate size. For the largest slates (20% < v < 60%), the share of new candidates almost reaches its maximum level at $r = 0.6$. The increase in novelty slows down considerably at $r = 0.2$ for 2% < v < 20% (two groups in Figure 3.8c), and around 0.15 for the smallest ones. This lends support to our approach of candidate weighting: those with a higher likelihood of getting elected tend to be less novel.

Another way to test this argument is to look at the relationship between the ratio of the relative list placement to the slate's vote share (r/v) and the share of new candidates. We would expect the fastest increase in novelty to occur

MEASURES MATTER 67

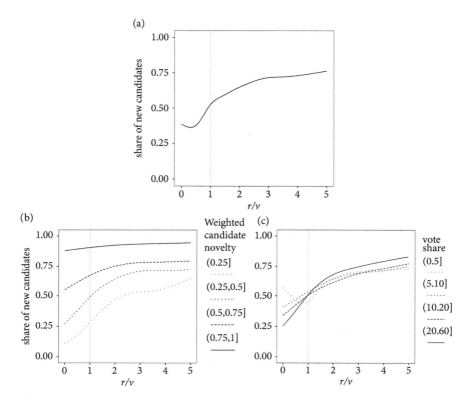

Figure 3.9 Candidate novelty and relative list position ratio to party vote share, by weighted candidate novelty and party size

around $r = v$, i.e. where the candidates are on a knife's edge of (not) getting elected. Figure 3.9 shows that candidate novelty increases fastest around the threshold for getting elected. This holds for parties at different levels of electoral support and across the different levels of overall novelty, apart from the genuinely new parties (novelty ≥ 0.75) whose candidates were new across the full range of r/v.

4
Determinants of candidate change

Candidate turnover between elections is inevitable. Many candidates run for office again, although not necessarily with the same set of people or in similar slates, to use our joint term for all electoral formations (parties, electoral coalitions, etc.). Others leave electoral politics voluntarily or involuntarily and are replaced by newcomers. Nevertheless, the rate of candidate change is not constant—periods of relative stability can alternate with major shifts—and does not affect all candidates and parties equally. Variation can be caused by internal party dynamics or external factors. Having outlined our perspective on candidate change and list formation in Chapter 2 and having presented our data and measures in Chapter 3, we now turn our attention to determinants of party change.

At the most basic level, candidate change is linked to the 'political life span' of candidates that determines the minimum rate of candidate replacement. As elaborated in our theoretical model in Chapter 2, turnover should vary considerably between 'feasible' candidates, i.e. those in electable positions, and their 'non-feasible' running mates. Larger parties with greater electoral appeal offer a larger number of promising positions, they have more feasible candidates and should experience lower rates of turnover than smaller parties. We find that the levels of candidate turnover are indeed different among feasible and non-feasible candidates and both candidate novelty and dropout are therefore significantly lower in larger slates. When parties experience increasing or decreasing levels of popular support this should affect candidates' incentives to return, join, or leave; similarly, it should affect parties' incentives to keep, attract, or repel them. We show that changes in party support are strongly correlated with levels of candidate novelty and dropout, although the patterns are different for the two types of turnover. Specifically, the absolute magnitude of change matters for dropout: we find similar levels of candidate dropout to be associated with vote increases and decreases of the same magnitude. In contrast, only increasing vote shares are associated with higher levels of novelty; here, parties that lose votes are similar to those with stable popularity. These results lend support to the key argument of this book: the level of candidate change provides useful insights into the working of political parties and party change in general.

The second part of the chapter suggests a practical application by examining other predictors of candidate change. Scholarship on Central and East European (CEE) party systems often emphasizes the importance of corruption as a driver of electoral change (Charron & Bågenholm 2016; Engler 2016; Hanley & Sikk 2016; Kostadinova 2009; Snegovaya 2020). Building on these insights, we analyse the impact of corruption perception on candidate turnover by testing two competing hypotheses: (1) rejuvenation, whereby increased corruption perception triggers renewal of candidate lists; and (2) renomination, whereby corruption leads to stagnation and the return of old candidates at the next election. Our preliminary findings are promising: increasing perception of corruption is associated with increased candidate dropout among governing parties. Moreover we find that economic growth attenuates candidate turnover among governing parties. Although a comprehensive analysis of determinants of candidate change and party change is beyond the scope of this book, this chapter offers a glimpse into the inter-electoral black box of candidate list formation (see Chapter 2) and illustrates how candidate change is associated with socio-economic developments.

A final note: attentive readers may already have noticed a subtle change in terminology in this chapter from 'slates' (a term for which we made a case in Chapters 2 and 3) to 'parties'. The reason lies in the definition of 'slates': an electoral list put forward by a political party or an alliance of parties (or any other political association) in one election. Hence, we cannot talk about 'slate vote change' as, strictly speaking, they exist for one election only; this chapter mostly focuses on parties that contest consecutive elections. However, we use slate congruences (introduced in Chapter 3) for estimating party vote changes between elections where party continuities are hard to pin down and may be overlooked in data sets on parties and electoral results. We extend this approach in Chapter 6, proposing a new method for the calculation of electoral volatility.

4.1 Party size, vote change, and candidate turnover

Party size is an obvious potential determinant of candidate turnover. In Chapter 2, we developed a basic model of candidate change that (a) derives the expected 'natural rate' of change based on the political 'life expectancy' of candidates, and (b) distinguishes between 'feasible' and 'non-feasible' candidates. Feasible candidates with a prospect of re-election can be expected to return to electoral lists in significantly greater numbers than non-feasible candidates. Given that larger parties have a greater number of feasible candidates than smaller ones, we predict higher levels of candidate turnover among parties with high vote shares than those with more limited electoral support. For the smallest of parties, we expect the average candidate turnover to be between 50% and 100% (see final sections of Chapter 2 for a fuller discussion), gradually decreasing for larger parties, reaching 7.7% for a hypothetical party that wins all votes and only features feasible candidates who are expected to change at the rate of natural replacement.

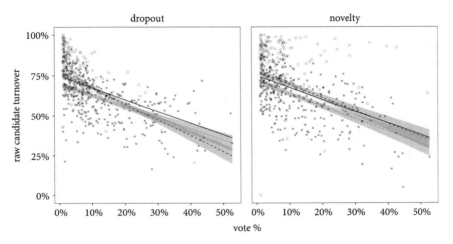

Figure 4.1 Electoral support and raw candidate turnover

Notes: solid line: theoretical expectation with feasible candidate turnover of 7.7% and non-feasible candidate turnover of 75%; dashed line: linear fit; dotted line: linear fit excluding slates without successors (for dropout) or predecessors (novelty); hollow markers: slates without easily identifiable successors/predecessors.

This baseline model is empirically substantiated in Figure 4.1 and Table 4.1. While there is variation around the central estimates, large slates experience substantially lower levels of raw (i.e. unweighted by candidate prominence) candidate dropout and novelty. The constants in Table 4.1 estimate turnover in slates made up exclusively of non-feasible candidates (all candidates approach non-feasibility as v approaches 0) and suggest a non-feasible candidate turnover around 75%, halfway between our two suggestions in Chapter 2. According to the regression models, the feasible candidate turnover (all candidates are feasible when $v = 1$), is around zero but not statistically significantly below the theoretically predicted 7.7% (except for model 3). Still, all extrapolations need to be taken with a pinch of salt as $v = 1$ is well outside the actual range of data. The estimates confirm our theoretical expectations even better in models that exclude small slates ($v < 5\%$, models 2 and 4).[1] These results, overall, corroborate our notions of feasible and non-feasible candidates and expectations of different rates of turnover among the groups; it also buttresses our formula for candidate weighting (Chapter 3) which assigns higher weights to feasible candidates.

Table 4.1 Electoral support and raw candidate turnover

	Raw novelty		Raw dropout	
	(1) $v \geq 1\%$	(2) $v \geq 5\%$	(3) $v \geq 1\%$	(4) $v \geq 5\%$
Vote	−0.82*** (0.07)	−0.69*** (0.10)	−1.00*** (0.06)	−0.73*** (0.07)
Constant	0.78*** (0.01)	0.75*** (0.02)	0.77*** (0.01)	0.71*** (0.01)
N	475	292	501	295
R^2	0.21	0.15	0.38	0.28

Notes: *p <.05; **p < .01; ***p < .001. Standard errors in parentheses.

The linear best-fit lines for candidate turnover are affected by genuinely new and genuinely disappearing parties. The line for candidate novelty, in particular, is pulled up by genuinely new political parties with many political novices as candidates, hovering at the top of the right panel in Figure 4.1. A considerable number of mostly small parties had no easily identifiable successor and pull up the linear fit line for candidate dropout (hollow markers in Figure 4.1). Identifying party continuities in CEE is a complicated task that will be discussed in some detail in Chapters 5 and 6. Here, we identify successors and predecessors using a 'three-code' strategy based on (a) party abbreviation, (b) party code in the MARPOR (Volkens et al. 2020), or (c) party code in the ParlGov database (Döring et al. 2022). We consider a party to continue if it is suggested by any of the three codes. The linear fit lines that exclude non-continuous parties (dotted lines in Figure 4.1) remain very close to our theoretical expectations and are, interestingly, virtually identical for candidate novelty and dropout.

The baseline model developed in Chapter 2 and empirically tested above considers the overall or raw candidate turnover without considering candidate importance. In the rest of the book, we are using the weighted versions of candidate novelty and dropout as introduced in Chapter 3. This assigns

---

[1] A regression model weighted by vote share—giving higher weight to larger slates that are much rarer than tiny ones and—would suggest a clearly positive turnover rate for feasible candidates.

higher weights to candidates with a higher list or district placement, i.e. those who are more feasible.[2] We expect the relationship between party size and weighted turnover to be more muted although not entirely absent. As discussed in the closing section of Chapter 2, large parties may be overall less susceptible to change and a stronger electoral potential carries the promise of attractive positions on electoral lists and jobs in government or party structures (Poguntke et al. 2020). Candidates are, therefore, more likely to return regardless of their immediate feasibility. Vice versa, smaller parties are likely to face higher candidate turnover because of meagre electoral and job prospects. Logged party size does, indeed, affect weighted candidate turnover, particularly dropout (Figure 4.2), possibly because of the reasons mentioned above but also because the highest-ranking candidates always contribute to the weighted turnover indices even though they are, practically speaking, non-feasible in smaller parties. Weighted turnover is nominally lower than raw turnover because feasible candidates, who are less likely to be newcomers or dropouts, carry more weight.

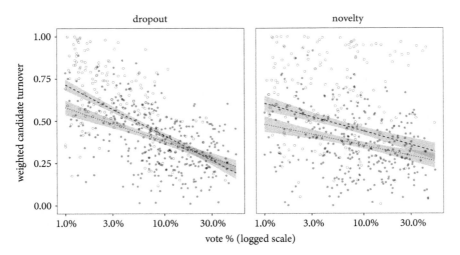

Figure 4.2 Electoral support and weighted candidate turnover
Notes: dashed line: linear fit; dotted line: linear fit excluding slates without successors (for dropout) or predecessors (novelty); hollow markers: slates without easily identifiable successors/predecessors.

The linear fit lines for weighted turnover change again (as they did for raw turnover) when we exclude slates with no easily identifiable successor or predecessor based on the three-code method described above (hollow markers in

---

[2] See Chapter 3 for details of the weighting scheme for single mandate district candidates in the mixed systems in Hungary and Lithuania.

Figure 4.2). However, Figure 4.2 also highlights some slates with remarkably low candidate turnover but without an identifiable successor or predecessor. This shows, on the one hand, the limitations of the three-code method: while the codes in the MARPOR and ParlGov databases flag continuities, their aim is not necessarily to flag *all* continuities. On the other hand, some continuities are evasive or debatable, especially where parties have split, merged, formed electoral coalitions, or have otherwise transformed. Continuities may be hard to spot for small parties that have found their way into the data sets. Distinguishing between continuing and non-continuing parties can be difficult (see Chapter 5), but many of the slates near the floor of Figure 4.2 were clearly not new or did not exit from electoral politics.

We can also expect the change in parties' electoral fortunes to influence candidate turnover. Increasing popularity makes parties more attractive to new entrants while a changed candidate line-up may also attract new voters. Equally, shrinking parties may struggle to attract new candidates or keep existing ones from leaving the sinking ship. Electoral losses can also lead to substantial transformations in other dimensions which, in turn, creates a potential for further change.[3]

Precise expectations on the link between changes in electoral support and candidate turnover are difficult to outline. On the one hand, we expect that increased electoral support attracts new candidates; on the other hand, the anticipation of enhanced electoral prospects could make old candidates more likely to stay and leave less room for newcomers. We expect more candidates to leave parties losing electoral support but, as their attractiveness to new incoming candidates should also be limited, the leavers are more likely to be replaced by previously running candidates further down the list. The relationship can also run in the opposite direction—parties can increase support because of attractive new candidates or lose support because of the dropout of certain candidates.

For the analysis of party support change, we look at the ratio between party vote share in a pair of consecutive elections (v_t/v_{t-1}). We analyse the impact of changes in electoral support on candidate turnover among continuing parties going beyond the 'three code approach' that overlooks some important continuities and very occasionally misidentifies successors

---

[3] Various other factors can affect candidate turnover: party change on other dimensions or changes in the institutional environment such as the electoral system or gender quotas (Aldrich & Daniel 2020; Gwiazda 2017). Also, the time between elections is positively associated with the turnover of MPs (Gouglas et al. 2020; Matland & Studlar 2004; Norris & Lovenduski 1995). However, exploring the full range of determinants is outside the scope of this volume.

or predecessors. Instead, we impute vote shares for slates—electoral formations in a given election—with successors (for novelty) or predecessors (for dropout) identified based on candidate congruences (explained in detail in Chapter 3), that in some cases involve combining or splitting the vote shares of multiple predecessors or successors. In contrast to the models for party size, we omit genuinely new and genuinely exiting parties, i.e. those without congruent slates in the preceding or subsequent election.

Figure 4.3 plots weighted candidate novelty and dropout against the vote change ratio. For ease of interpretation, we have logged the vote change ratio so that the absolute value of vote gains would equal that of vote losses: e.g. $\log_{10}(20/10) = -\log_{10}(10/20) = 0.301$. We only include parties with $\min(v_t, v_{t-1}) \geq 5$ to avoid the overpopulation of the extreme ends of the scale by small parties with high ratios but trivial changes in support.

The local estimated smooth (loess) patterns in Figure 4.3 suggest that the impact of party support change is different on candidate dropout and novelty. Both positive and negative changes in party vote share increase candidate dropout. Therefore, we use the absolute value of the logged ratio of vote shares in a pair of elections in our regression models (Table 4.2). In contrast, candidate novelty only increases when party popularity rises; vote losses are not systematically associated with candidate turnover. Therefore, in candidate

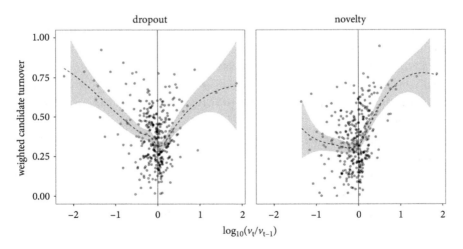

Figure 4.3 Electoral support change and weighted candidate turnover
Notes: dashed lines show loess fits.

Table 4.2 Electoral support change and weighted candidate turnover

	Weighted novelty		Weighted dropout	
	(1)	(2)	(3)	(4)
$\log_{10} v$	−16.6*** (2.51)	−8.57*** (2.28)	−30.3*** (1.79)	−15.9*** (2.72)
zerofloor$(\log_{10}(v_t/v_{t-1}))$[a]		42.2*** (4.44)		
abs$(\log_{10}(v_t/v_{t-1}))$				18.0*** (2.89)
Constant	60.4*** (2.34)	40.2*** (2.38)	71.4*** (1.62)	49.9*** (3.33)
N	474	317	499	317
R^2	0.083	0.229	0.365	0.262

Notes: *p < .05; **p < .01; ***p < .001. Standard errors in parentheses. Parties with $v \geq 5\%$ in t_0 or t_1.

[a] $zerofloor(x) = \begin{cases} x \text{ if } x \geq 0 \\ 0 \text{ if } x < 0 \end{cases}$

novelty models, we use a 'floored' transformation where reduced vote shares are levelled up to 0 (i.e. $v_t/v_{t-1} = 1$).

Regression models for party size and change in electoral support using weighted turnover (Table 4.2) continue to suggest that larger slates experience less turnover. The predicted novelty decreases from 34% to 26% for slates with 5% and 50% of votes, respectively. Candidate dropout decreases even more substantially from 39% to 23% (model 3). Changes in party vote share yield a considerable additional effect. Controlling for slate size ($v = 15\%$), novelty drops from 37% when party support stays stable to 31% when it doubles or halves (model 4). Changing electoral fortunes have an even stronger impact on candidate novelty: the model suggests 45% for parties that double their support compared to 30% for those that fail to increase their vote share (model 2).

We suspect that candidate novelty, unlike dropout, is immune to vote losses because fresh candidates are less likely to be attracted by ailing or stagnant formations. Hence, when party support wanes, winnable list positions become scarcer and even though more candidates drop out, the old guard clings on to the remaining attractive spots. Alternatively (or additionally), parties that fail to rejuvenate their candidate lists may be less attractive to voters. A similar logic would also explain the elevated levels of dropout among parties with *either* decreasing or increasing popularity: the loss of support can repel existing candidates or candidate flight can signal weakness to voters; conversely, the pruning of candidate lists can help parties to win over voters; this argument is corroborated by our analysis of the impact of corruption below.

While electoral support and vote change clearly impact candidate turnover, other party-external determinants also deserve our attention. In the remainder of this chapter, we first discuss push-and-pull factors behind candidate change at a theoretical level. We then assess empirically to what extent change in socio-economic factors—perceptions of corruption, GDP, and unemployment—affects parties and is associated with candidate change.

4.2 Corruption and socio-economic factors as drivers of candidate change

The nomination of candidates for public office is one of the core functions of political parties and other electoral formations (Gallagher & Marsh 1988; Hazan & Rahat 2010; Lundell 2004; Rahat 2007). In Chapter 2, we conceptualized this 'slate-making' as an iterative process involving two sets of active agents doing their bidding: (a) potential candidates and (b) parties or proto-slates, i.e. electoral lists in the making. For candidates, running again is usually the default option but its attractiveness may change as parties change, e.g. as their electoral support rises or falls. Similarly, the attractiveness of candidates to their running mates can fluctuate over time—highly publicized scandals can quickly turn hot assets into liabilities, but other kinds of political, economic, and societal changes can affect the calculations of candidates and running mates alike.

In modern democracies, regular elections serve as a crucial accountability mechanism, allowing the public to evaluate their representatives. Voters can reward parties and candidates for good performance or to punish them, for example, for failing to deliver on campaign promises (McDonald & Budge 2005), or scandals and revelations of malfeasance and corruption (Bågenholm 2013b). Several studies have analysed the electoral impact of corruption and the effectiveness of elections as mechanisms of vertical accountability (Costas-Pérez et al. 2012; Ferraz & Finan 2008; Peters & Welch 1980). Voters' perceptions of corruption in political parties have been shown to determine voting behaviour (Deegan-Krause et al. 2011; Ecker et al. 2016; Slomczynski & Shabad 2012), and high and rising levels of perceived corruption have been crucial for the breakthrough of new anti-establishment parties in CEE (Hanley & Sikk 2016). This suggests that the perceptions of corruption may also lead parties to change their candidate line-ups. However, comparative large-N studies on this topic are rare (Bågenholm 2013b remains an exception), and we know little about the impact of corruption on candidates before parties face voters at the polls.

Parties can respond to rising levels of corruption in two equally plausible ways. The first of these is a strategy of *rejuvenation*, i.e. a large-scale renewal of candidate lists. Voters are, *ceteris paribus*, more likely to vote for less corrupt parties and candidates. Therefore, both parties and candidates should try to appear as 'clean' as possible.[4] Parties can most visibly distance themselves from corruption by 'throwing out the rascals'. Since voters tend to blame individual politicians rather than parties for corruption (Slomczynski & Shabad 2012), replacing old and ostensibly corrupt candidates can be an effective way for a party to distance itself from the sins of its former corps. Clean candidates can also distance themselves from tainted parties by joining different slates or leaving electoral politics altogether.

Despite some mixed findings from Italy (Asquer 2014, 2015; Chang et al. 2010), the idea that corruption drives turnover among candidate slates has been supported by studies of the 2009 UK expenses scandal (Eggers & Fisher 2011; Larcinese & Sircar 2017; Pattie & Johnston 2012) and corruption scandals involving members of the US Congress (Banducci & Karp 1994; Basinger 2013). Moreover, the offering of novel candidates untainted by scandals has associated with the success of new anti-corruption and anti-establishment parties (Bågenholm 2013a; Bågenholm & Charron 2014, 2015; Bochsler & Hänni 2022; Engler 2016, 2020; Engler et al. 2019; Hanley & Sikk 2016). Even when scandals do not directly implicate a party or its candidates, voter perceptions of increasing corruption and malfeasance should still induce parties to drop old candidates or introduce new faces (or both) to boost their electoral chances. This leads to our rejuvenation hypothesis: *rising corruption perceptions are associated with increased candidate turnover as parties refresh their candidate lists by introducing new faces or dropping old ones.*

The second possible strategy for parties in the face of rising corruption is *renomination* i.e. filling candidate slots with loyal existing cadres. The underlying logic of this strategy stems from the fact that electoral list positions—especially the safe ones—are scarce commodities. In highly institutionalized parties, these are often awarded for long-term commitment to the party, involvement in grassroots activism, canvassing, committee work, etc. (Gallagher & Marsh 1988; Manow 2013; Norris 1997). As parties become more institutionalized, such traditional recruitment channels become stronger and

---

[4] Programmatic reorientation or organizational changes such as relabelling, or splits and mergers can also help to cleanse one's image.

more stable (Bolleyer & Bytzek 2013; Pettai & Kreuzer 1999). However, strong institutionalization can also constrain political recruitment by reinforcing clientelist practices within parties, which in turn are often associated with political corruption. For candidate recruitment, this can mean that parties trade attractive list positions for favours or clientelistic or corrupt revenues instead of making meritocratic appointments (Protsyk & Matichescu 2011). This puts candidates with more limited resources at a disadvantage compared to those with wealth or influence. Most importantly for our purposes, returning candidates are at an advantage because they are most likely to command resources (e.g. through clientelist channels) for the benefit of the party.

Rising corruption may also reduce parties' incentives to replace old candidates for other reasons. While a new set of candidates may be attractive to voters, even implicated incumbents outperform new candidates due to name recognition, track record of electoral success, and the incumbency effect (Larcinese & Sircar 2017). Meanwhile, the departure or removal of old candidates following corruption scandals may be seen as an admission of guilt by the party, further highlighting inappropriate practices and deterring voters. Furthermore, as MPs often enjoy immunity from prosecution that can only be lifted by a parliamentary majority, parties may seek to protect their own by keeping them in safe list positions (Protsyk & Matichescu 2011). Finally, even if parties see advantages in introducing new candidates, as perceptions of corruption increase, parties may struggle to attract new 'clean' candidates. Hence, parties may have to stick with existing candidates as they cannot—rather than will not—rejuvenate under increasing corruption. This leads to our renomination hypothesis: *increasing perceptions of corruption are associated with a decrease in candidate turnover as parties protect incumbents and the pool of 'clean' candidates is limited.*

Overall, government participation is likely to amplify the effects of rising levels of corruption. On the one hand, ruling parties have ample opportunities to engage in clientelist exchanges, reproducing corrupt networks, and favouring renomination over rejuvenation. On the other hand, governing parties should also face greater pressure to renew their slates when perceptions of corruption increase. Ecker et al. (2016) argue that voters evaluate governing parties not only on the basis of economic performance (economy, unemployment rate, etc.) but also on corruption performance. This should be particularly relevant in CEE where corruption tends to be one of the most important issues for voters (see also Singer 2011: 293). Therefore, ruling parties will be under particular pressure to renominate or rejuvenate. Not only do they have access to public goods but they also have the power to prevent their misuse for private gain. High or rising levels of corruption will increase the pressure on these parties either to rejuvenate their candidate lists in anticipation of electoral punishment or to renominate candidates in order to benefit from their resources and shield them from prosecution.

Finally, we expect socio-economic factors to have a broadly similar impact as changes in corruption perceptions. Deteriorating conditions lead potential candidates to expect a decline in governing party's popularity and make them less likely to join their electoral lists. However, existing cadres need more secure list placements for the same reason, but also because opportunities outside of politics may deteriorate in a negative economic climate.

4.3 Analysing determinants of candidate turnover

In this section, we build upon the models discussed above to analyse a fuller model of candidate turnover that incorporates the impact of corruption and socio-economic variables. We start by discussing variable measurement, then consider the bivariate relationship between corruption performance and candidate turnover, and finish with multiple regression models.

The measurement of weighted candidate turnover was discussed in Chapter 2 and we outlined our approach to party size and party vote change variables earlier in this chapter. We measure perceived levels of corruption using Transparency International's corruption perception index (CPI). We calculate weighted averages of CPI in the election year and the preceding year so that the more recent index gains gradually more weight over the course of the year. Although the index does not necessarily reflect 'real' levels of corruption or clientelism, it is arguably a meaningful indicator of societal perceptions of such exchanges, including among political parties. We analyse both the level of CPI and the change in CPI over an electoral term.[5] Hanley and Sikk (2016) demonstrate that socioeconomic developments affect the chances of new party breakthroughs. Even though these are not the main factors of interest in this chapter, we tentatively expect them to influence levels of candidate turnover and include unemployment and GDP per capita change in our models as control variables. We incorporate the percentage point change in the unemployment rate and the rate of economic growth (GDP per

---

[5] We cannot include all elections as CPI changed methodology after 2012, making the more recent indices not comparable to earlier ones. However, we use CPI as it is more sensitive to changes in corruption perception than potential alternatives that often show very limited or no changes between elections (e.g. the V-Dem index of political corruption or the World Bank control of corruption index).

capita) over an electoral term, both weighted by the month of election similarly to CPI.

As discussed above, we expect the impact of corruption and socio-economic factors to be mediated by parties' participation in government. In CEE, parties have often switched in and out of governing coalitions during a parliamentary term, particularly in the early years of democratization. A simple dummy variable for all parties that have been present in the government over the legislative term cannot always adequately capture how involved a party was in executive affairs. Some only count parties that were included in government in the run-up to elections (see Bågenholm 2013b) but that can leave out important governing parties during a parliamentary term. Therefore, we coded the governing status for all parties using data from the ParlGov database (Döring et al. 2022), adding data on portfolio allocation for each government from the EJPR's *Political Data Yearbook*, Blondel and Müller-Rommel (2001), and Ismayr (2010). On that basis, we constructed a measure of weighted cabinet participation that ranges from 0 (no portfolios held during the parliamentary term) to 1 (the party held all portfolios), depreciated by the time between when a party was in government and elections so that participation towards the end of the parliamentary term carried more weight than participation at the beginning of the term (see Sikk & Köker 2016: 27 for further technical details). In the current analysis, we use a 0.1 threshold of weighted cabinet membership, hence including all large or long-term cabinet parties but excluding some marginal governing parties, those with a short government tenure or one limited to an early part of an electoral term.

Table 4.3 shows descriptive statistics for variables included in our regression models, broken down by governing status of parties. Governing parties experienced lower levels of candidate change than other parties with a candidate novelty of 28.7 (in contrast to 38.8 for non-governing parties) and an average dropout of 33.7 (40.8). This suggests some support for the renomination hypothesis or at least that parties that managed to enter the government were attractive enough to retain their candidates and rely less on the influx of new people. While the average vote shares of governing and non-governing parties are similar, the average levels of vote change are markedly lower for governing parties. The average logged ratio of vote change of governing parties was around −0.2, corresponding to a loss of about one-third of votes. This aligns with the previously identified phenomenon of hyper-accountability in CEE where governing parties have incurred a significant lump 'cost of ruling' regardless of their success in governing (Roberts 2008). Non-governing parties only saw very slight increases in voter support on average.

Table 4.3 Descriptive statistics

	N	Mean	SD	Min	Max
CPI change	81	1.72	6.06	−12.09	13.40
CPI	81	49.64	8.50	34.27	66.73
GDP change	81	1.16	0.16	0.90	1.50
Unemployment change	81	−0.24	5.01	−7.62	11.55

	\multicolumn{4}{c}{Governing parties}		\multicolumn{4}{c}{Non-governing parties}
Novelty models	N	Mean	SD	Min	Max	N	Mean	SD	Min	Max
Weighted novelty	81	28.69	15.72	1.90	66.60	115	38.81	18.27	3.76	94.77
$\log_{10} v$	81	0.99	0.43	−0.19	1.65	115	1.01	0.35	−0.19	1.72
zerofloor($\log_{10}(v_t/v_{t-1})$)	81	−0.21	0.32	−1.16	0.25	115	0.049	0.35	−0.99	1.87

Dropout models	\multicolumn{4}{c}{Governing parties}		\multicolumn{4}{c}{Non-governing parties}
	N	Mean	SD	Min	Max	N	Mean	SD	Min	Max
Weighted dropout	86	33.72	17.13	1.51	84.46	106	40.78	18.29	1.95	92.44
$9\log_{10} v$	86	1.19	0.26	0.72	1.72	106	0.98	0.39	−0.96	1.63
abs($\log_{10}(v_t/v_{t-1})$)	86	−0.20	0.32	−1.25	0.34	106	0.0048	0.42	−1.74	1.87

As suggested above, the dynamics of candidate turnover in governing and non-governing parties can differ, and therefore, we run regression models separately for the two groups of parties. To avoid our data being contaminated by numerous small extra-parliamentary parties, we only include those that won at least 5% of votes. This decision is also supported by our finding in earlier analyses (see above) that candidate novelty is strongly dependent on other variables, particularly party size and vote change that we include in the models as controls.[6]

In the bivariate analysis, the change in corruption perception only appears to affect candidate dropout among governing parties (Figure 4.4b) with

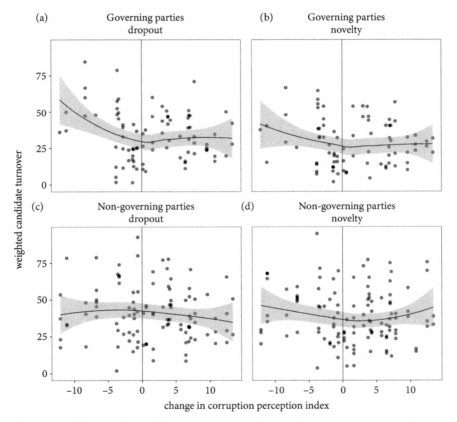

Figure 4.4 Weighted candidate turnover and change in corruption perception
Notes: black lines show loess fits. Slates with no identified successor/predecessor excluded

---

[6] For novelty analysis, we use the vote share in the more recent one in a pair of elections. For dropout analysis, we use the earlier election, i.e. when the candidates who dropped out used to run. While we might be even more interested in the vote share in the more recent election, determining these vote shares is often impossible because of the fluidity of CEE party systems.

no clear effect on other parties. Furthermore, only rising corruption seems to increase governing party candidate dropout while it is not affected by improved corruption perceptions. Therefore, we recode in regression models any CPI increases (i.e. decreasing perceptions of corruption) to zero. This 'zeroceil(ing)' function is similar to the 'zerofloor' function that we use for vote change and candidate novelty.

According to our multiple regression models (Table 4.4), deteriorating corruption perception (i.e. decline in CPI) increases candidate dropout among governing parties; a ten-point decrease in CPI over an electoral term—close to the maximum change in the data set—increases dropout by a notable 10%. This finding lends support to our rejuvenation hypothesis, whereby governing parties respond to increased perceptions of corruption by replacing their candidates or candidates themselves react by leaving electoral slates. The effect is considerably noisier for novelty but still points in the same direction. Remarkably, a similar mild effect materializes for novelty among opposition parties: increased corruption perception increases the share of new candidates. This is possibly because corruption not only provides a platform for new anti-establishment parties (Hanley & Sikk 2016) but also for political novices entering existing opposition parties and partially new parties (see Chapter 5).

The level of CPI is mildly statistically significant for candidate novelty (model 1 in Table 4.4) and a ten-point difference in CPI (roughly its standard deviation) decreases novelty by almost four percentage points. The coefficient for dropout (model 3) has a similar magnitude and standard error while it is only slightly less statistically different ($p = 0.064$ vs $p = 0.046$); the standard thresholds of statistical significance do not do justice to the similarity of the effect here. This suggests that for governing parties, lower levels of corruption overall (i.e. higher CPI) are associated with a more open and competitive environment that allows for more candidate turnover; no effect materializes for opposition parties.

The effect of GDP change on governing parties is similar to that of CPI change: an improved economic outlook lowers candidate turnover. The effect is clearer for dropout than for novelty (model 1 vs model 3 in Table 4.4) although the coefficient for novelty is still borderline statistically significant ($p = 0.068$). Economic growth of 10% over an electoral period—well within the actual range of the variable—compared to a standstill would reduce candidate turnover by about three percentage points among governing parties while the impact on opposition parties is negligible.

Table 4.4 Determinants of weighted candidate turnover

	Weighted novelty Governing parties (1)	Weighted novelty Non-governing parties (2)	Weighted dropout Governing parties (3)	Weighted dropout Non-governing parties (4)
zeroceil(CPI change)[a]	−1.00 (0.66)	−1.32** (0.50)	−1.94** (0.61)	−0.22 (0.53)
CPI	0.39* (0.19)	0.27 (0.18)	0.35 (0.18)	−0.18 (0.19)
GDP change	−27.36 (14.79)	15.00 (13.58)	−32.22* (14.13)	−7.90 (15.40)
Unemployment change	−0.23 (0.49)	−0.24 (0.45)	−1.14* (0.48)	−0.28 (0.48)
$\log_{10} v$	−8.27** (3.92)	−12.67** (4.02)	−3.51 (5.82)	−16.26*** (4.78)
zerofloor($\log_{10}(v_t/v_{t-1})$)[b]	83.67** (28.76)	36.23*** (5.36)		
abs($\log_{10}(v_t/v_{t-1})$)			25.33*** (6.19)	15.41** (5.58)
Constant	44.89* (19.77)	13.85 (18.77)	48.02* (20.91)	70.18** (20.79)
N	81	115	86	106
R^2	0.26	0.36	0.41	0.32

Notes: *p<0.05; **p<0.01; ***p<0.001. Standard errors in parentheses.

[a] $zeroceil(x) = \begin{cases} x \text{ if } x < 0 \\ 0 \text{ if } x \geq 0 \end{cases}$

[b] $zerofloor(x) = \begin{cases} x \text{ if } x \geq 0 \\ 0 \text{ if } x < 0 \end{cases}$

Interestingly, the change in unemployment) has only a slight impact on governing party candidate dropout (but none on novelty) and in a counterintuitive direction: a massive, ten-percentage-point increase in unemployment levels would reduce dropout by about eleven percentage points, but the standard error of the estimate is high. The relationship between unemployment and party system change can be complex. Previous research has shown that it can either boost new anti-establishment parties or curtail them, presumably because voters err on the safe side (Hanley & Sikk 2016). We speculate that candidate dropout may decrease under increasing levels of unemployment because it affects candidates' career prospects outside of politics; therefore, established candidates may prefer to stick to politics under poor labour market conditions.

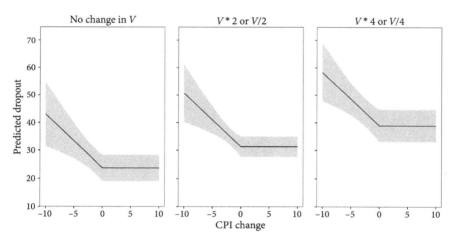

Figure 4.5 Predicted effect of CPI change and vote change on weighted dropout in governing parties

Notes: based on model 3 in Table 4.4; $v = 15\%$, other variables are set at means. The panel variable refers to the ratio of vote shares in two elections: $v_t/v_{t-1} = 1$ (i.e. no change); $v_t/v_{t-1} = 2$ or $v_{t-1}/v_t = 2$ (i.e. a doubling or halving of the vote share), $v_t/v_{t-1} = 4$ or $v_{t-1}/v_t = 4$ (a fourfold increase or decrease).

The effects of party size and vote swings—the basic determinants of candidate turnover discussed at the beginning of this chapter—hold up in models with corruption and socioeconomic developments. The bigger the swing in party popularity—regardless of the direction—the higher the candidate dropout; however, only increased popularity increases candidate novelty.[7]

---

[7] We make no strict assumptions about the direction of causality: high candidate novelty (inclusion of new, presumably attractive, faces) can increase party popularity and high dropout can lead to *either* increased or decreased popularity (depending on whether the exiting candidates were popular or unpopular).

Notably, the coefficients for vote change variables are higher for governing than for non-governing parties: i.e. governing parties are more responsive or vulnerable to swings in popularity. Governing parties on the rise could be more open and enticing to new candidates. They are likely to re-enter the cabinet after elections, providing opportunities for jobs and access to power, making it easier for the old guard to accept newcomers. It is also understandable that languishing parties—whether in opposition or government—may not be particularly attractive to new candidates. The effect on governing parties is particularly robust on candidate dropout (see Figure 4.5), which more than doubles when we compare a party significantly losing votes under severely increased corruption to one with stable electoral support under improved or stable CPI. Deteriorating electoral prospects make returning to the ballot less attractive and, under increasing perceptions of corruption, parties are also more likely to purge tainted candidates.

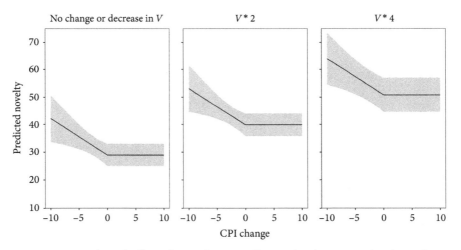

Figure 4.6 Predicted effect of CPI change and vote change on weighted novelty in non-governing parties

Notes: based on model 2 in Table 4.3; v = 15%, other variables are set at means. The panel variable refers to $v_t/v_{t-1} = \{1; 2; 4\}$ where 1 refers to no decline in vote shares (note the zerofloor function used in models in Table 4.4); 2 to a doubling of the vote share, and 4 to a fourfold increase.

When it comes to candidate novelty, the combined effect of party vote change and CPI change is particularly robust for non-governing parties (see Figure 4.6). It is obvious why new candidates might be attracted to up-and-coming opposition parties for which fighting corruption is often a key manifesto pledge. The parties can be less tainted than governing parties by corruption allegations because of their limited access to relevant networks alone.

Ultimately, they are likely to be governing parties in waiting which makes it more palatable for existing elites to accept newcomers as enhanced prospects offer a promise of more abundant parliamentary seats and jobs within the gift of parties. In a virtuous circle, the inflow of new faces themselves can also improve parties' electoral prospects.

Party size retains the effect seen in more limited models, but it becomes weaker for governing parties, which can largely be explained by the narrower range of electoral strength: large parties are much more likely than small parties to enter government (see Table 4.3). Even though larger parties may have a larger pool of potential candidates—that could increase dropout as candidates are easier to replace—they often also have a stronger party organization and more developed hierarchy. These, in turn, favour the nomination of party elites or tighten their grip on the process, which can benefit existing candidates.

4.3 Conclusion

What have we learned in this chapter about the determinants of candidate turnover? First, we have shown that party size and vote changes affect levels of overall candidate turnout. Larger parties tend to be considerably more stable than their smaller counterparts owing to (the theoretically expected) differential turnover of feasible and non-feasible candidates, i.e. among those with a realistic chance of getting elected and among those with dim prospects. However, the impact of party size persists when we consider weighted candidate turnover that assigns higher weights to the most feasible candidates and lower weights to non-feasible ones (see Chapter 3 for the discussion of our weighting method). Larger parties tend to have lower levels of candidate turnover than small parties; possibly owing to their better chances of parliamentary representation and holding executive office, larger parties offer better long-term electoral and political office prospects even for non-feasible candidates. The effect is more pronounced for candidate dropout than for novelty, i.e. while large parties attract electoral newcomers at somewhat lower rates than small parties, candidates running in small slates are considerably more likely to leave electoral politics than those running for larger ones. We propose this may be because even those large party candidates who fail to get elected are more integrated into party structures and may be holding non-parliamentary offices, or are content with waiting for their turn until more highly ranked candidates retire. This argument is further supported by the fact that governing parties have lower levels of candidate turnover than non-governing parties and are more immune to the effect of party size, again, particularly regarding candidate dropout.

We also find that candidate turnover is associated with changes in parties' electoral support. Improved electoral fortunes are associated with both increasing novelty and dropout but increased candidate novelty is only associated with improved electoral performance while any vote losses or stable support are associated with similar lower levels of turnover. Furthermore, governing parties are more responsive than non-governing parties to changes in their electoral fortunes, both in terms of candidate novelty and dropout.

Second, alongside party size and changes in their electoral support, socioeconomic conditions, and changes in corruption perception also matter. We found that increased societal perception of corruption leads to higher candidate dropout among governing parties which suggests that the logic of rejuvenation prevails over renomination. As expected, governing parties are generally impacted more strongly because corruption is associated primarily with those in government; they also bear the brunt of the blame for macroeconomic difficulties and can claim credit when things are looking up. Determining which governing parties the voters hold accountable is complicated in countries with multi-party cabinets (most of our cases), a problem highlighted in the rich 'clarity of responsibility' literature on economic voting (see Anderson 2000; Hobolt et al. 2013; Royed et al. 2000; Whitten & Palmer 1999; also see Schwindt-Bayer & Tavits 2016 and Tavits 2007 on the impact of clarity of responsibility on corruption). In this chapter, we have considered all governing parties, only excluding those with a marginal number of cabinet seats or smaller parties that dropped out of the government early in the parliamentary term. While some of our findings are suggestive rather than strong—partly because our models do not yet consider many country- or party-specific factors—it is reassuring to discover that factors known to affect party popularity and new party success, also impact change within parties.

This chapter has presented the first large-scale cross-country analysis of candidate turnover in modern democracies. We believe that focusing on electoral candidates not only sheds light on political parties' responses to corruption but also furthers our understanding of political parties and party system change more broadly. Electoral candidates are a central part of a party's organizational structures: the selection of candidates is a core function of political parties and candidates nearly always enter elections through parties or their coalitions. Therefore, change *within* parties needs to be taken seriously even for understanding changing party systems that are markedly fluid in CEE but also increasingly so in many Western European countries. The analysis of candidate change helps us to better understand party system dynamics as demonstrated in the next two chapters on new parties and electoral volatility. This chapter has also shown that the dynamics of intra-party change are, to an extent, guided by similar factors as are changes in party systems such as corruption perception and economic developments.

5
Old, new, and partially new parties

Once formed, political parties seldom remain unchanged or disappear completely; usually, they find themselves somewhere in between. Akin to the evolution of species of seabirds (or plants or bacteria) over time, parties evolve and transform in various ways over the course of several elections. Parties often conceal their limited genuine novelty and palpable links to old parties under shiny new overcoats. Some parties—often highly successful ones—sit uneasily in either the 'old' or 'new' camps (see Barnea & Rahat 2011; Litton 2015; O'Dwyer 2014; Sikk & Köker 2019). Examples of new parties with irrefutable ties to previously existing ones are plentiful. The Polish Law and Justice (PiS) and the Civic Platform (PO) stormed onto the political scene in 2001 sprouting from the Solidarity Electoral Action (AWS). The Austrian Team Stronach in 2013 drew some of its top brass from the Alliance for the Future of Austria (BZÖ). The Danish People's Party (DFP) broke off from the Progress Party (FP) in 1995. As a stump FP survived, DFP looked like a newcomer; however, it amassed a large slice of its members alongside a former leader (Sikk & Köker 2019). More recently, the Brexit Party (renamed Reform Party in 2020) was largely a reboot of the United Kingdom Independence Party (UKIP); set up by Nigel Farage, the face of UKIP, it attracted many former leaders and members. Genuinely new parties have been much rarer than such spin-offs: notable recent examples include the Italian Five Star Movement, and the Party of Miro Cerar in Slovenia (Emanuele & Sikk 2021). At the same time, disappearing parties do not always fade away for good but often split up, transform, or adopt a new name (Beyens et al. 2016; Bolleyer et al. 2019a; Haughton & Deegan-Krause 2015). In addition to such drastic changes, a more subdued evolutionary clock keeps ticking, gradually yet perpetually replacing electoral candidates and altering parties.

Studies of new parties and electoral volatility—where distinguishing between new, exiting, and continuing parties is critical—seldom problematize party change. Mostly for practical reasons, the political world is often reduced to one populated solely by 'old' and 'new' parties. However, this often clashes with political reality and ignores partial novelty (Chapter 2) that, we suggest, can be measured by candidate novelty and dropout (Chapter 3). Throughout this book, we argue that the evolution of the 'big' (i.e. parties and party systems) can best be understood by disaggregating and following the 'small' (i.e. candidates). In this chapter, we use candidate data to shed light on one core aspect of party system change—party entry, exit, and continuity. For the benefit of the readers who may have found the formulas in some of the previous chapters taxing, this chapter is kept as accessible and non-technical as possible. To do that, we illustrate our argument with clear, relevant, and well-known examples from party politics in Central and Eastern Europe (CEE).

We start the chapter with an outline of an ideal–typical relationship between aggregate party entry and exit and candidate turnover. Our starting point is that only some fresh-looking parties with high candidate novelty are genuinely new and substantively change party politics, whereas many others are de facto continuations of old parties (see Sikk 2005). Likewise, genuinely exiting parties are only those that leave the party system and take most of their significant candidates with them. The degrees of novelty and continuity among parties can be assessed by looking at candidate novelty and dropout.

We analyse candidate novelty and dropout using five authoritative data sets on party entry and exit (Döring et al. 2022; Mainwaring et al. 2016; Powell & Tucker 2014; Tavits 2008b; Volkens et al. 2020). We find higher candidate novelty among parties classified as new compared to continuing ones, yet some of them have remarkably low levels of candidate novelty; other important parties are neither here nor there. In particular, parties rarely exit the political scene completely and nearly always leave behind swathes of important candidates. The rarity of genuine entry and exit as well as the abundance of imperfect cases explains why agreement on party entry and exit is far from perfect in existing data sets, leading to considerable differences in aggregate measures of party system change. In the final section of this chapter, we propose a new way to distinguish between entering, exiting, and continuing parties based on candidate turnover. This approach reduces arbitrariness and provides a more nuanced assessment of party system change. The particular cases of entering, exiting, and partially new parties that we examine throughout this chapter largely validate our approach.

This chapter has three key messages. First, we show that a casual reading of party histories and identities can overlook important continuities and affect (usually inflate) the impression of overall party system instability. Second, party continuities can be complex; sometimes it is impossible to pin parties down over time as they vary from the genuinely new and partially new to the not so new. Finally, candidate dropout measures reveal that parties seldom 'genuinely exit'. Even those that experience proper breakdowns leave behind candidates in significant numbers. These lessons are significant for the study of new parties, the emergent study of party demise, and, by extension, for the study of party system development, particularly if it relies on electoral volatility, which is the subject of our next chapter.

5.1 Candidate turnover, party entry, and exit

Most analyses of party system evolution focus on the aggregate level without much drilling down into individual parties. Some studies distinguish between changes caused by the entry of new parties and the fluctuating fortunes of continuing ones (Mainwaring et al. 2016; Powell & Tucker 2014; Tavits 2008a). However, measures such as new party vote share and electoral volatility aggregate the change among all parties. Existing studies reduce messy political realities to a simplified world of perfectly old and entirely new parties. This approach was not unreasonable when classic studies on party system innovation in Western democracies were published (Bartolini & Mair 1990; Daalder & Mair 1983; Harmel & Robertson 1985; Hauss & Rayside 1978; Hug 2001; Kitschelt 1988; Lucardie 2000; Pedersen 1979, 1980; Willey 1998). Electoral change usually took the form of swings between existing parties, interrupted by occasional, often minor, breakthroughs by new parties. In this political Garden of Eden, it was safe to assume the existence of just two kinds of parties: new and old. In a perfect world, new parties only enlist new candidates and exiting parties do not leave any candidates behind. Let us assume for a moment that the candidate lists of continuing parties remain intact and unchanged. Under such ideal conditions, the overall weighted candidate novelty (WCN) would perfectly correspond to new parties' vote share. Likewise, the vote share of parties exiting at the next election would correspond to the overall weighted candidate dropout (WCD; see Figure 5.1).[1]

However, as we will see below, the paradise of tidy party competition has been lost or, in fact, it never existed for two reasons. First, even if entering and exiting parties are genuine items, continuing parties experience natural candidate turnover as explained in our theoretical model in Chapter 2. This lifts overall candidate novelty and dropout above the diagonals in Figure 5.1. Second, many new parties enrol candidates who contested elections before and exiting parties can leave behind candidates who run for other (new or continuing) parties. This pulls candidate turnover down from the diagonals.

---

[1] The calculation of WCN and WCD is explained in Chapter 3.

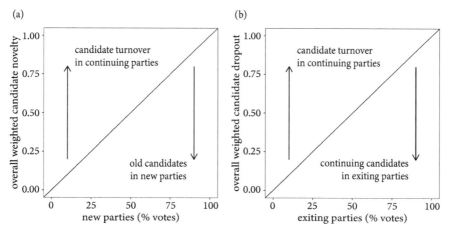

Figure 5.1 Hypothetical relationship between support for new/exiting parties and overall candidate novelty/dropout

Hence, elections are not expected to line up neatly on the diagonals even if the distinction between genuinely new, old, and exiting parties was very clear. However, large deviations from the diagonals would suggest that: (a) continuing parties experience extensive change, casting doubt on their 'oldness', (b) ostensibly new parties enlist old candidates, calling into question their 'newness', or (c) exiting parties leave behind swathes of candidates, calling into question whether exit really means exit. In other words, this suggests that party continuity can be overestimated (scenario a) or significant continuities overlooked (scenarios b and c).

Figures 5.2 contrasts data on candidate turnover in CEE with data on party entry and exit based on Powell and Tucker (2014, P&T), generously shared with us by the authors. P&T is one of the largest and most widely used data sets on electoral volatility and is particularly useful for our purposes as it distinguishes between two types of volatility: Type A (fluctuations in the support of continuing parties) and Type B (volatility stemming from party entry and exit). The correspondence between candidate turnover and electoral support for entering and exiting parties is clearly imperfect. As noted above, we expect candidate novelty always to be above zero: even if no new party entered, natural candidate turnover would still occur. However, candidate novelty can be significant if returning parties experience considerable internal change. When entering parties are weak (total support under 20%), WCN is still often close to 0.50 (top-left triangle in Figure 5.2a). Likewise, candidate dropout can be significant even when party exit is limited (top-left triangle in Figure 5.2b).

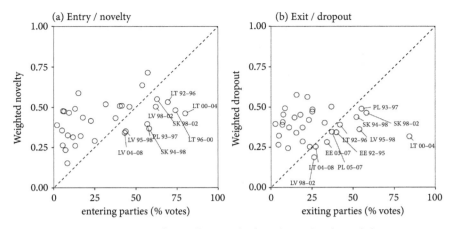

Figure 5.2 Party entry/exit (Powell & Tucker) and weighted candidate turnover

Deviations below the diagonals in Figure 5.2 are more problematic as they cannot be explained by natural candidate turnover. In several elections, WCN hovered around 0.50 even though new parties won a majority of votes. This implies that the ostensibly 'new' parties must have fielded old candidates: if all of them were genuinely new in terms of their candidates, the overall candidate novelty would rise above the diagonal. In several elections, this was far from the case, particularly in three Lithuanian elections, Poland in 1997, and Slovakia in 1998. Yet all elections below the diagonal are problematic, suggesting new parties were 'contaminated' by old candidates.

Similar problems appear in the relationship between exiting parties and WCD (Figure 5.3). In some elections with medium-low WCD (0.25–0.5), the vote share of exiting parties was considerably higher. The 2000–4 electoral cycle in Lithuania is the most notable: nearly all of the 2000 parties (91% of votes) seemingly exited by 2004 but WCD was only moderate (0.31). In other words, roughly two-thirds of candidates returned even though their parties were supposedly gone.

We return to the puzzles in the aggregate picture later in this chapter. Before doing so, we contrast and discuss existing approaches to party entry and exit. We then zoom in on candidate turnover among individual slates and see that many parties in CEE poorly fit a strict three-way distinction between genuinely new, old, and exiting parties. Finally, we propose a new candidate-based method for distinguishing between continuing and discontinuing parties.

5.2 Entering and exiting parties: comparing existing approaches

How do you spot a new party? The easiest way is to rely on the work of other scholars and use existing data sets on elections and parties. For example, the MARPOR (Volkens et al. 2020) and ParlGov (Döring et al. 2022) data sets cover all countries and all elections in our ECCEE data set and assign codes for individual parties. We can pin down continuing parties using these codes in consecutive elections: a new code identifies a new party and a repeated code a continuing party. The approach is not infallible, as tracking party continuities was not the principal aim of either MARPOR or ParlGov. MARPOR relies on available information on party continuities but does not appear to have explicit rules for introducing new party codes or sticking with old ones. ParlGov has clearer instructions and sets a higher threshold for introducing new codes, e.g. by coding mergers as continuations of the largest party (Döring 2016: 539). Nevertheless, both data sets require new codes or drop old ones in certain situations, e.g. the code of the minor partner in a merger disappears.

This party-code-based 'basic approach' identifies new and continuing parties rather well. Three authoritative data sets with an explicit focus on party entry—by Powell and Tucker (below: P&T, also considers exit), Mainwaring, Gervasoni, and España-Najera (2016, MGE), and Margit Tavits (2008a, MT)—are expected to perform even better as the study of new parties and party system change requires meticulous attention to party continuities and discontinuities. For this analysis, we connected ParlGov and MARPOR data sets and raw data generously shared by the authors of the other three data sets. The coverage of the data sets varies. First, the data sets differ in vote share thresholds: P&T considers all parties that won less than 2% in the previous election new; MT sets the threshold at 0.3% (either in PR or SMD for mixed electoral systems) and MGE does not specify an explicit threshold. MT covers party entry in CEE from the early 1990s until 2004, MGE until 2006, and P&T until 2009.

Figure 5.3 shows the total vote shares of entering parties over time according to the basic approach and the three data sets. In most elections, entering parties won less than a majority of votes with a median of 23% according to the basic approach and P&T, and 13% according to MT and MGE. P&T and the basic approach suggest that entering parties won more than 40% of votes in about one-third of elections while they managed that in fewer than one in every six elections according to MGE and MT. Regardless of the data source, well-known earthquake elections stand out, e.g. Bulgaria in 2001 and 2009,

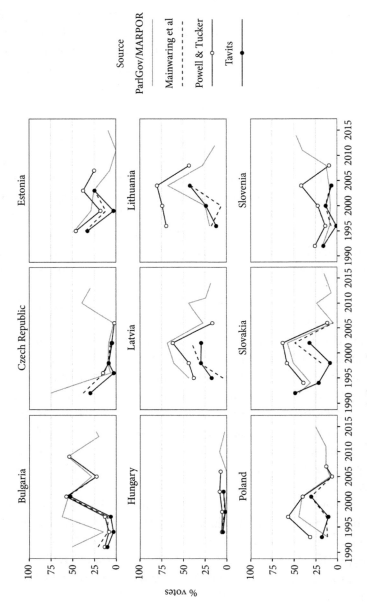

Figure 5.3 Party entry according to different data sets

Latvia in 2002, Poland in 2001, and Slovakia in 2002. Also apparent is the general stability in Hungary, stabilization in Estonia and Slovakia, and increased turbulence in the Czech Republic and Slovenia since 2010.

The four approaches agree on general trends, but there are significant discrepancies. For example, the indices suggest that in the 2004 election in Lithuania, nearly all (P&T) or less than half (MT and MGE) of the parties were new. Indeed, for that electoral cycle, P&T records the second highest volatility among the nearly 100 post-communist elections included in their data set that includes earthquake elections in countries like Ukraine or Georgia. Remarkably, no major disruption occurred in Lithuanian politics: Prime Minister Algirdas Brazauskas returned to the office together with almost half of his cabinet, including both the foreign and the finance ministers.

The level of disagreement between the four approaches is laid bare on the scatterplot matrix in Figure 5.4. The indices are clearly correlated—as expected, given that they measure the same thing—yet, one would expect the data to fall close to the central diagonals. The highest correlation (between MT and MGE) is a respectable 0.88, but even there we find significant deviations for individual elections. The correlations between P&T and others are still lower. For many elections, the factor of disagreement between indices is more than two, i.e. new party support in one is more than twice the support in another (observations outside the solid grey lines in the bottom-left half of Figure 5.4). For still a significant number of elections, the magnitude of disagreement is even higher: one-third of the elections deviate in P&T and MT by a factor of four (dashed grey lines). These are extraordinary discrepancies for indices measuring the same phenomenon.

Figure 5.5 shows party exit over time according to P&T and the basic approach as neither Mainwaring et al. (2016) nor Tavits (2008a) studied party exit and their data sets do not provide detail on exiting parties. Disagreements are expected, as Powell and Tucker (2014) were specifically interested in exit, unlike the two data sets behind the basic approach. Strikingly, P&T reports that parties that garnered the majority of votes disappeared by the next election in five out of forty elections. Most of these electoral cycles also stood out in terms of new party entry: for example, in the 2000–4 electoral cycle in Lithuania, parties previously supported by 84% disappeared. However, high levels of exit do not necessarily entail high levels of entry: party demise can benefit surviving parties (Poland 2005–7 and the Czech Republic 1992–6) or

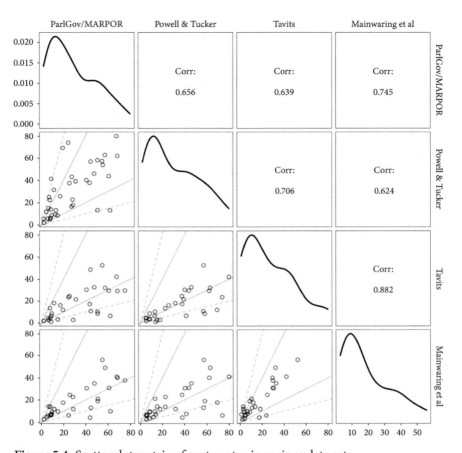

Figure 5.4 Scatterplot matrix of party entry in various data sets

Note: Distribution of new party vote shares on the diagonal. The top half shows correlation and the bottom half scatterplots between the measures. Solid grey lines demarcate disagreement by a factor of two and dashed grey lines by a factor of four.

new parties weaken rather than exterminate old parties (Bulgaria 1997–2001). However, high correspondence between entry and exit can also suggest non-genuine turnover, where seemingly exiting parties are replaced by . . . themselves.[2] To explain these striking discrepancies in different data sources and some inexplicably high levels of overall party entry and exit, we now turn our attention to the levels of candidate novelty and dropout in individual slates.

---

[2] See Appendix in section 5.7, for further analysis.

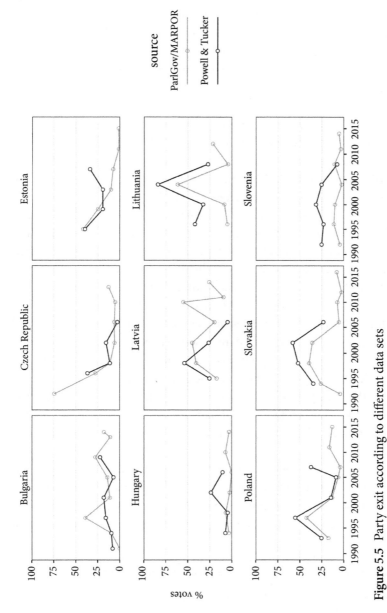

Figure 5.5 Party exit according to different data sets

Note: The election year refers to the more recent one in a pair of elections; the vote share reflects the combined vote of dropped-out parties in the preceding election. For example, Bulgaria 2014 reflects the vote share in 2013 of parties that dropped out by 2014 or the dropout in the 2013–14 electoral cycle

5.3 Party entry and candidate novelty

How new are individual slates in terms of their candidates? The WCN indices among the twenty most successful entries (according to P&T) show that only seven of them exhibit novelty above 0.75 (see Table 5.1).[3] All seven were genuinely new and classified as new by P&T, MT, and the basic approach.[4] For others, there were several differences between P&T and the basic approach, and even more between P&T and MT. In fact, MT classifies only two of the twelve slates with WCN < 0.75 as new. Such disagreements notwithstanding, the overall effect of candidate novelty on the agreement is remarkable: all sources concur where candidate novelty is high while disagreement increases as we move further down the list.[5]

Two-thirds of slates in Table 5.1 had a WCN below 0.75 and failed the test of genuine novelty. Several of them were newly formed electoral coalitions, dominated by previously existing parties which explains their low levels of candidate novelty. Three others were successors to coalitions. The Lithuanian Homeland Union (TS, 1996) emerged from the independence movement that competed in the 1992 elections as a loose coalition; the new party was led by the movement's leader and retained many of its candidates. The Slovak Democratic and Christian Union (SDKÚ, 2002) was the successor party to the Slovak Democratic Coalition (SDK, 1998), an electoral coalition also included in Table 5.1.[6] After the coalition was transformed into a party, many—though not all—candidates returned to their original parties and new faces filled the vacancies. Finally, the Slovak Party of the Democratic Left (SDL', 1998) had been the runner-up in the 1992 parliamentary elections and the leading member of the left-wing 'Common Choice' (SV) coalition in 1994. After the coalition was dissolved, SDL' established its own parliamentary group and ran independently again in 1998.

Three of the slates in Table 5.1 were partially new parties. The Latvian People's Party (TP, 1998) of Andris Šķēle, a former non-partisan prime minister, brought in new faces but also siphoned off candidates from other parties. The Estonian Reform Party (ER, 1995) absorbed the Liberal Democratic Party that

---

[3] Our analysis mostly focuses on P&T as it covers more elections included in the ECCEE data set than the others do and is explicitly concerned with both party entry and exit. However, the issues identified also apply to the other data sets.

[4] We did not have detailed individual party data for MGE.

[5] This pattern is analysed in more detail in the Appendix in section 5.7 where we find that apparent (i.e. non-genuine) exit and entry are more common in smaller (or less familiar) countries. The data sets converge in the coding of large parties and diverge in the coding of smaller parties.

[6] Legally, the SDK was a political party, yet the participating parties did not merge and retained their organizational integrity.

Table 5.1 Candidate novelty: the largest entering parties

Election	Slate	Vote %	WCN	Entry, according to: MT	Basic	Origin
LV2002	JL New Era	24.0	0.97	+	+	GNP[a]
LT2008	TPP National Resurrection Party	15.1	0.95	+	+	GNP
BG2001	NDSV National Movement Simeon II.	42.7	0.93	+	+	GNP
BG2009	GERB Citizens for European Development of Bulgaria	39.7	0.91	+	+	GNP
LT2004	DP Labour Party	28.4	0.90	+	+	GNP
EE2003	RP Res Publica Union for the Republic	24.6	0.89	+	+	GNP
LT2000	NS New Union (Social Liberals)	19.6	0.85	+	+	GNP
LT2000	LLS Lithuanian Liberal Union	17.3	0.67	–	–	Borderline GNP
LT1996	TS Homeland Union	31.3	0.55	–	–	Coalition successor
EE1995	ER Reform Party	16.2	0.55	+	+	Partially new party
SI2004	SDS Slovenian Democratic Party	29.1	0.54	–	–	Name change
LV1998	TP People's Party	21.3	0.52	+	+	Partially new party
LV2002	PCTVL For Human Rights in a United Latvia	19.1	0.50	–	+	NEC
SK2002	SDKÚ Slovak Democratic and Christian Union	15.1	0.48	–	+	Coalition successor
PL1997	AWS Electoral Action 'Solidarity'	33.8	0.47	–	+	NEC
SK1998	SDL' Party of the Democratic Left	14.7	0.42	–	+	Breakaway from a coalition
LT2000	BSDK A. Brazauskas Social Democratic Coalition	31.1	0.25	–	–	NEC
SK1998	SDK Slovak Democratic Coalition	26.3	0.20	–	+	NEC
EE2007	IRL Pro Patria and Res Publica Union	17.9	0.17	–	–	Merger
LT2004	UdL Working for Lithuania	20.6	0.14	–	+	NEC

Notes: Entry based on Powell and Tucker (2014).
[a] GNP: genuinely new party, NEC: new electoral coalition.

had been part of an electoral coalition in 1992. The Lithuanian Liberal Union (LLS, 2000) was an existing parliamentary party that still carried more novelty than many others in Table 5.1. It experienced major changes and, together with TP and ER, represents a true borderline genuinely new party.[7] Pro Patria Union and Res Publica Union (IRL, 2007) was a merger between Res Publica (a genuinely new party in 2003) and the well-established Pro Patria (IL), hence the low level of candidate turnover. Finally, the Slovenian Democratic Party (SDS, 2002), a sizable parliamentary party since 1990, merely changed its name in 2003.

Of the thirty-three highly novel slates of significant size (WCN ≥ 0.75 and $v > 5\%$, Table 5.2), only two were classified as continuing parties by both the basic approach and P&T: the Czech Rally for the Republic (SPR–RSČ, 1996) and the Slovenian Democratic Party of Pensioners (DeSuS, 2008); the Slovak party Ordinary People and Independent Personalities (OĽaNO, 2012) was not classified as novel by the basic approach but was not covered by the P&T time span.[8] All had novelty scores just above the 0.75 threshold and are rare instances of parties that experienced a substantial influx of new candidates. Only half of the high-novelty slates in Table 5.2 appeared during the nineteen years covered by the P&T data set and the other half stems from a period of mere seven years after 2010. In other words, high candidate novelty among electorally successful parties has become more common over time. Interestingly, overrepresented among the recent cases are Slovenia and the Czech Republic: countries that once used to boast seemingly the most consolidated party systems in the region (e.g. O'Dwyer 2014). The increased turbulence in these two countries suggests that apparent party system consolidation can be fleeting or, perhaps, partial, confined to the 'established party sub-system' (Deegan-Krause & Haughton 2018: 490), and may not herald the end of party system evolution.

Most of the largest continuing parties recorded a WCN below 0.40 (Table 5.3). Only two of the twenty largest parties covered by the P&T data set scored above 0.5, both from the mid-1990s when novelty among continuing parties tended to be higher.[9] However, their candidate novelty remains a far

---

[7] Former Prime Minister Rolandas Paksas joined LLS and became its leader. As a result, the party increased its number of seats in the parliament from one to thirty-four. It was classified as absent in 1996 according to P&T as it fell just below the two per cent inclusion threshold. It would have probably been classified as a continuing party had it won only 1,000 additional votes.

[8] MT adds to the list the Self-Defence of the Polish Republic (2001), a party that was classified as new in P&T due to a very poor result in the previous election.

[9] The mean WCN for continuing parties (as defined by P&T) until 2000 was 0.52, dropping to 0.44 since (see Figure 3.3 in Chapter 3). The trend persists when controlling for party size that reduces candidate novelty.

Table 5.2 High candidate novelty slates

Election	Slate	Vote %	WCN	P&T	Tavits	basic
EE1995	MKOE 'Our Home is Estonia'	5.9	0.99	+	+	+
SK1998	SOP Party of Civic Understanding	8.0	0.98	+	+	+
HU2010	LMP Politics Can Be Different	7.5	0.97			+
LV2002	JL New Era	24.0	0.97	+	+	+
PL2015	N Modern	7.6	0.97			+
SK2002	SMER-SD Direction-Social Democracy	13.5	0.96	+	+	+
SK2010	SaS Freedom and Solidarity	12.1	0.96			+
BG2001	NDSV National Movement Simeon II	42.7	0.95	+	+	+
EE2007	EER Greens	7.1	0.95	+		+
LT2008	TPP National Resurrection Party	15.1	0.95	+		+
PL2011	RUCHP Palikot's Movement	10.0	0.95			+
SK2016	SR We are Family	6.6	0.95			+
SI2014	SMC Party of Miro Cerar	34.5	0.94			+
LV1998	JP New Party	7.3	0.93	+	+	+
SK2002	ANO Alliance of the New Citizen	8.0	0.93	+	+	+
BG2009	GERB Citizens for European Development of Bulgaria	39.7	0.91	+		+
LV2011	ZRS Zatlers's Reform Party	21.0	0.91			+
PL2015	KUKIZ15	8.8	0.91			+
LT2004	DP Labour Party	28.4	0.9	+	+	+
CZ2013	ANO 2011	18.7	0.89			+
EE2003	RP Res Publica–Union for the Republic	24.6	0.89	+	+	+
PL2001	SRP Self-Defence of the Polish Republic	10.2	0.88	+	−	+
SI2011	LGV Gregor Virant's Civic List	0.4	0.88			+
LT2012	DK The Way of Courage	8.3	0.87			+
LT2000	NS (Social Liberals)	19.6	0.85	+	+	+
CZ2010	VV Public Affairs	10.9	0.84			+
SI2011	PS Positive Slovenia	28.5	0.83			+
CZ2013	ÚSVIT Dawn	6.9	0.8			+
SK2012	OL'aNO Ordinary People and Independent Personalities	8.6	0.78			−
BG2005	ATAKA National Union Attack	8.1	0.77	+		+
CZ1996	SPR–RSČ Rally for the Republic Republican Party of Czechoslovakia	8.0	0.76	−	−	−
LV2014	NSL For Latvia from the Heart	6.9	0.76			+
SI2008	DeSuS Democratic Party of Pensioners	7.4	0.75	−		−

Note: WCN ≥ .75, $v > 5\%$

Table 5.3 Candidate novelty: the largest continuing parties

Election	Slate	Vote %	WCN
EE1995	KMÜ Coalition Party and Rural Union	32.2	0.57
HU1994	MSZP Hungarian Socialist Party	33.0	0.53
BG1997	ODS United Democratic Forces[a]	52.2	0.48
SI2008	SD Social Democratic Party	30.4	0.48
CZ1996	ODS Civic Democratic Party	29.6	0.42
CZ2006	ODS Civic Democratic Party	35.4	0.40
CZ2006	ČSSD Czech Social Democratic Party	32.3	0.40
PL2001	SLD–UP Coalition of the Democratic Left Alliance and Labour Union	41.0	0.40
CZ2002	ČSSD Czech Social Democratic Party	30.2	0.37
HU2006	Fidesz–MPSz–KDNP Fidesz–Hungarian Civic Union–Christian Democratic People's Party	42.0	0.35
SI2008	SDS Slovenian Democratic Party	29.3	0.32
PL2007	PO Civic Platform	41.5	0.31
SK2006	Smer–Social Democracy	29.1	0.27
BG2005	KzB Coalition for Bulgaria	31.0	0.24
CZ1998	ČSSD Czech Social Democratic Party	32.3	0.22
HU2002	MSZP Hungarian Socialist Party	42.1	0.18
PL2007	PiS Law and Justice	32.1	0.14
HU1998	MSZP Hungarian Socialist Party	32.9	0.12
HU2002	Fidesz–MPP–MDF Alliance	41.1	0.10
HU2006	MSZP Hungarian Socialist Party	43.2	0.08

Notes: Continuing parties based on Powell and Tucker (2014).
[a] classified as new by the basic approach.

cry from the typical levels among new parties. The Estonian Coalition Party and Rural Union (KMÜ, 1995) was an electoral coalition with an equivocal link to a 1992 electoral coalition KK (Safe Home), the precursor identified by P&T, although only two of its five component parties overlapped with KK. The high novelty of the Hungarian Socialist Party (MSZP, 1994) is more surprising as it was clearly a continuing party. After a lacklustre performance in the first democratic elections, this communist successor party changed in terms of ideology and personnel. Its subsequent success in 1994 catapulted many new candidates to winnable list places which increased WCN.

Overall, candidate data confirms that new and continuing parties are distinct species. The level of candidate novelty is clearly higher among most new parties; where this is not the case, the different sources tend to disagree on coding. Even though continuing parties can experience an influx of new candidates, this pales compared to the freshness of faces on the slates of genuinely new parties. While most entering and continuing parties can be classified rather easily, an impish group of slates with medium levels of candidate novelty stands out. Such partially new parties—new parties with conspicuous links to past party politics or old parties undergoing major transformations—blankly refuse to agree with the dichromatic world of new and old parties (see also Sikk & Köker 2019). Their abundance poses a direct challenge to binary classification that we challenge in later chapters of this book. Later in this chapter, we show how candidate turnover can be utilized for a more meaningful and standardized identification of new (and exiting) parties.

5.4 Party exit and candidate dropout

Strikingly, among the twenty biggest exiting parties (as defined in P&T) only two saw most of their candidates drop out in the following election (Table 5.4). In half of the cases, more than two-thirds of candidates returned. While most of the parties did lose an independent electoral presence, this often involved the creation or break-up of electoral coalitions where the dominant party often either led the new coalition or absorbed most candidates after a break-up. For instance, the fizzled-out coalitions Slovak Democratic Coalition (SDK, 1998) and Common Choice (SV, Slovakia 1994) returned about half of their candidates to their home parties when these ran independently again. The party with the lowest WCD—clearly only *seemingly* exiting—was the Working for Lithuania coalition (UdL, 2004). It was a one-off alliance led by the Social Democratic Party (LSDP) that ran on its own in 2008. The electoral coalitions Popular Front (RR, Estonia 1992) and Sąjūdis (SK, Lithuania 1992) broke up and their dominant parties contested elections independently. Conversely, the Polish Democratic Left Alliance (SLD, 2005) became the leading party in a new left-wing electoral coalition in 2007. Finally, the Social-Democratic Party of Slovenia (SDSS, 2000) was a simple case of a name change.

Some parties experienced a cleaner break: Res Publica (RP, Estonia 2003) and the Polish Democratic Union (UD, 1993) were both involved in mergers. The Lithuanian Liberal Union (LLS, 2000) split following a bitter leadership contest. Yet in all three cases, there was a clear organizational and candidate continuity between successors and predecessors. Overall, the main message in Table 5.3 is that few important parties have ever disappeared without a clear trace.

High levels of candidate dropout are surprisingly rare given the ubiquity of apparent exits. Out of the 296 slates in our data set with $v \geq 5\%$, only eight recorded dropout levels above 0.75 (see Table 5.5). The reasons for their high dropout rates vary. The Hungarian Alliance of Free Democrats (SZDSZ, 2006) probably anticipated electoral losses after participating in the scandal-ridden

Table 5.4 Candidate dropout: the largest exiting parties

Electoral cycle	Slate	Vote % (t₀)	WCD	Exit according to basic approach	Comments
SK1994–8	SV Common Choice	10.4	0.52	+	Fizzled out coalition
SK1998–2002	SDK Slovak Democratic Coalition	26.3	0.50	+	Fizzled out coalition
SK1998–2002	SDL' Party of the Democratic Left	14.7	0.46	–	*
PL2005–7	SRP Self-Defence of the Polish Republic	11.4	0.46	–	*
LT1992–6	LKDPK Lithuanian Christian Democratic Party Coalition	12.6	0.45	–	Coalition break-up
HU1998–2002	FKgP Independent Smallholders' Party	13.8	0.40	–	*
PL1993–7	UD Democratic Union	10.6	0.40	–	Merger
EE2003–7	RP Res Publica	24.6	0.37	–	Merger
SI2000–4	SDSS Social-Democratic Party of Slovenia	15.8	0.36	–	Name change
LT2000–4	NS New Union (Social Liberals)	19.6	0.33	–	Entered a coalition
LT1992–6	SK Sajudis Coalition	21.2	0.34	–	Coalition break-up
LV1995–8	DPS Democratic Party 'Saimnieks'	15.2	0.32	–	*
PL2005–7	SLD Democratic Left Alliance	11.3	0.32	–	Entered coalition
LT2000–4	LLS Lithuanian Liberal Union	17.3	0.30	+	Split and merger
EE1992–5	RR Popular Front	12.2	0.25	+	Coalition break-up
CZ1992–6	LB Left Bloc	14.0	0.23	–	*
LT2000–4	BSDK A. Brazauskas Social Democratic Coalition	31.1	0.19	+	Coalition break-up
LV1995–8	TKL-ZP Popular Movement for Latvia-Zigerista Party	15.0	0.18	–	*
LV1998–2002	TSP National Harmony Party	14.2	0.15	+	Entered coalition
LT2004–8	UdL Working for Lithuania	20.6	0.11	–	Coalition break-up

Notes: Exiting parties based on Powell and Tucker (2014).
* Excluded from P&T as fell below 2% of votes in the following election.

governments of Ferenc Gyurcsány (MSZP) as a popular backlash affected both parties. The electoral appeal of the Liberal Democracy of Slovenia (LDS, 2008) also waned. Having dropped from 23 to 5% of votes between 2004 and 2008, it lost hope of entering parliament again and candidates quit. The Czech Public Affairs (VV, 2010) and the Slovenian Gregor Virant's Civic List (LGV, 2011) were 'one-hit wonders' whose candidates disappeared as quickly as they had surfaced. Both had been genuinely new parties that joined the government immediately after their first election. After VV's leading figures were accused of corruption (ironically, for an anti-corruption party), the party chose not to run again. Similarly, LGV's leader Gregor Virant was criticized for receiving unemployment payments after leaving the government, which caused the party's support to collapse. Following disastrous European elections and the leader's resignation, many candidates with limited political experience and weak incentives to stay in politics deserted. The more established Czech Civic Democratic Alliance (ODA, 1996) was also damaged by scandals; it skipped the 1998 election and flopped upon return in 2002.

Table 5.5 Slates with the highest candidate dropout ($v \geq 5\%$)

Electoral cycle	Slate	Vote % (t_0)	Vote % (t_1)	WCD	Exit, according to: P&T	Basic
HU2006–10	SZDSZ Alliance of Free Democrats	6.5	(10 joint candidates with MDF)	0.92	+	
SI2008–11	LDS Liberal Democracy of Slovenia	5.2	1.5	0.84	–	
CZ2010–13	VV Public Affairs	10.9	–	0.79	+	
SI2011–14	LGV Gregor Virant's Civic List	8.4	0.6	0.79	–	
SI2000–4	NSi New Slovenia	8.6	9.1	0.78	–	–
PL1993–7	BBWR Non-Partisan Bloc in Support of Reforms	5.4	–	0.78	+	+
CZ1996–8	ODA Civic Democratic Alliance	6.4	(skipped one election, then 0.5)	0.76	+	+
PL2001–5	AWSP Solidarity Electoral Action of the Right	5.6	–	0.76	+	+

The two genuinely exiting Polish cases in Table 5.5 were unstable from the start. The Non-Partisan Bloc in Support of Reforms (BBWR) was founded to provide parliamentary support to president Lech Wałęsa in the run-up to the 1993 election. However, Wałęsa quickly fell out with the party. His failed re-election bid in 1995 deprived BBWR of its *raison d'être* and its deputies scattered into five different party groups. The Solidarity Electoral Action of the Right (AWSP) succeeded the similarly named Solidarity Electoral Action (the winner of the 1997 elections) but suffered from internal rifts and lost prominent candidates to important new parties (Civic Platform, PO, and Law and Justice, PiS) by 2001. New Slovenia (NSi) is unusual among the parties in Table 5.5: despite high candidate dropout it increased its vote share in 2004 even though five of its nine MPs did not run for re-election.

Our main message here is that parties seldom simply disappear. Even when a party becomes extinct, it usually leaves behind traces of its former elites. Some 'dead' parties have stayed very much 'alive' when seen through the prism of candidates; some that remained 'alive'—if on life support—experienced considerable dropout. This chimes with the variation in the forms of party death as noted by Bolleyer et al. (2019a: 4). However, our analysis suggests that their proposed distinction between 'merger death' and 'dissolution death'—as a proactive or reactive choice of the party elites, respectively—is not always straightforward. In particular, 'dissolution death' is not necessarily a reaction to the failure of a party to fulfil its basic functions, but like 'merger' death, can be part of a proactive strategy to ensure the survival of the party 'genes' (see also examples in Chapter 1).

Notably, the continuing parties exhibit some of the highest candidate dropout levels, such as five of the slates in Table 5.5. The asymmetry between candidate dropout and novelty is remarkable: there have been many genuinely new parties but genuine disappearance is much rarer, at least among parties with significant electoral support. However, some of the largest continuing parties did lose many candidates, as shown in Table 5.6. The vote shares here are much higher than among the largest exiting parties in Table 5.4: successful parties persevere, even in the tempestuous electoral climate of CEE. In 1997, the Bulgarian Socialist Party-led coalition (BSP 1994) lost more than half of its candidates[10] and a few others came close to 50%. However, low dropout clearly dominates, with most parties losing no more than one-third of candidates—and often much less (extended tables are available on the book website https://osf.io/nm5ek/).

---

[10] The party collapsed due to an economic crisis and the fall of a BSP-led cabinet in 1996–7.

Table 5.6 Candidate dropout: the largest continuing parties

Electoral cycle	Slate	Vote % (t_0)	WCD
BG1994–7	BSP–BZNS–AS–PKE	43.5	0.59
PL2001–5	SLD Coalition of the Democratic Left Alliance and Labour Union	41.0	0.47
SI2000–4	LDS Liberal Democracy of Slovenia	36.3	0.47
BG1997–2001	ODS United Democratic Forces	52.2	0.44
BG2009–13	GERB Citizens for European Development of Bulgaria	39.7	0.43
CZ2006–10	ODS Civic Democratic Party	35.4	0.42
PL1997–2001	AWS Electoral Action 'Solidarity'	33.8	0.36
PL2011–15	PO Civic Platform	39.2	0.35
SK1994–8	HZDS Movement for a Democratic Slovakia	35.0	0.33
LT1992–6	LDDP Lithuanian Democratic Labour Party	44.0	0.32
HU2010–14	FIDESZ–KDNP Fidesz Christian Democratic People's Party	52.7	0.29
PL2007–11	PO Civic Platform	41.5	0.27
BG2001–5	NDSV National Movement Simeon the Second	42.7	0.26
HU2006–10	MSZP Hungarian Socialist Party	43.2	0.25
HU2002–6	FIDESZ–MDF Fidesz–Hungarian Democratic Forum	41.1	0.24
HU2006–10	FIDESZ–KDNP Fidesz–Christian Democratic People's Party	42.0	0.21
HU2002–6	MSZP Hungarian Socialist Party	42.1	0.18
HU1994–8	MSZP Hungarian Socialist Party	33.0	0.18
SK2012–16	Smer–Social Democracy	44.4	0.15
SK2010–12	Smer–Social Democracy	34.8	0.04

5.5 Candidate-based entry and exit

Our analysis so far has shown that 'new' parties often lack novelty and 'old' parties can experience significant change. Likewise, seemingly exiting parties often leave swathes of their candidates behind. In this section, we show how to use candidate turnover for a more nuanced and standardized coding of party entry and exit.

Figure 5.7 shows the overall distribution of candidate novelty and dropout among continuing and exiting parties (as defined in P&T). There is a clear distinction in the distribution of candidate novelty but substantial overlap in terms of dropout. While candidate novelty in continuing parties is usually limited (WCN < 0.5 in 86% of cases), entering parties often exhibit low novelty.

Exiting parties lose more candidates than continuing ones, yet a clear majority of their candidates return even when their party does not: only 28% of exiting parties have a WCD above 0.5. Nevertheless, only one continuing party had WCD > 0.66, i.e. high dropout clearly is the preserve of exiting parties.

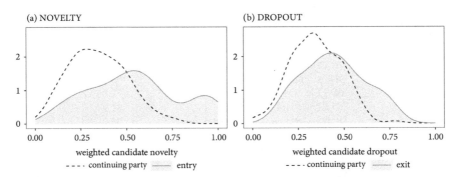

Figure 5.6 Distribution of candidate turnover among continuing and not continuing parties
Note: Entry and exit as defined in PT; $v > 5\%$

The overlap in the distributions notwithstanding, Figure 5.6 suggests that WCN and WCD can be used to operationalize party entry and exit. Based on the empirical cut-offs suggested by the discussion above, we use WCN ≥ 0.75 and WCD ≥ 0.66 as thresholds for entry and exit, respectively. Compared to existing indices, the CEE electoral scene looks on average distinctly less eventful through the lens of candidate-based party novelty (thick grey lines in Figure 5.7): in 80% of elections, more than 75% of the votes were cast for slates dominated by seasoned candidates. The nine elections where new parties won more than a quarter of the vote are well-known cases of genuinely new party breakthroughs.[11] Novelty-based entry is correlated with the other indices to a varying degree: most strongly with MGE and MT (r = 0.8) and least strongly with the basic approach (r = 0.51). The levels of new party entry are generally lower compared to the basic approach and P&T but the deviation from MT and MGE has no clear overall direction. Some elections saw considerable corrections. New party entry decreased compared to all four existing indices by more than twenty percentage points in Estonia 1995, Latvia 1998, and Poland 2001, all elections marked by very successful

---

[11] Bulgaria 2001 and 2009, Czechia 2013, Estonia 2003, Latvia 2002, Lithuania 2004, Poland 2015, Slovenia 2011 and 2014.

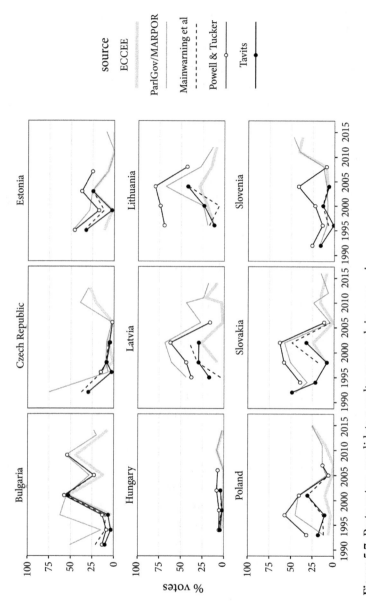

Figure 5.7 Party entry: candidate novelty approach in comparison

Note: Slates with WCN ≥ 0.75 are defined as new parties.

partially novel parties.[12] The first two saw a breakthrough of a single successful partially new party (see Table 5.1) and the 2001 Polish election no fewer than three of them: the Civic Platform (PO, v = 12.7%), Law and Justice (PiS, 9.5%), and the League of Polish Families (LPR, 7.9%), all with medium WCN just over 0.6.[13]

As shown above, candidates very seldom leave politics even when their parties disintegrate. Adopting a threshold of WCD = 0.66 for a dropout-based exit, we again see significant deviations from the basic approach and P&T (see Figure 5.8). In about one-quarter of elections, the dropout-based estimates slightly exceed P&T. The most dramatic differences are in the other direction: Lithuania 2000–4 and Latvia 1995–8 stand out, each with two seemingly exiting parties with very low candidate dropouts (see Table 5.3). The central message of Figure 5.8 is one of stability: an overwhelming majority of voters nearly always vote for slates that lose fewer than two-thirds of their candidates in the following election.

We believe that candidate-based entry and exit provide highly intuitive correctives to estimates of overall party system turnover. However, any candidate turnover threshold for entry will always remain somewhat arbitrary and either fully includes or fully excludes partially new parties. Lowering the entry threshold would open the door to parties that are not novel enough, increasing the risk of overlooking important changes in party systems. The exact threshold value can have a significant impact on results. Exit is even more problematic as most 'seemingly exiting' parties leave behind many—often most—of their candidates while parties that continue to exist occasionally experience substantial candidate dropout. We contend that party exit is a rather elusive phenomenon and concur with Mainwaring et al. (2016) that focusing only on new parties might be more fruitful for assessing party system change. However, even then a dichotomous approach to new parties is bound to remain inadequate. Forcing all parties into 'new' and 'old' baskets would mean succumbing to the 'tyranny of the discontinuous mind' (Dawkins 2011) where clarity trumps empirical diversity but is ultimately based on arbitrary categories. In the next chapter, we suggest a new approach to measuring electoral volatility that explicitly accounts for degrees of party novelty and candidate movement between parties.

---

[12] The difference between the basic approach and candidate-based party novelty was also substantial for Latvia 2010, which is only covered by the basic approach. The two slates classified as new by the basic approach but not the candidate-based approach, were Unity (Vienotība) and PLL (Par Labu Latviju!), two coalitions that drew in complex ways from earlier slates (see Lilliefeldt 2010).

[13] See Sikk and Köker (2019) for a more extensive discussion.

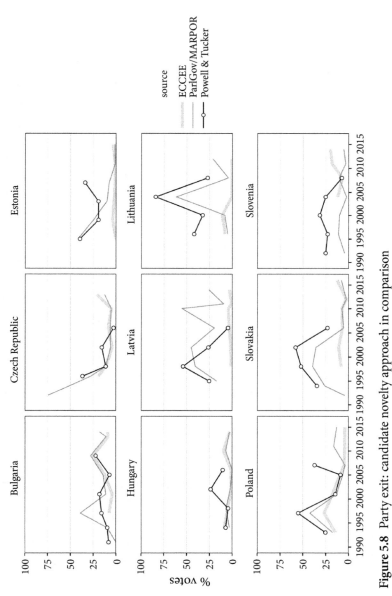

Figure 5.8 Party exit: candidate novelty approach in comparison

Note: Slates with WCD ≥ 0.66 are defined as exiting. The years on the horizontal scale refer to the latest in the pairs of elections. For example, Bulgaria 2014 reflects the vote share in 2013 of parties that dropped out by 2014.

5.6 Conclusion

Party continuity, novelty, and disappearance all come in various forms: they can be genuine, bogus, or anything in between. The analysis of party system stability hinges upon telling them apart, regardless of whether we are looking at the success of new parties or electoral volatility. This is not always easy: for example, the coalition Working for Lithuania (UdL, 2000) carried some novelty but certainly less so than many other slates in Table 5.1 and not only in terms of candidates. Powell and Tucker (2014) count it as new alongside smaller and more complicated cases in that same election which results in a record electoral volatility above 85%. Others report significantly lower but still high electoral volatility: MGE 59% and others just below 50% (including some data sets not discussed here). The volatility indices by various authors show remarkable differences well beyond this extreme case. Casal Bértoa et al. (2017) find an average correlation of 0.73 between electoral volatility indices for CEE from different sources. We fully concur that this is 'shockingly low for results that are intended to measure the same phenomenon' (145). In this chapter, we have seen that similarly imperfect correspondence affects measures of party entry and exit.

What explains these discrepancies between the measures of volatility and party entry? The analysis above suggests that—in addition to different inclusion thresholds—analysts sometimes pay too much attention to superficial changes and can overlook important continuities between parties.[14] Many of the problematic elections are from smaller countries (Latvia, Lithuania, Slovakia, Slovenia) on which information is presumably scarcer. As our analysis in the Appendix to this chapter suggests, such ignorance may play a role as a smaller country and party size weakens agreement on the classification of party entry. We, therefore, suggest considering candidate turnover for making any coding decisions. This information is fairly easily available for most recent elections and does not require extensive expertise about all individual parties and countries.[15] While smaller countries may feel substantively less 'significant' than bigger countries, in quantitative analysis each data point carries the same weight and, therefore, requires the same level of precision, regardless of how important we may deem an individual distant election or any particular party from a small country.

---

[14] This is partly linked to the necessity in dichotomous coding schemes to decide on a single successor/predecessor in case of splits and mergers.

[15] In the absence of candidate data, MP turnover can be an acceptable proxy, although it is problematic for smaller countries, smaller parties, and parties moving in and out of parliament. See further discussion in Chapter 2.

However, we would go even further and argue that a meaningful coding of parties as either continuous or non-continuous is often impossible. As we have seen, many partially new parties defy a clear-cut classification. Coding them as new rather than continuing parties can severely increase volatility measures (Barnea and Rahat 2011; Sikk and Köker 2019). Therefore, in the next chapter, we propose a new approach to electoral volatility that considers candidate turnover as well as the movement of candidates between parties (based on slate congruence introduced in Chapter 3).

Our readers might find the complexity of party novelty slightly intimidating—as do we. Degrees of change are much more challenging to use in empirical research than binary categories. However, the choice is not always between simple and complex—it is sometimes between more and less misleading. Seemingly complex ideas—like degrees of party change—may sound alien and carry the risk of alienating audiences beyond party researchers and political scientists. Still, black-and-white indicators of party system change that poorly chime with real-life experiences may, in the longer run, have even more critical downsides.

5.7 Appendix: candidate turnover and party entry/exit classification

Could the agreement between P&T and novelty-based entry depend on slate and country size? Generally, more information about the background of political parties is available for larger slates and countries which can increase confidence in their classification. Figure 5.9a suggests that the correspondence between P&T entry and novelty-based entry increases as party size increases. At $v = 2\%$, there is only a fifty–fifty chance of agreement that increases to 85% at $v = 50\%$ (bold overall line in Figure 5.9a). We also see that the correspondence between the two measures is poorer for smaller than for larger countries, though only for larger parties: naturally so, as we would not expect the agreement to fall even below 50% for smaller parties.

The correspondence of novelty-based entry to Margit Tavits's data set (MT) is significantly better (Figure 5.9b), particularly for small parties and in smaller countries that may even slightly 'outperform' larger countries. However, the agreement still increases with slate size. Contrasting P&T and MT (Figure 5.9c), we see that they disagree more regarding smaller countries and smaller parties. Disagreement generally means that P&T spots entry where MT does not (with just one exception). Overall, slightly more than half of P&T entries are not classified as entries by MT.

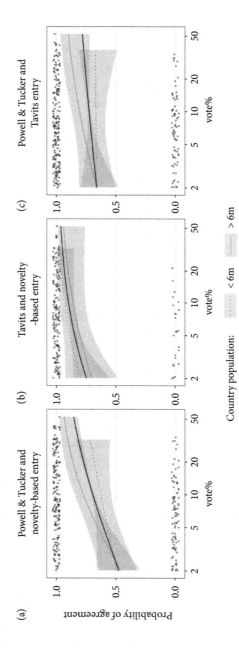

Figure 5.9 Probability of agreement between classifications of party entry over slate size and country size
Note: novelty-based entry threshold WCN > 0.75

6
Getting volatility right

For decades after the Second World War, most West European party systems were peaceful pastures where stable parties or party blocks roamed the electoral landscape. Although they regularly conceded some ground to each other and occasionally to smaller new parties, the patterns of competition echoed the social and cultural conflicts of the nineteenth century (Lipset & Rokkan 1967). To capture change in such party systems, one could simply add up parties' gains or losses at each election, known as Pedersen's volatility index (1979). Even as cleavages thawed and gave rise, for instance, to Green parties, the volatility index remained an elegant and effective tool for understanding party systems of increasing yet still limited complexity (Bartolini & Mair 1990).

However, the fall of the iron curtain revealed a dramatically different scenery. During its hold over Eastern Europe, the glacier of communism had all but wiped away traditional party affiliations (if they ever were as strong as in Western Europe) and dug its own deep furrows through society. Its melting uncovered a fertile ground for diverse political groups vying for electoral support. They often resembled parties in established democracies, yet their organization, membership and patterns of competition eschewed Western blueprints. Although some parties proved durable, new parties have cropped up regularly, winning elections and entering government, often only to split up, merge with others or seemingly vanish into thin air (Haughton & Deegan-Krause 2020). Meanwhile, West European party systems have gradually been losing their steadiness in recent years. In many places, the popularity of traditional parties has dwindled, with new parties gaining ground, suggesting that the East European-style instability could herald the new normal rather than presenting an anomaly (Emanuele et al. 2020; Emanuele & Sikk 2021).

To understand complex developments, one must try to reduce the complexity; however, established methods and measures can fail to do this in a consistent and reasonable fashion. The challenges of adapting old measures to new settings are familiar to students of party politics. For example, it is widely accepted that a unidimensional left–right index of party positions is of limited value in Central and Eastern Europe (CEE, Mölder 2016; Tavits & Letki 2009). Some—such as the Chapel Hill Expert Survey (Jolly et al. 2022)—have adopted a different, explicitly multidimensional approach to party positions in response. In a similar vein, scholars have tweaked the volatility index. While 'block volatility' was an important concern for Pedersen—partly because of the prominence of left and right blocks in the Nordic party systems—the recent mushrooming of new parties has prompted a distinction between intra- and extra-system volatility (Mainwaring et al. 2016; Powell & Tucker 2014; Sikk 2005). Yet, as our analysis of candidate change and party novelty in the previous chapter shows, a crisp distinction between new and old parties is often problematic.

We believe that a single index could meaningfully capture the level of party system change; however, any composite measure is sensitive to how it is calculated and the quality of underlying data. This chapter aims to redeem the volatility index and to show how to overcome the challenges it faces—in particular, the ever-present difficulty of identifying parties or their successors or predecessors. Building on our candidate-based (electoral/genetic) view of party change and our earlier ideas (Sikk & Köker 2019), we present a new approach to calculating electoral volatility that accounts for partially new and partially exiting parties and complex links ('congruences') between electoral slates—to use our term for any electoral formations (parties, electoral coalitions, etc.) in a particular election. The approach removes the need to pin down strict continuities in party development and, thereby, offers a robust way of measuring substantive change in party systems. We compare our scores to the main existing data sets of electoral volatility and discuss a range of individual slates and elections, illustrating how our adjusted index yields meaningful results. In particular, it avoids considerably overestimating or underestimating volatility because of difficult-to-code organizational changes that are a major issue in existing approaches and perhaps the main cause of the low agreement between volatility indices from different sources. We conclude by using our volatility scores to test the impact of GDP change on party system change. Although an effect has been reported in other world regions it has so far remained elusive in CEE; we find that the economic performance of a country does indeed affect electoral volatility.

6.1 Problems with volatility

The idea at the heart of the electoral volatility index is elegantly simple: the changing electoral fortunes of individual parties reflect the overall extent of party system change. This can easily be summarized in an index that sums up parties' respective gains or losses, or, as is often done in practice, dividing the sum of the absolute values of vote changes by two (Pedersen 1979). When parties' electoral support is stable, party systems are considered stable; when parties experience considerable gains or losses, party systems are considered unstable. The electoral volatility index ranges from 0, i.e. total stability and no changes in parties' vote shares, up to 100, i.e. a complete change of the party system and replacement of extant parties by newcomers. The index 'only' presumes that we correctly identify a party in one election and the next. Spotting party continuity between elections and distinguishing between old and new parties was largely uncomplicated when the index was devised and remains easy in some countries. However, party continuity can be evasive in complex political environments or elections for which detailed data or expertise is lacking. Yet, when continuity among major parties is ignored, misinterpreted or—most typically—wide open to interpretation, the index can easily climb to vertiginous heights.[1]

Let us imagine that archaeologists unearthed a clay tablet inscribed with electoral results for the ancient assembly of Philistia. Although using fictional ancient elections as an example may seem far-fetched, political scientists often analyse a wide range of countries, for some of which they cannot be expected to claim in-depth expertise. Relying on published election results—be they on clay tablets, paper, or screen—is often the only way to gather information on a large number of elections. The results (Table 6.1) appear straightforward: the David Party lost to the Goliath Party in 950 BC and disappeared from the electoral scene two years later. While Goliath's support remained stable, a new formation, the Amnon Coalition, entered the scene out of nowhere.

Table 6.1 Electoral results in Philistia, 950–948 BC

Slate	950 BC	948 BC
Goliath Party	70%	70%
David Party	30%	
Amnon Coalition		30%

Two years after the expedition, additional detail about the electoral slates surfaces on scrolls in the British Museum archives.[2] It transpires that after the David Party failed to defeat the Goliath Party, its ageing leader David

---

[1] Much less commonly, researchers assume continuity where there is none or little, reducing total volatility.
[2] The discovery of new data on candidates millennia later is not unheard of: see Evans's (1991) study on candidates and competition in Roman consular elections, 218–48 BC.

Jesseson retired from politics and disbanded the party. However, the candidates, most of whom were David's children and grandchildren, craved a second shot and rallied around his oldest son, Amnon. Prime Minister Goliath cunningly exploited the brief panic among the opposition by calling a snap election. Amnon failed to register a party in time and only a loose coalition of his followers materialized; while all of David's children ran again, several of his wives also joined the slate.

The added evidence suggests a dramatically different picture of party system change. At first, the continuity—or congruence, to use our technical term—between the David Party and the Amnon Coalition was obscured by limited knowledge of the prehistoric election. Based on the information available, the overall volatility reached 30%: significantly higher than the long-term average of Western Europe (10.3% between 1946 and 2015, Chiaramonte & Emanuele 2017: 380). However, once we consider the strong link between the David Party and the Amnon Coalition, volatility drops to zero. As Chapter 5 showed, continuities between real parties can be elusive even when we rely on prints and screens rather than clay tablets or papyri for information. Even more importantly, the example of the David Party and the Amnon Coalition also suggests that some parties may be neither perfectly novel nor perfectly 'old', further complicating the calculation of volatility. Clearly, the Amnon Coalition was not exactly the same as the David Party, but it was neither a genuinely new entity, similar to Kadima in nearby Israel almost three millennia later (Barnea & Rahat 2011). Hence, zero volatility might be too low and 30% too high; a score in between would reflect the extent of party system change more accurately.

Alas, the complexity of the Philistian party system pales in comparison to many contemporary democracies, particularly in CEE and other complex party systems. Besides the issue of party continuity, researchers need to grapple with splits and mergers (also known as fissions and fusions) and thresholds of inclusion in fragmented elections where many parties only win a small share of votes. In the following, we use the real example of the Estonian party system between 1992 and 1995 to illustrate all of these three thorny matters.

6.1.1 What happened to the Estonian party system between 1992 and 1995?

The finer details of the Estonian party system development in the early 1990s may not be household knowledge but are much less veiled by the fog of history than the fictional Philistian election. Still, as we will see, different interpretations of seemingly trivial details are at the heart of a considerable scholarly disagreement over the level of volatility between the 1992 and 1995 Riigikogu elections. Some readers may be tempted to skip this section about some obscure election in an inconsequential country, but we urge them to stay tuned. For comparative studies of electoral volatility, all elections are equal. The scores for all elections matter for any meaningful causal analysis; it is perhaps even most critical to get lesser elections right where unusual (or even dubious) coding choices may go unnoticed by peer scrutiny.[3]

In this section, we offer qualitative scrutiny of a volatility score for a single election. While aggregate indices from different sources have been compared before (see Casal Bértoa et al. 2017), the dissection of individual scores have been rare in literature (but see Sikk & Köker 2019). Yet, zooming in on individual slates is important as they have the power to significantly alter aggregate volatility that is, after all, an aggregation of vote changes between individual parties. The disagreement over how individual party fortunes changes underlies the large variation in the reported volatility score for the Estonian 1992–5 electoral cycle. Data sets disagree not only over the exact value of the score but also over whether the election recorded a high, moderate, or low volatility by CEE standards (see Figure 6.1). Meleshevich (2007) and Powell and Tucker (2014) suggest that the election witnessed one of the highest

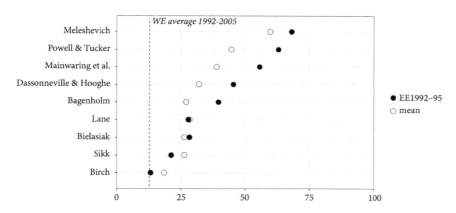

Figure 6.1 Volatility scores for Estonia 1992–5 compared to CEE means
Notes: Based on Casal Bértoa et al. (2017), the West European average from Chiaramonte and Emanuele (2017). The means are based on elections analysed in this book; not all data sets include all of the elections.

---

[3] The Appendix to Chapter 4 demonstrates that ignorance of smaller countries and smaller parties may affect coding decisions and, by extension, index scores and results of any analysis based upon them.

levels of volatility in the region; Birch (2003) and Sikk (2005) consider it a low-volatility election, reporting an electoral volatility index of about three times lower, close to the West European average. Other authors settle for anywhere between, neatly covering the full spectrum of values between the extremes.

How can academics—often experts on the region—suggest scores so different, using a formula so elegant and simple that it can be comprehensively explained in one line? Casal Bértoa et al. (2017) propose two main reasons for differences in volatility scores: different inclusion thresholds of parties and different approaches to party continuity. Thresholds for only including parties above a certain vote share (due to lack of information on smaller parties) partly explain the differences. Excluding everything under 5%, the volatility contribution would decrease to 4.8 or 7%, depending on whether we use a 'transition pairs' or 'individual points' approach (Casal Bértoa et al. 2017). 'Transition pairs' includes all parties that appear above the threshold in either of the elections (i.e. both results for Kun and PE-EK in Table 6.2 would be recorded), 'individual points' only the individual results above the threshold (Kun and PE-EK only recorded for 1992, the vote share of zero recorded for 1995). While these differences in volatility may look considerable, a 5% threshold is unusually high, and the highest explicit threshold used by authors covered by Casal Bértoa et al. (2017) is only 2%. A lower threshold would bring the contribution to the volatility score much closer to the 15.2% figure: around 9 or 15% with 3 and 2% inclusion thresholds, respectively.

Hence, high thresholds do matter, but the low thresholds used by the authors included in Figure 6.1 cannot explain the big differences in volatility scores. Whether and how to use aggregation (i.e. combining the vote shares of successors and/or predecessors) and specific decisions on party continuity play a bigger role, especially when party system development is as eventful as in the early 1990s Estonia. A key reason why this election (among several others) is so contentious is the abundance of electoral coalitions, their breakups, and party mergers. Pro Patria (IL), the winner of the 1992 election, was an electoral coalition of five centre-right parties budding from the moderately radical wing of the independence movement. The three runners-up were also electoral coalitions comprising three, four and two parties or organizations, respectively.

Among the names of front runners in 1995, only Pro Patria and the National Independence Party (ERSP) suggest a relationship to two 1992 slates. Yet, it

Table 6.2 Elections to Riigikogu, Estonia 1992–5

	Vote % 1992	Vote % 1995
Pro Patria (IL)*	22.0	
Safe Home (KK)**	13.6	
Popular Front (RR)***	12.2	
Moderates (MD)	9.7	6.0
National Independence Party (ERSP)*	8.8	
Royalists (Kun)	7.1	0.8
Better Estonia–Estonian Citizen (PE-EK)	6.9	3.6
Coalition Party and Country People's Union (KMÜ)**		32.2
Reform Party (ER)*		16.2
Centre Party (K)***		14.2
Pro Patria and National Independence Party (I-ERSP)*		7.9
Our Home is Estonia (MKOE)		5.9
The Right Wingers (PP)*		5.0
Others	19.6	8.4

Notes: Sets of asterisks indicate groups of linked slates discussed in text.
Source: Döring, Huber, and Manow (2022).

was anything but a simple merger between the moderately nationalist (IL) and somewhat more radical formations (I-ERSP). In the process, IL lost several MPs from its constituent organizations: most notably from the Liberal Democratic Party (ELDP) which merged with the newly founded Reform Party (ER) and the Right Wingers (PP). As discussed in Chapter 5, ER was an archetypal partially new party. Many of its prominent candidates were new but many others originated from ELDP that merged with ER just hours after it was established in 1994 (Muuli 2013: 146). The victorious Coalition Party and Country People's Union (KMÜ) was another mixture of continuity, novelty, and fusion. Two of its constituent parties had been included in 'Safe Home' (KK) in 1992, two had run on their own, and one was a new formation. The Centre Party (K) was the leading member of the Popular Front (RR) in 1992 but also attracted candidates from other slates.

Similarly, the IL/ERSP–ER/I-ERSP/PP nexus is the knottiest issue here. Sikk (2005) lumps together all successors of Pro Patria and ERSP. Powell and Tucker (2014) (a) disregard continuity between RR and K, and (b) connect only IL to I-ERSP and classify ERSP as an exit as a direct consequence of their 'strict linkage' approach to party continuity, to use the terminology from Casal Bértoa et al. (2017).[4] Yet, while the link between RR and K was far from explicit in their names, it was still strong—the congruence between them was around 0.5—surpassing that between I–ERSP and IL (0.4). Mainwaring et al. (2016) share Powell and Tucker's approach regarding IL and ERSP but link RR and K, hence arriving at a volatility score of thirteen percentage points lower. Dassonneville and Hooghe (2011) use 'inclusive aggregation' by adding together vote shares of parties linked to a common successor or predecessor and combining the vote shares of IL and ERSP in 1992; they arrive at a volatility score of 45.4%, i.e. nearly ten points lower than Mainwaring et al. and over twenty points lower than Meleshevich.

Bielasiak (2002) and Lane and Ersson (2007) follow a similar approach to Sikk but use different thresholds and treat 'others' differently. Remarkably, the general principle of 'inclusive aggregation'—where splits and mergers are aggregated—still results in large discrepancies in scores: from 21.3 (Sikk) to 45.4 (Dassonneville and Hooghe). This is because some authors interpret ER and/or 'the Right Wingers' (PP, a party that, somewhat paradoxically, later merged with the centre-left Social Democrats) as splinters from IL while others do not. As discussed above, ER was clearly a merger involving a splinter from the electoral coalition. Likewise, PP was clearly a splinter: IL provided as many candidates to PP as to its formal successor (I–ERSP). However, this is easy to miss because it was not a splinter in a formal, organizational sense. PP was not based on any individual organization from the 1992 coalition but draw members from several IL's constituent parts. Several more or less formal mergers complicate the picture further: the Farmers' Assembly joined the KMÜ coalition, several candidates from the small Entrepreneurs' Party joined K, and the Greens merged with the Royalists (Kun) who unsuccessfully campaigned for crowning Prince Carl Philip of Sweden as the King of Estonia.

While this may already sound complicated in the extreme, we have only scraped the surface of continuities, splits, mergers, and defections. KMÜ's list in 1995 included candidates from no fewer than eleven slates from 1992, yet none of its top four candidates had run three years earlier. Hence, KMÜ combined (a) splits, candidates or proto-parties abandoning their erstwhile comrades, (b) a merger, various parties and organizations coming together in KMÜ, and (c) defections, although it was not always clear whether organizations 'lost' candidates or simply joined KMÜ, with (d) a considerable

---

[4] Meleshevich's seems to have made the same choices but treated 'others' differently so that they add to the overall level of volatility.

degree of electoral novelty. This variety of candidates was not unique to KMÜ: K and PE–EK drew their candidates from seven, and MD and PP from five 1992 slates each. Many of these would count as defections but some were closer to actual splits and mergers: e.g. when a part of an electoral coalition breaks free but then joins another electoral coalition. Unsurprisingly, given all the frenzy, electoral coalitions were banned in Estonia before the 1999 parliamentary elections.

Thresholds, approaches to identifying the main successors and predecessors and methods of aggregation are all important but as the example of Estonia 1992–5 shows, even similar thresholds (no more than 2%) and approaches to aggregation, volatility scores greatly vary between authors. The complexity of the early 1990s Estonian party system poses impossible choices to researchers. Even though we might question some of the more unconventional coding decisions by fellow volatility-watchers, it is hard to disagree with any of them completely. A measure that results in wildly different values when researchers do not really disagree about the evidence at hand needs to be fixed. Many of the complicated coding choices involve knife-edge decisions that should not affect a measure to the above extent. Hence, 'correct' coding is often impossible. In the following, we will outline our suggestion for taming the beast of volatility with a different approach that disaggregates individual slates based on their novelty and congruence with various predecessors and successors. Admittedly, it complicates the calculation of volatility somewhat but, importantly, standardizes the approach to party change. We do away with detailed coding manuals that outline and justify critical knife-edge decisions and for practical reasons usually omit some of the less important though still relevant detail.[5] While our algorithm may seem a bit technical it could be outlined fully and precisely on about one page, as done below omitting illustrations and clarifications.

To reiterate, we are proposing a novel approach rather than challenging any existing data—details in excessively complex countries are very easy to overlook, and some party continuities are incredibly complex or open to diverse yet equally plausible interpretations. The problem is that simple rules inspired by classic works fail under the extreme fluidity of contemporary CEE party systems. Also, as the Appendix to Chapter 5 shows, increasing levels of obscurity (small parties, small countries) make different authors disagree more; CEE party systems are incredibly complex, and accounts of party life histories can

---

[5] All authors contacted very generously offered their raw data but even with very detailed protocols for dealing with new parties, mergers, splits, etc. it did not allow us to reproduce the volatility scores fully.

be patchy. In a nutshell: decisions matter and if we want an index that is reproducible, reliable, and can be implemented in a standardized way in all settings, we need an approach that allows for complex linkages between electoral slates. No matter how extensively we study, for example, the Estonian Reform Party, one could never unequivocally classify it as a continuation of IL rather than a new actor—or vice versa. But the decision—as many such decisions across CEE are required under strict linkage approaches—makes a critical difference to the estimated level of volatility.

6.2 Redeeming electoral volatility

The quality of research can never be higher than the quality of the indicators that feed into it. The discussion above underscores that volatility as a measure needs standardization to be used meaningfully in analyses as a dependent or independent variable. We believe that data on candidate change and movement (at least as a proxy for overall party change) can help deal with the thorniest issue: the tyranny of dichotomous decisions regarding party continuity, entry, and exit. Our approach—technically speaking a split-by-congruence approach (SBC, originally outlined in Sikk & Köker 2019)—offers a way forward. As emphasized earlier, classifying parties bluntly as new or old, and identifying a singular successor or predecessor can misconstrue party development. Partially novel parties are common in CEE and often defy 'correct' dichotomous coding, yet such coding decisions can lead to very different volatility scores.

The core innovation in our approach is to split up a slate's vote between successors or predecessors—based on their respective congruences—and novelty or dropout. The latter two are effectively congruences to a pool of 'non-running candidates'. To start with a very simple example: if only one-quarter of Amazing Party ($v = 60\%$) candidates return in the following election, its vote share is split between two virtual components—one a successor to the Amazing Party (virtual $v = 15\%$), the other a 'successor of non-running candidates' ($v = 45\%$, see Figure 6.2).

Assuming that the vote share of the Amazing Party and all other parties remains the same, the traditional approach would yield a volatility score of zero. This would overlook the fact that the Amazing Party had undergone a significant transformation reflected in candidate dropout. Let us also assume that three-quarters of Amazing Party candidates in election 2 were new; we then split its election 2 vote into two virtual components: one for the continuation

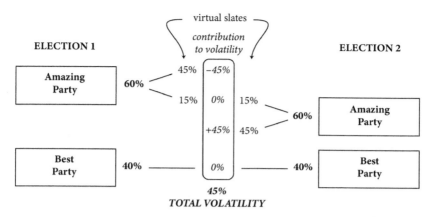

Figure 6.2 A simple example of split-by-congruence volatility

of Amazing Party (v = 15%) and one for the novel component (v = 45%). When we consider this rejuvenation of the Amazing Party, volatility rises to 45%, in contrast to zero based on the traditional approach that is misleadingly low considering the significant turnover of candidates. That degree of turnover may, indeed, lead one to treat the Amazing Party in election 2 as a new party and report a volatility of 60 based on the traditional approach. That only highlights the fundamental issue with the traditional approach: a (qualitative) threshold is needed for considering a party new rather than a continuation. Different researchers may focus on different aspects of the party and end up with an extremely low (0%) or extremely high (60%) volatility while all values in between are impossible. Just small changes around the threshold would have a seismic effect on the volatility score: add just a pinch of extra novelty such as a cosmetic name change to the Amazing Party and the electoral cycle would soar from the rock bottom of the volatility table to the very top of elections ever.

Were the Amazing Party to split, our approach would also consider the candidate-based congruence with all successors, i.e. to all slates that include candidates that ran for the Amazing Party in election 1 (Figure 6.3). If three-quarters of the Amazing Party's candidates join the Awesome Party, 45% of votes are assigned to its virtual predecessor, leaving 15% for the Amazing Party's virtual predecessor. Assuming, for simplicity's sake, that no new candidates were involved and no candidates dropped out, we end up with a total volatility score of 35%. This is again an example where traditional approaches would struggle and suggest much lower or higher volatility scores. If a researcher were to prioritize the continuation of the name or the largest

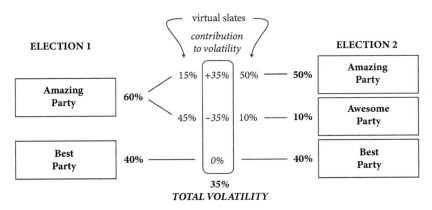

Figure 6.3 Fission and split-by-congruence volatility

successor, the total volatility for the election would be just 10%. However, noticing the significant personnel overlap between the Amazing Party in election 1 and the Awesome Party—with a congruence that high, it must be dominated by some high-profile defectors—one may be tempted to assign the Awesome Party as its heir despite the different name and the electoral flop. This would result in a very high electoral volatility score of 50%, a whole forty percentage points higher than for those prioritizing the name or electoral performance. Most importantly, traditional approaches do not offer any middle way in such cases, apart from what Casal Bértoa et al. (2017) call 'inclusive aggregation' that combines the vote shares of the Amazing and Awesome Parties in election 2 and gives us a highly dubious volatility score of zero. Once again, minuscule differences in the assessment of party development can lead traditional approaches to produce wildly different volatility indices. Our approach treats mergers—that are, in fact, more common than splits (see Chapter 7)—in a similar, mirrored fashion.

How can we deal with a defection of a group of prominent politicians from one party to another or a party moving from one electoral coalition to another? To the best of our knowledge, traditional approaches either ignore such defections or, those based on 'inclusive aggregation',[6] pool vote shares. Again, virtual slates provide an elegant solution to this thorny issue. Imagine that a third of candidates—a self-declared 'Be Amazing!' group—leaves the Amazing Party to join the Best Party, where they make up one-quarter of the candidates

---

[6] These '[aggregate] all predecessor and successor parties treating them as a single party' (Casal Bértoa et al. 2017: 148).

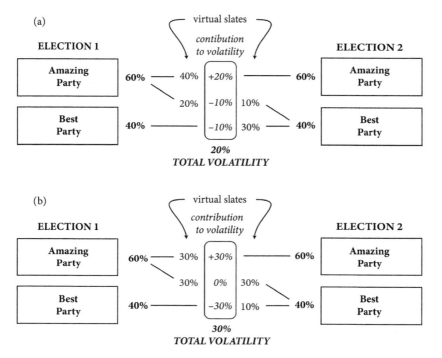

Figure 6.4 Collective defection and split-by-congruence volatility

(Figure 6.4a).[7] Traditional approaches would register zero volatility despite a considerable substantive change in the party system; this is reflected in the SBC volatility of 20%. The second scenario (Figure 6.4b) presents a more drastic change in the party system where half of the Amazing Party candidates effectively take over the Best Party, representing three-quarters of its candidates. Total SBC volatility would be 30%, while the traditional approach would be stuck at zero. Unless, of course, the researcher notices the changed face of the Best Party and classifies it as a new party with an old name (Best Party 1.0 disappears and Best Party 2.0 enters) propelling volatility to 40%: a hair-thin difference in circumstances can lead to a huge difference in the volatility score.

While some of these scenarios may appear fancifully complicated, they are tame compared to reality in many East European elections. Partial novelty and exit often coincide with splits, mergers or collective defections, as shown by the automatically drawn party evolution trees based on candidate turnover

---

[7] This is possibly due to the weighting of candidates: even if a party lost 90% of its candidates, they could only constitute 10% in their new home party if they were placed at the tail end of the electoral list.

and movement (see Appendix in section 6.6). Focusing on candidates, we can calculate volatility without studying the intricate and often obscure details of party evolution to determine all linkages. Candidate lists allow us to calculate congruences between slates in consecutive elections as well as the rates of candidate novelty and dropout. To calculate SBC volatility in practice, we must adjust the general principles discussed above for the baseline levels of candidate turnover. As the first step, we deduct from novelty and dropout the logically derived 'baseline' rate of candidate turnover, as outlined in Chapter 4: $R = 0.5 - v[0.5 - \sqrt{(t/l)}]$ where v is slate's vote share, t the length of electoral term and l the effective 'electoral life expectancy' of candidates (we use a ballpark figure of $l = 70 - 18 = 52$ years); under a typical electoral cycle of four years, this simplifies to $R = 0.5 - v[0.5 - \sqrt{(4/52)}] = 0.5 - v(0.5 - \sqrt{0.0769}) = 0.5 - 0.223v$. The adjusted novelty and dropout are floored at zero as, obviously, they cannot be negative.

As the second step, all congruences and novelty or dropout rates—that are actually special types of congruences to the 'party of non-running candidates'—are standardized so that they add up to 1. For example, take slate C ($v = 20\%$) with a novelty of 0.55 and congruences of 0.35 and 0.1 to slates A and B from the previous election. We first adjust novelty to 0.55–R = 0.55– (0.5–0.223*0.2) = 0.09. The adjusted congruences are 0.65 for A (0.35 divided by 0.35 + 0.1 + 0.09) and 0.19 for B; the adjusted novelty is 0.17. If slate F ($v = 40\%$) is congruent to D and E (0.18) has a novelty of 0.59, novelty is adjusted to 0.18 and all three scores are standardized to 0.33.

Our approach is based on a standardized way of dealing with various forms of party change, completely eradicating the need for qualitative decisions. As we have shown in the hypothetical and Estonian examples, these can be knife-edge choices resulting in substantial fluctuations in volatility scores. Figure 6.5 shows the size of virtual slates related to candidate novelty and dropout (the first column and first row with a dotted pattern, respectively) and the congruences between all slates with at least 3% of the vote in the Estonian electoral cycle of 1992–5. For example, nearly all of KK's votes in 1992 (13.6%) were assigned to KK as the virtual predecessor of KMÜ (12.6%). Meanwhile, about half of KMÜ's votes in 1995 (32.2%) were allocated to KMÜ as a virtual successor of KK (15.3%) and about one-quarter to KMÜ as a new slate (8.3%). Thus, KMÜ was a partially new slate, its novelty contributing |+8.3%/2| = 4.15% to the overall volatility level and the link to KK further |+2.7%/2| = 1.35%. With the contributions of minor parties added (not all are shown in Figure 6.5), the total contribution of KMÜ and KK is similar to that of a strict linkage between

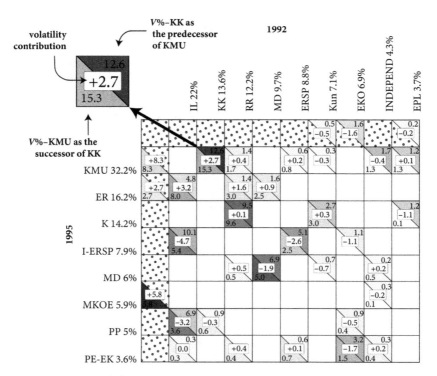

Figure 6.5 Virtual slates, Estonia 1992–5

Notes: A virtual slate's contribution to volatility in white boxes in the centre of cells. The top-right corner of cells: the vote share of a virtual predecessor; the bottom-left: the vote share of a virtual successor. Triangle shading indicates congruence between pairs of slates. Novelty and dropout in the first column and row, respectively

the two slates. However, the downfall of IL is toned down because ER was a partial successor to one of its integral components (the Liberal Democratic Party). Because of its clear linkages to 1992 slates (IL, but also RR and MD), ER appears less successful than it would if it were considered a new entrant, with a contribution to volatility |+8.4%/2| = 4.2% instead of |+16.2%/2| = 8.1%. However, our approach does not necessarily reduce volatility through aggregation. The pairs of 'near continuity' (RR was a clear predecessor of K, and MD of MD) saw their volatility increase: the absolute value of their vote changes is smaller than the sum of vote changes between the virtual slates in respective columns and rows, e.g. the RR column and K row, some smaller slates missing from the figure.

Other motifs from the discussion of the Estonian electoral cycle above—that did not consider candidates at all—appear. We can see the links between

IL and its successors in 1995 (I–ERSP, partial successors ER and PP). About half of IL votes and ERSP votes were assigned to the slates as predecessors of I–ERSP; as a merger, it was fairly uncomplicated but several 'quasi-parties' based on IL formed in the parliament after the 1992 election went their own way. K was a fairly straightforward successor of RR—albeit with links to other slates—and MD was one of the most clear-cut successors of itself; MKOE is the only unequivocally genuinely new party in Figure 6.5.

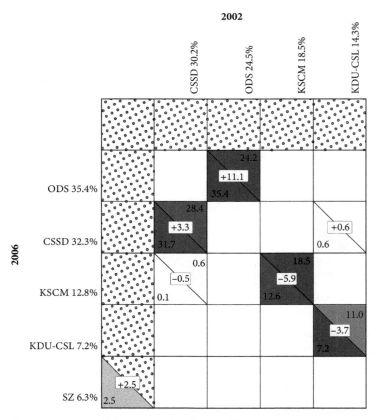

Figure 6.6 Virtual slates, the Czech Republic 2002–6

Many CEE countries did have extremely complicated patterns of party system development in the early 1990s. The congruence matrices for some other elections look considerably more stable. Figure 6.6 shows a remarkable continuation of Czech slates between 2002 and 2006 that allowed for some volatility but, in contrast to many other elections, there was a reasonable agreement among authors (see below).

6.3 Volatility in CEE

How do our volatility scores look against the cacophony of volatility scores in existing data sets? Our approach does not systematically increase or decrease the level of volatility: the scores are often close to the median of others (Figure 6.7). Despite factoring in many linkages between slates, our scores are seldom at the lower end of the scale. Only for a few elections is our score outside of the range of indices covered by Casal Bértoa et al (2017). In two Czech electoral cycles (ending in 1996 and 1998) this results from high candidate turnover among returning parties. The Czech Social Democratic Party (ČSSD) experienced considerable change before the 1996 election when Miloš Zeman became the party's leader (also see Chapter 8 on leadership change). It was an example of a partially new returning party—in contrast to more common new formations that include substantial numbers of previously running candidates—with a higher candidate novelty than in several parties commonly classified as new (see Chapter 5). Candidate novelty was also high in two other major returning parties: Rally for the Republic—Republican Party (SPR–RSČ) and the Communist Party of Bohemia and Moravia (KSČM). In 1998, the candidate turnover in the embattled Civic Democratic Party (ODS) pushed up the volatility score.

Our score for Bulgaria 1997 is also higher than most existing indices, mostly because of significant candidate dropout from the Bulgarian Socialist Party (BSP, ran as the Democratic Left, DL, in 1997) and novelty in the Union of Democratic Forces (SDS). Poland 1997 is unusual: some data sets propose considerably higher volatility than we do, while lower scores prevail in those based on 'inclusive aggregation'. The election saw many parties and organizations join the Solidarity Electoral Action (AWS). While we agree that some aggregation is justified, AWS also experienced notable new candidate inflow and some of its predecessors experienced considerable candidate dropout.

For four elections, our score is much lower than the median of others or outside of their range. First, Lithuania 2004 experienced complex reconfigurations of its parties while prominent political faces remained unchanged, with the important exception of the arrival of the Labour Party (DP). The link between the Social-Democratic Coalition of Algirdas Brazauskas (BSDA) and 'Working for Lithuania' (UdL) is discussed in detail in Chapter 5. For Order and Justice (UTT), a new formation around the impeached president Rolandas Paksas, attracted candidates from the New Union (NS) and the Liberal Union (LLS) while UdL and the Liberal and Centre Union (LICS) were the

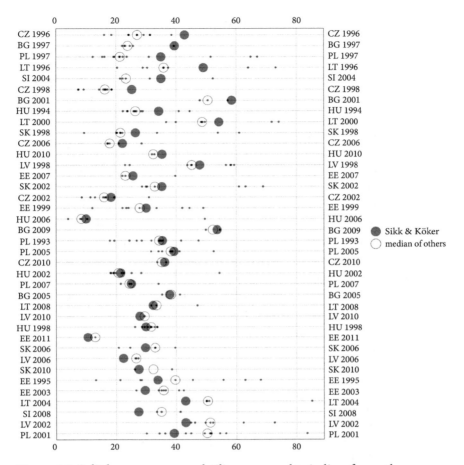

Figure 6.7 Split-by-congruence volatility compared to indices from other sources

Notes: Data sorted by the difference between our scores and the median of others; other indices based on Casal Bértoa et al. (2017).

main successors of the two, respectively (see Figure 6.8, other slate matrices are available online at https://osf.io/nm5ek/).

Second, the main culprit for our lower volatility score in Latvia 2002 is the break-up of JP (New Party) that, as far as we can tell, most sources classify as an exit. However, Raimonds Pauls, a famous composer and the founder of the party, joined the newly founded People's Party (TP) while many of its top candidates continued in the Latvia First Party (LPP).

Third, our volatility score for Slovenia 2008 is low because returning parties had clear links to various slates. The Liberal Democracy of Slovenia (LDS)

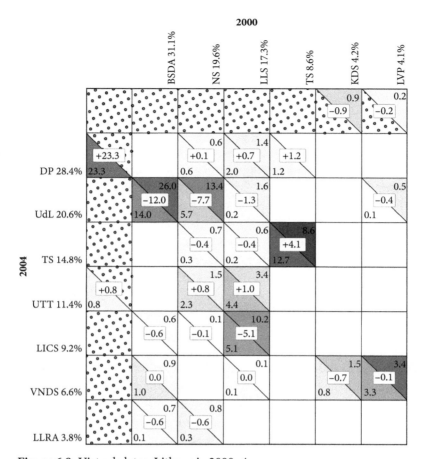

Figure 6.8 Virtual slates, Lithuania 2000–4

returned severely weakened but not only did it spawn a splinter (Zares–Social Liberals) but also suffered a collective defection to Social Democrats (SD, including former Prime Minister Anton Rop) in March 2007. Only three out of LDS's top candidates in 2004 ran again for LDS in 2008 while many joined SD and many more Zares. While the link to Zares may be accounted for by followers of 'inclusive aggregation' approaches, collective defections—even the highly significant ones—completely escape the radar of traditional approaches to electoral volatility.

Fourth, our score for Poland 2001 is at the lower end of the range of existing volatility scores. We are closer to the 'inclusive aggregation' camp because we recognize the linkages of all successors to the umbrella Solidarity Electoral Action (AWS); yet, we also recognize the significant novelty in three key splinters: the Civic Platform (PO), Law and Justice (PiS) and the League of Polish Families (LPR). Volatility is also reduced because we consider the candidates that PO inherited from Freedom Union (UW), a returning party, including Iwona Śledzińska-Katarasińska, the only Polish MP serving in all Sejms from 1991 to early 2020s, thereby reducing the extent of UW's decline.

Finally, our approach offers a robust solution to the complicated pattern of party change in Estonia 1992–5 discussed earlier in the chapter. Our score is well within the range of existing indices but considerably higher than some of the lower scores, highlighting a problem with aggregation: for example, aggregating all predecessors of Pro Patria/National Independence Party (IL and I-ERSP) and various successors parties of these predecessors (as done by Sikk 2005). When linkages between slates are complex, aggregating both successors and predecessors can lead to artificially low volatility scores. In a hypothetical election where all major slates had some links to all others in the preceding election, it can result in zero volatility even if there was a considerable change in parties' electoral support or significant candidate turnover. On the other hand, ignoring linkages in complex elections can lead to significantly overestimated electoral volatility.

Our data includes all slates without any exclusion thresholds; candidate linkages give us the necessary information about connections, even between slates we may know little about. Because our approach is based on virtual rather than actual slates, it is difficult to test what impact inclusion thresholds might have. However, as an indirect test, we can exclude slates based on 'individual points' or 'transition pairs' thresholds, i.e. excluding all slates below the threshold or excluding pairs of slates where both are below the threshold (Casal Bértoa et al. 2017). The impact is very mild: a threshold of 3% reduces volatility by 2.1% on average (individual points) or just 0.8% (transition pairs), this is reduced to just 1.7 and 0.5, respectively, with a 2% threshold. The potential impact of 2%, the highest threshold used in practice, pales in contrast to the average standard deviation in volatility scores for elections considered in this chapter (9.4%). Thresholds matter but much less than aggregation and dichotomous choices in thorny cases.

6.4 The impact of economic growth on electoral volatility

Little is known about the determinants of electoral volatility in CEE (Powell & Tucker 2014). This could be because researchers have yet to find the correct set of determinants, the theoretical specifications of models need improvement, or the available data is limited. However, we contend that data reliability could be a significant contributing factor, considering the wide discrepancies in the volatility scores used by different authors. In the following analysis, we test some potential key determinants of electoral volatility using indices based on our proposed method of volatility calculation. Our modelling choices here differ somewhat from those used by others. First, we modify the dependent variable in two steps (see Equation 6.1):

(a) divide the volatility score by the number of years between elections to account for the possibility that changed electoral allegiances can accumulate over time, and then multiply it by four to obtain a volatility score corresponding to a typical four-year electoral cycle; and
(b) calculate the ratio of the volatility score to the country mean to account for the impact of various country-specific factors that are difficult to include in the model.[8] The resulting index is 1 if volatility in a given election is at the country mean, 2 if it is double the country mean, 0.5 if half of the country mean, etc.

Because we incorporate the electoral gap and (largely constant) country-specific factors on the right-hand side of the regression equation, we do not need to include them on the left-hand side.

$$\frac{v_{adj}}{\bar{v}_{adj}} = X\beta + \varepsilon \qquad (6.1)$$

where $v_{adj} = 4 \frac{volatility}{electoral\ gap\ in\ years}$

Considering that the political impact of economic developments may take time to materialize, we have lagged the variable of GDP per capita by one year, calculate the ratio to the GDP per capita at the time of the previous election and annualize it (dividing by years since the previous election).[9] In contrast to Powell and Tucker (2014), we are not using the ratio of GDP per capita to its level in 1989. The countries had a fairly similar starting point and, more

---

[8] For example, the electoral promiscuity of voters; this also yields redundant variables related to the political and electoral system (a crude distinction between semi-presidential/parliamentary systems, and mean district magnitude that is difficult to conceptualize in multi-tier and mixed electoral system) and ethnic fractionalization used by Powell and Tucker.
[9] We adjust GPD per capita according to the month of the election: for January elections, we use the GDP recorded two years before the election year and for December elections we use the GDP recorded in the preceding year; for elections between, we use a weighted average of the two values.

importantly, reliable data for 1989 on per capita GDP is difficult to find, considering that half of our countries were not even independent at the time and the statistics from a period of economic turbulence are not particularly reliable. We do, however, include time since the start of the transition (year–1989) and the logged effective number of parties (based on Armingeon et al. 2021, via Coppedge et al. 2022; descriptive statistics for all variables are shown in Table 6.3).

Table 6.3 Descriptive statistics

	Mean	SD	Min	Max
Dependent variables				
Volatility ratio to country mean:[a]				
Total	1	0.411	0.318	2.41
Extra-system	1	0.614	0.187	2.9
Intra-system	1	0.386	0.209	2.21
Independent variables				
Gap between elections (years)	3.57	0.813	0.958	4.16
GDP per capita	6070	2540	1940	12100
GDP change (%)	3.73	3.47	−4.49	11.2
Time = Year–1989	12.9	3.2	4	15
Effective number of parties	5.47	1.57	2.7	9.8
ln(Effective number of parties)	1.66	0.292	0.994	2.28

[a] Standardized for a four-year electoral cycle.

Following Powell and Tucker (2014) and Mainwaring et al. (2016), we also split our volatility index into intra- and extra-system volatility. Extra-system volatility is calculated as the sum of volatility components in the first rows and columns of congruence matrices (the dotted cells in Figures 6.5, 6.6, and 6.8).[10] Intra-system volatility is the rest of total volatility, i.e. the volatility between components that involve slates in both elections.

While full explanatory models of volatility are difficult given the relatively small number of elections under analysis, we did detect a robust effect of economic growth. The effect of GDP change is statistically significant, corroborating findings in studies on other regions (Lee & Casal Bértoa 2021; Mainwaring et al. 2016; Mainwaring and Su 2021) but has proved elusive in CEE (see Powell & Tucker 2014; Tavits 2008a); the effect is clearer for total volatility and on extra-system volatility than intra-system volatility (Table 6.4).

[10] Mainwaring et al. (2016) only consider new parties for extra-system volatility. That would yield similar and only slightly less statistically significant results in our analysis.

Table 6.4 Determinants of electoral volatility

	Total volatility[a] (1)		'Extra-system'[a] (2)		'Intra-system'[a] (3)	
GDP per capita	−0.00	(0.00)	−0.00	(0.00)	−0.00	(0.00)
GDP change[b]	−4.78 ***	(1.32)	−7.17 ***	(2.02)	−3.58 **	(1.31)
Year−1989	−0.02	(0.01)	−0.01	(0.01)	−0.02	(0.01)
lnN	0.25	(0.18)	0.41	(0.27)	0.17	(0.18)
Constant	1.09 **	(0.34)	0.94	(0.52)	1.15 **	(0.33)
N	51		51		51	
R2	0.292		0.259		0.215	

Notes: *p<0.05 **p<0.01; ***p<0.001. Standard errors in parentheses.
[a] Ratio of volatility adjusted to a four-year electoral cycle compared to the country mean.
[b] Ratio to GDP per capita at the time of the previous election lagged and annualized (see text).
Source: Data based on Coppedge et al. (2022) unless otherwise noted in text.

The level of per capita GDP or time since the start of the democratic transition does not impact the level of volatility. The relationship between the logged effective number of parties and volatility is in the correct direction with more parties leading to higher volatility, but the data is noisy and part of the effect might be subsumed in our adjustment by country means as the number of parties changes little between elections.

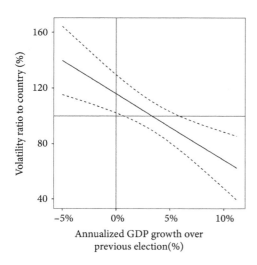

Figure 6.9 The effect of GDP change on electoral volatility
Notes: Dashed lines indicate 95% confidence intervals. Other variables set at means.

The regression model predicts total volatility at the national mean at around 3.3% annualized GDP growth, arguably a mild level of growth during the period in CEE (Figure 6.9, everything apart from GDP change is fixed at the mean). The magnitude of the impact of economic growth or decline is remarkable. With a 5% recession, volatility stands at 40% of the national mean (e.g. from the mean of 40 to 56%). When the economy grows by 10% annually (within the range of the data), volatility drops to only 68% of the national average (e.g. from 40 to 27%). These findings are based on one region and time period dominated by high growth and punctuated by the sharp recession in the late 2000s. Yet, they suggest that economic growth does ameliorate electoral volatility, especially its 'extra-system' component. Further validation is needed with larger data sets, but it suggests that economic factors may affect electoral volatility in CEE after all and that the effect could have been elusive so far due to inconsistent data.

6.5 Conclusion

This chapter tackles a constant headache in the studies of electoral volatility in CEE: the wide discrepancies in volatility indices, that cannot be explained by differences in coding rules, yet none of which appear 'wrong'. We offer a solution to the often impossible choice of coding parties as either strictly new or strictly exiting, and of having to establish strict linkages between successors and predecessors. So far, the only alternative to strict linkages has been to aggregate successors/predecessors that, as we have seen, carries its own risks. We check the validity of our measure by looking at particular electoral slates (parties and all other electoral formations in a pair of elections) and individual elections. It is encouraging to discover a relationship between our volatility index and economic growth between elections, a variable long reported for other regions that has been elusive in CEE, possibly because measuring electoral volatility has been particularly bothersome in the region. Our approach might be computationally more complex than traditional approaches, but offers exact recipes for dealing with party linkages between elections (that the readers are welcome to fine-tune in the future). The algebraic complexity is only relative: the mathematics behind even the most basic regression methods widely used in political research is considerably more complicated.

Admittedly, candidate change is just one aspect of party change, but it is a good starting point as a proxy for overall change and a tool that allows connecting parties with complex evolutionary paths between elections. We are astounded by how well the automatically drawn candidate-based evolutionary trees in the Appendix to this chapter reflect party system evolution while doing away with the need to consult party life histories in extortionate detail. As the following chapters demonstrate, candidate change is also linked to other main dimensions of party change, even if not always perfectly. We will suggest ways to operationalize change in other dimensions, but candidate change carries clear advantages in terms of data availability and susceptibility to quantitative measurement.

More fundamentally, our approach of breaking down parties into virtual slates raises the question of whether a party is necessarily the appropriate unit of analysis for understanding party system dynamics, echoing the question raised by this book whether a party as a legally registered entity with its organization, membership, etc. is always the best unit of analysis for understanding party development. We will return to these more fundamental questions in the conclusion of this volume.

6.6 Appendix: candidate-based view of party evolution

The candidate-based party evolution trees in Figure 6.10 provide ample examples of why choosing a single predecessor or successor for a party is often problematic. It also demonstrates that good approximations of party system evolution can be automatically derived from candidate lists.

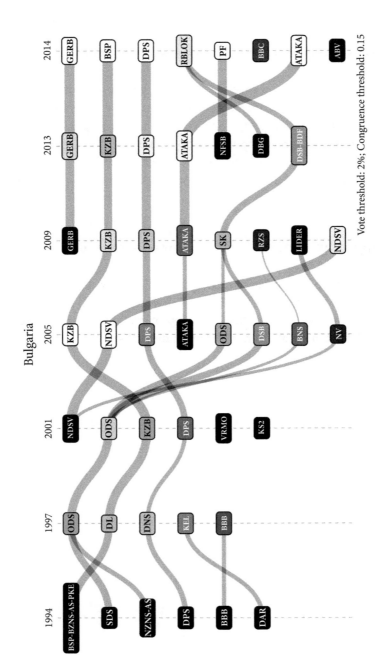

Figure 6.10 Trees of party evolution

Notes: The thickness of lines between electoral slates is proportional to their pairwise congruences. The shading of labels indicates candidate novelty: darker hues stand for higher novelty. The slates are ranked in the order of votes won.

Vote threshold: 2%; Congruence threshold: 0.15

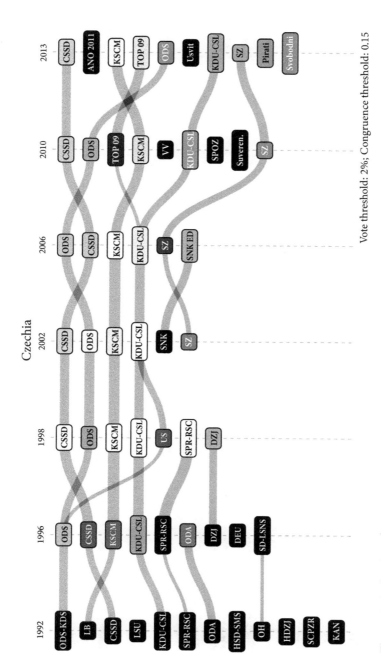

Figure 6.10 *Continued*

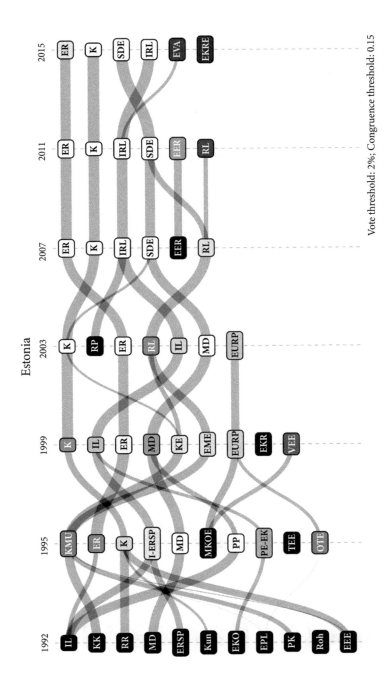

Figure 6.10 *Continued*

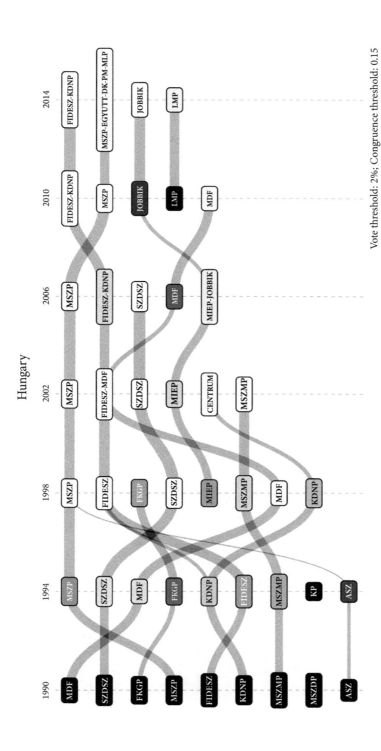

Figure 6.10 *Continued*

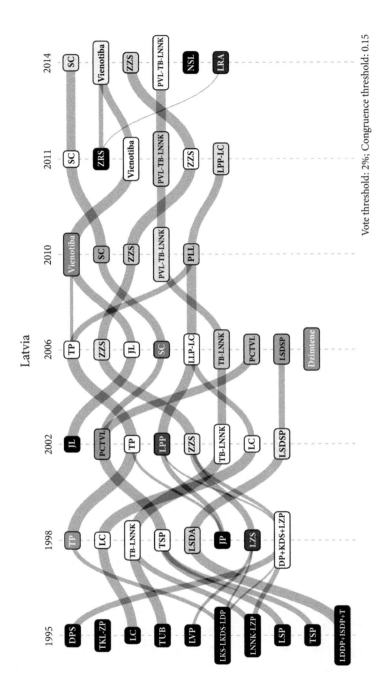

Figure 6.10 Continued

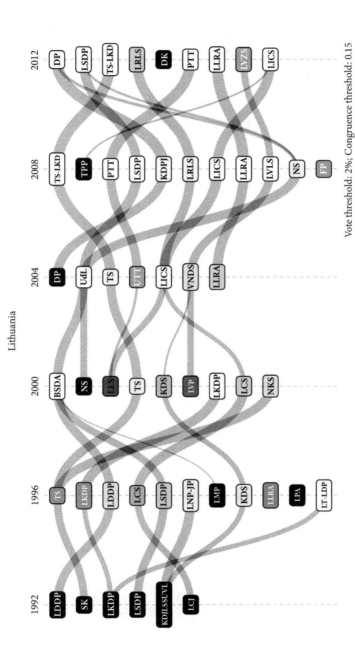

Figure 6.10 *Continued*

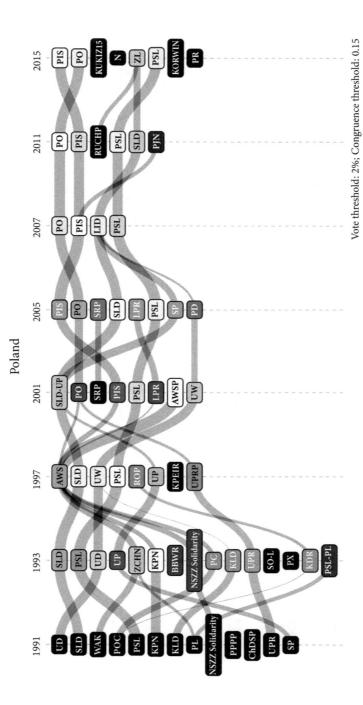

Figure 6.10 *Continued*

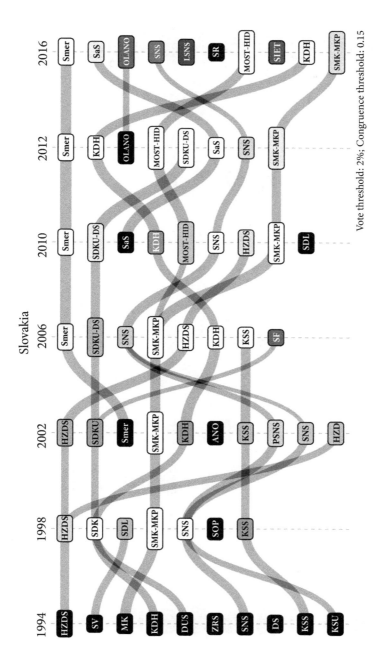

Figure 6.10 *Continued*

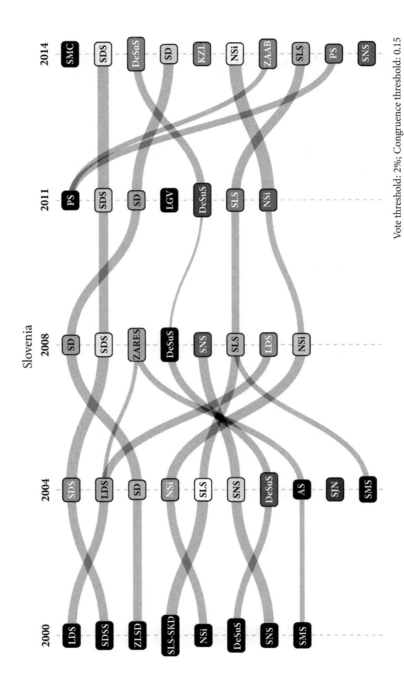

Figure 6.10 *Continued*

7
Fission and fusion

Parties seldom freeze to stone between elections. More often than not, they alter their organization, leadership, or programme to replace some candidates. The central argument of this book is that overall party change is reflected in high candidate turnover and party stability in more return candidates. Party change can be internal or external: internally, a new leader can be elected, a manifesto revised, popular support gained or lost, members recruited or lost; external change involves interaction with other parties as parties can merge and split up or establish and abandon electoral coalitions. Central and Eastern Europe (CEE) is a fertile ground for studying these changes because of numerous organizational changes and the ubiquity of electoral coalitions (Ibenskas 2016a; 2016b, 2020; Marinova 2015). Indeed, 'many so-called parties [in CEE] are actually electoral alliances or blocs that consist of multiple parties and other groups' (Ibenskas & Sikk 2017: 45). All five electoral slates to enter the Latvian parliament in 2010 were electoral coalitions, but coalitions have also been a mainstay in other countries. Electoral alliances take many shapes: some are makeshift, others more institutionalized; some disappear quickly while others persist for several elections, yet others morph into parties.

Because of its diversity, external party change is difficult to capture fully using existing terminology. The concept of 'slates' that we introduce in this book focuses on electoral units unique to each election and eliminates the need for the fuzzy distinction between coalitions and 'proper' parties. For a similar reason, we prefer the terms 'fission' and 'fusion' (F&F) to 'splits' and 'mergers'. These terms are less common; nevertheless, they have been used by several political scientists, even if the reasons for their choice of terminology were seldom explained (see Ceron 2015; Döring 2018; Giannetti & Laver 2001; Grofman et al. 2000; Kreuzer & Pettai 2003; Laver & Benoit 2003; Laver & Kato 2001; Mair 1990). The terms 'split' and 'merger' may be more common but they do not fully fit the analysis of some changes, in particular those related to electoral coalitions. F&F do not always involve the kind of organizational changes commonly invoked by 'split' and 'merger'. Indeed, we propose embedding the analysis of defections, especially those of a collective nature, in a joint framework with splits and mergers. Electoral slates can also experience F&F simultaneously which sometimes involve intricate combinations of events.

Most importantly, we argue that internal and external change is a continuous and gradual phenomenon. Like the irregular ticking of the molecular clock in genes, sedate party evolution can be punctuated by bursts of sudden changes. Hence, F&F can be glacial processes that may sometimes speed up, leading to seismic events (splits and mergers). The extent of change can range from the quiet defection of a candidate to the formation of a major electoral coalition or a merger of several political parties. The extent to which candidates from one slate are dispersed across several slates at the next election, or the background of candidates on electoral slates (coming from one or more predecessors) can give an indication of how common *fissionary and fusionary tendencies* are, even without having to document specific cases of F&F.

What happens to candidates amidst F&F? Where do they go when their slates fissure and where do fusions get their candidates from? In this book, we argue that parties are vehicles—'survival machines' to use our genetic analogy—serving the people that create them. Cooperation ensures candidates' collective (political) survival, yet ultimately they prioritize their own destiny over the survival of their 'survival machines'. Hence, parties can be cast aside when candidates feel better served by other existing or new machines. Some fellow candidates may carry on in the original party, others may follow the defectors, join other renegades, or leave politics altogether. If so, fissions and fusions should register in candidate movements and turnover: merged parties should mix candidates from several precursors and splits should scatter candidates among several successors. The same holds for the F&F of electoral coalitions. In contrast, continuing parties should not lose many candidates to others. However, if our argument is wrong and candidates are a mere sideshow in party politics, the candidate background of slates involved in F&F compared to other slates should look similar. While this chapter focuses on candidate movement between slates, we also analyse candidate novelty and dropout. We compare candidate novelty among slates emerging from fission and candidate dropout among slates entering a fusion to other slates and expect the disruption caused by F&F to increase candidate turnover.

Our analysis broadly confirms our expectations and rather neatly flags up known cases of F&F in CEE, upholding candidate turnover as a rich and valid indicator of party change. Fused slates mix candidates from two or more past slates; following fission, candidates tend to part company. In the absence of fission, candidates return under the same banner, albeit possibly under a changed name. In the absence of fusion, candidates usually stem from one previous slate. We discover some seeming anomalies, yet, on closer inspection, these pose more challenges to the concepts of party merger and split than to our approach. Finally, we find that external party change, in particular fission, has become less prevalent in CEE since the early 1990s.

The contributions and insights of this chapter go beyond the analysis of candidates' fates under F&F. We provide an original definition of F&F for electoral coalitions and propose new ways of thinking about electoral coalition change. Throughout the chapter, we also illustrate the sheer variety of forms that external change can take, whether in party splits and mergers or in electoral coalition transformation. Candidate movement data demonstrates how slates involved in F&F can vary in importance. Fission can split a party right through the middle or cast out a mere splinter off the parent party. A fusion can be an equal merger or a coalition of two parties, or a flourishing party swallowing a floundering one. Some coalitions contest several elections with member parties unchanged, others participate once and then break up; some coalitions bring together new parties while others assemble old ones, or mix new and old formations. When coalitions break up, constituent parties can run independently, join other coalitions, or disappear from the electoral scene altogether. Finally, our approach spotlights simultaneous F&F, an overlooked but common phenomenon throughout CEE and beyond. Parties often leave one coalition to enter another, and several politicians can collectively defect from one party to join another. Events like that remain undetected in the traditional schema of splits and mergers, simply because they are neither when an 'interim party'—often an unregistered and sometimes unnamed organization if it exists at all—does not feature among lists of registered parties or in electoral results.

7.1 Concepts, measures, and expectations

Party F&F usually result from strategic considerations: party elites (including candidates) may feel that they will fare better by joining forces with others or competing on their own (Ceron 2015; Giannetti & Laver 2001; Ibenskas 2016b; Mair 1990). F&F can be straightforward when a party simply splits into several or when several parties merge into one. Often, F&F are more complicated, especially when they involve electoral coalitions where some parties remain together while others move in or out of the alliance. In this section, we propose a standardized terminology of F&F, define what we mean by new coalitions (a form of fusion) and coalition break-ups (fission), and outline candidate-based indicators used in our analysis. We start by outlining our general expectations regarding the relationship between F&F and candidate movement.

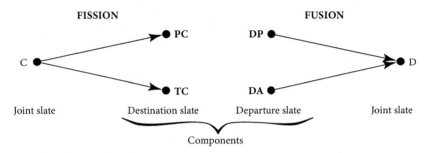

Figure 7.1 Electoral slate fission and fusion

Let us consider what we expect to happen to candidates during a simple case of F&F (see Figure 7.1). An equal fission of Conservatives (C) into two—Progressive Conservatives (PC) and True Conservatives (TC)—would result in the same number of C's candidates in both PC and TC. Here, C is a *joint slate* and PC and TC are the *components*. Conversely, an equal fusion of two components—the Democratic Party (DP) and the Democratic Action (DA)—into Democrats (D) would draw the same number of candidates from both DP and DA. In other words, D would be equally *congruent* with DP and DA, and C would be equally congruent with PC and TC (for the definition of congruence, see Chapter 3). Under unequal F&F, a dominant successor or predecessor would be more congruent to the joint slate than the lesser components. In the absence of F&F, we would expect a slate to have only one highly congruent component in the following or preceding election.

How do you identify F&F in parties and coalitions? The logical first step is to use existing data sets, as we do in our analysis of party entry and exit (see Chapter 4). To study the link between candidates and F&F, we use Raimondas Ibenskas's (RI) authoritative data set that spans from the early 1990s to around 2010 and includes 51 mergers, 75 splits, and 98 electoral coalitions relevant to the elections covered by this book (Ibenskas 2016a; 2016b, 2020). The RI data lists the joint and component parties for each merger and split. We exclude from our analysis mergers based on electoral coalitions in previous elections: for our purposes these are continuing slates with more institutionalized cooperation.[1]

---

[1] For example, the Czech Civic Democratic Party (ODS) merged with the Christian Democratic Party (KDS) after running in a joint coalition in 1992. Similarly, the Lithuanian Union of Political

FISSION AND FUSION 155

The RI data set identifies party splits and mergers but only gives member parties for coalitions, hence not specifying whether they were newly created or break-ups (Ibenskas 2016a). To identify fissions and fusions involving coalitions, we had to specify some qualifying conditions.

We assumed all coalitions to be fusions, except when:

(a) the components of a coalition were identical to those of a coalition in $t-1$ (based on party names), or
(b) a coalition with an identical name contested the previous election and, if it included any new components, these had not been present in $t-1$ (either independently or in any coalition); coalitions *expanded* by components previously running independently or in a coalition separately from the others were considered fusions, or
(c) all components were new parties (i.e. not present in $t-1$).[2]

Similarly, by default we assumed fission—i.e. that all coalitions in $t-1$ break up in t—except when:

(a) the composition of a coalition perfectly overlapped in two elections, or
(b) a coalition continued under the same name, though not necessarily including all previous components, and none of its components ran separately in t; if any of the components ran independently or separately from the others, the coalition would be *reduced* (fission), or
(c) the coalition 'consolidated' into a party—i.e. the components merged.

These nuanced rules are necessary because complex developments in electoral coalitions are far from purely hypothetical. In new democracies, party changes and coalition dynamics are often complicated and go well beyond simple splits, mergers, and the formation or dissolution of electoral coalitions. All of these can even occur simultaneously. Consider the example of the electoral coalition For Human Rights in a United Latvia (PCTVL) and its successors after the 2002 election (Figure 7.2). PCTVL consisted of three parties: National Harmony Party (TSP), Latvian Socialist Party (LSP), and Equal Rights (L). When the first two left in 2003, PCTVL continued as an alliance of L and Free Choice in People's Europe (BITE), founded by defectors from

Prisoners and Deportees (LPKTS) merged with the Homeland Union (TS) before the 2004 election, having been in a coalition in 2000.
[2] We found instances of coalitions of new parties, but also some that only looked new (because of name changes). Such coalitions involving only seemingly new parties will be identified in the analysis below.

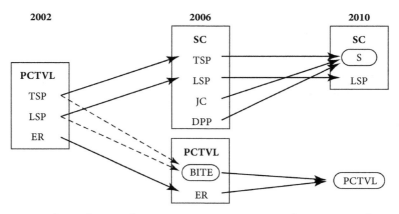

Figure 7.2 The evolution of successors to For Human Rights in a United Latvia (PCTVL)

Notes: Rectangles indicate coalitions, rounded rectangles merged or new parties. Solid arrows indicate party continuities or formal mergers, dashed lines indicate defections. BITE: Free Choice in People's Europe, DPP: Daugavpils City Party, ER: Equal Rights, JC: New Centre, LSP: Latvian Socialist Party, PCTVL: For Human Rights in a United Latvia, S: Harmony, SC: Harmony Centre, TSP: National Harmony Party.

TSP and LSP. TSP and LSP themselves formed a new coalition, the Harmony Centre (SC), with two smaller parties. TSP and some smaller parties later merged into Harmony (S) that still contested elections as part of SC. PCTVL was transformed into a party in 2007. This example includes the dissolution of one electoral coalition (PCTVL), the formation of another (SC), complicated splits (defectors from two parties joining into BITE) and two mergers (Harmony and PCTVL).

Candidate movements would here reflect changes in *slates*, but some *party* changes can slip through the net. Parties—such as the LSP in Figure 7.2— can glide effortlessly from one coalition to another, coyly absent from election results. Nevertheless, we believe that our focus on slates and candidates compensates by providing a richer picture of fissions and fusions than basic notions of parties coming together or moving apart, which may require hard-to-obtain details on the parties involved to code. Sometimes parties and electoral coalitions are difficult to distinguish in electoral records; coalitions can also morph into parties and are sometimes in transition at the time of an election. For example, the Estonian Pro Patria and Res Publica Union (IRL) officially merged shortly before the 2007 elections but retained two leaders, representing the constituent parties (Sikk and Köker 2019). Similarly, the Polish Citizen's Platform (PO)—a 'civic electoral committee' at the time of its first election in 2001—was treated as a party under electoral law but not under party law (e.g. it did not receive subsidies

FISSION AND FUSION 157

allocated to registered parties, see Szczerbiak 2007). Furthermore, electoral slates of parties can include members of other parties in the absence of formal coalitions, and 'dummy parties' can mix candidates without a formal merger (e.g. SDK in Slovakia in 1998, where electoral rules banned electoral coalitions).

We expect fused/fissioned electoral slates to have a connection to several past/future slates and other slates to be mostly linked to just one. We explore the fragmentation among the components by calculating their congruences vis-à-vis the joint slate. Fragmentation is high if the joint slate is significantly congruent to more than one component and fragmentation is low if congruence with one dominates. Congruence can roughly be interpreted as a share of candidate overlap between slates, i.e. congruence of 0.33 suggests that about one-third of candidates were overlapping.

We use three key indicators:

- $cong_1$—congruence with the most congruent component,
- $cong_2$—congruence with the second most congruent component, and
- $cong_{2+} = \Sigma(cong_2 + ... + cong_n)$—congruence with all but the most important component.

In our analysis below, we use $cong_{2+}$ as some fissions and fusions are diverse but have low $cong_2$. For example, if a medium-sized party (75% of candidates) merges with three small ones (5% each), $cong_2$ is low (0.05), yet $cong_{2+}$ is considerable (0.15). The combination of low $cong_1$ and high $cong_{2+}$ indicates high fragmentation, something we expect to see for slates that experienced F&F. To visualize the impact of F&F on fragmentation and candidate turnover, we plot $cong_{2+}$ against $cong_1$ for F&Fs and other slates.

The expected locations of various slates are shown in Figure 7.3. We expect no single component to dominate F&F slates: these should be placed in the upper portion of the triangle. We expect perfectly equal F&Fs to be placed at the very top of the triangle (where $cong_1 \leq cong_{2+}$). We expect little fragmentation where no F&F occurs and expect the slates to fall under the dashed line in Figure 7.3 (where $cong_1$ is much higher than $cong_{2+}$). Below the dashed line, the main successor/predecessor dominates as its congruence ($cong_1$) is several times higher than the congruence of all other congruent components combined ($cong_{2+}$). The bottom-left corner beyond the dotted line is reserved for genuinely new parties with high novelty and limited congruence with past slates or, respectively, party breakdown with massive candidate dropout and little congruence with future slates. Slates with many return candidates populate the opposite edge of the triangle.

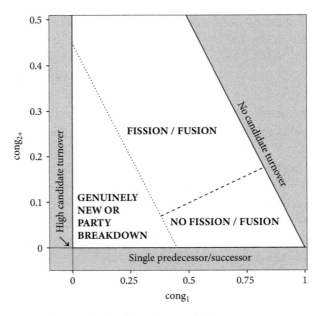

Figure 7.3 Expected relationship between candidate congruences, turnover, and fission and fusion

Note: The exact placement of the lines is different for F&Fs and is empirically determined so that it best discriminates between F&Fs and other slates in RI data set.

We do not only expect F&Fs to be captured by the movement of candidates between elections but also expect F&Fs to affect candidate novelty and dropout because they can be messy and can thus affect candidates' decisions to stay or go. Some may give up electoral politics altogether, bitter about policy shifts or nomination politicking as mergers mean fewer plum spots on electoral lists. Splits increase uncertainty about one's electoral prospects, yet also signal a new beginning and hence an opportunity for political novices.

7.2 Fission

Electoral coalitions and alliances, and even parties, are not always made to last. While some coalitions are so strongly institutionalized that they could well be parties, other coalitions and even some parties are impromptu. Not all splits are the result of candidates' desperation or the weakness of the parent slates: candidates can leave successful parties if their goals are better served elsewhere, and parties can maintain electoral vigour even after significant splits. For example, when Geert Wilders left the Dutch People's Party for Freedom and Democracy (VVD) in 2004, he cast off the shackles of both VVD policies (e.g. on Turkey's EU accession) and membership interference by creating his memberless Party for Freedom (PVV, see Mazzoleni & Voerman 2017). Notable splinter parties failed to wreck the Civic Platform (PO) and Law and Justice (PiS) in Poland's 2011 elections as only Palikot's Movement (RUCHP), a splinter from PO, entered parliament while Poland Comes First (PJN), a splinter from PiS, flopped (Szczerbiak 2013). Fissions are not always sparked by turncoats as candidates can also be deselected or expelled by their parties. When candidates become an electoral liability for the party, or the party becomes an ideological straitjacket for candidates, a break-up may better serve the political survival of both the party and the defectors.

Splits and coalition break-ups have been very common in CEE. The RI data set includes data on fifty-five splits covered by the ECCEE elections. Some of the earliest elections experienced the highest number of splits—four following the 1991 election in Poland and the 1990 election in Slovakia—but otherwise splits have become neither more nor less common over time.[3] The average electoral support was very low (3.4%) among the thirty-four splinters for which vote shares were available; most of the others joined electoral coalitions while some disappeared from the radar altogether. Only seven won more than 5% of votes and just two exceeded 10% (Czech TOP09 in 2010 and Polish Civic Platform in 2001). While fourteen of the parent parties won more than 5% of votes in the following election (six won more than 10%) very few increased their support. In fact, splinters often fared better than their parent parties, challenging the notions of 'parent' and 'splinter', usually inferred from party names.[4] However, changes in support are difficult to analyse as the parent party vote share in the following election was unavailable for nineteen splits, almost always because it had entered a coalition. We also identified twenty coalition break-ups: these are rarer than coalition creation because they have to be formed before they can be dissolved while some coalitions persist or even become parties. Somewhat surprisingly, electorally successful coalitions were more likely to dissolve than less successful ones as the average vote share of fissioned coalitions was higher than for all coalitions (19.6 and 15%, respectively).

Fissioned slates had a significantly lower congruence with the largest successor ($cong_1$) than slates not involved in fissions (medians 0.43 versus 0.66, respectively; see Figure 7.4).[5] However, $cong_1$ can be low either because

---

[3] Throughout, we refer to fissions taking place following an election as the RI data set records the year of election preceding the fission.
[4] For example, the Danish People's Party (DFP) that split from the Progress Party (FP) in 1998 can lay a claim to equal inheritance to the party because of high leadership and candidate congruence (Sikk & Köker 2019). While the DFP continues to enjoy electoral success, the FP dropped out of the Danish parliament in 2001.
[5] The differences are statistically significant unless otherwise noted.

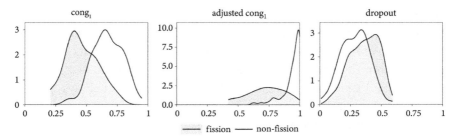

Figure 7.4 Distribution of the fragmentation of successors: fissions vs other slates

Note: $v \geq 10\%$

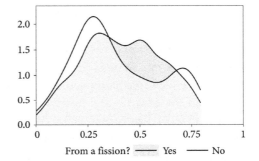

Figure 7.5 Candidate novelty: post-fission slates and other slates

Note: high novelty (> .75) slates excluded. $v \geq 10\%$

candidates are spread over a large number of successors or because candidate dropout is very high. To control for the effect of dropout, we calculate *adjusted congruence* ($acong_1$) based exclusively on continuing candidates: $acong = cong/(1-dropout)$. Thus, for a slate with $dropout = 0.3$, $cong_1 = 0.5$ the adjusted congruence would be $acong_1 = 0.71$. The adjusted congruence points at a very pronounced difference: non-fissioned slates are almost perfectly congruent to their largest successor (0.97) while congruence is much more limited for fissioned slates (0.73). Fission slightly increases the overall candidate dropout (median 0.36 compared to 0.29 for other slates). The difference between means is small (0.074) but statistically significant (t = 3.52, p = 0.001). Equally, slates emerging from fission typically have higher levels of novelty (see Figure 7.5).[6]

---

[6] Because of the bimodal distribution, the difference in the means is statistically not significant (0.42 and 0.40, t = −1.36, p = 0.176), but the difference in medians is (0.40 and 0.33; Mood's median test: Chi-squared = 11.658, p-value = 0.001).

7.2.1 Candidate movement in fissions

We have seen that candidate destinations following fissions are more diverse than those of other electoral slates; to get a more detailed picture and to check the validity of our approach we now turn our attention to individual slates. Figure 7.6 shows where different slates from elections covered by RI data fall in terms of their congruence with the largest successor ($cong_1$) and their combined congruence with all other successors ($cong_{2+}$). (The congruence scores for all slates discussed in this chapter are available in supplementary materials on the book website, https://osf.io/nm5ek.) The top panels show individual slates with labels for those in unexpected locations (i.e. differently classified by RI and our candidate data) and a couple of examples of fissions discussed in the text. The bottom panels show the two-way density distribution of slates with darker areas showing higher concentrations of slates. Non-fissioned slates occupy the bottom right of the triangle (panels b and d in Figure 7.6) as nearly all (86%) of them were dominated clearly by one successor. Similarly, 92% of the fissions identified by RI are in the expected area, higher up on the left panels of Figure 7.6. Fission comes in different forms, ranging from an equal parting of ways (at the top in the scatterplot) and mere slivers breaking off (lower down) as suggested by the bimodal two-way density distribution in Figure 7.6.

The Estonian Pro Patria electoral coalition (I 1992) demonstrates how candidate movements illuminate patterns of party change. This quintessential fission escaped our criteria for coalition break-up but classified it exceptionally as a fission. Its constituent parties underwent major changes. Four of them merged to form the Pro Patria party, which soon emitted a splinter (the Right Wingers). The fifth member, the Liberal Democratic Party (ELDP), merged with the newly founded Reform Party (ER). In 1995, the Pro Patria party formed an electoral coalition with the National Independence Party (ERSP), setting the scene for a later merger. Although all original party names had vanished by 1995 after three fusions and two fissions, three slates were clear successors to I 1992. A casual look at electoral results and even coalition composition would miss much of this complex story. Remarkably, candidate movement data places it at the very top of the triangle in Figure 7.6a and individual congruences expose all key developments: the three-way split in I, the merger with ERSP, and the link between the partially new ER and I (through ELDP).

Candidate data also highlights the diversity among other fissions. For example, the break-up of the Slovak Democratic Coalition (SDK 1998) was

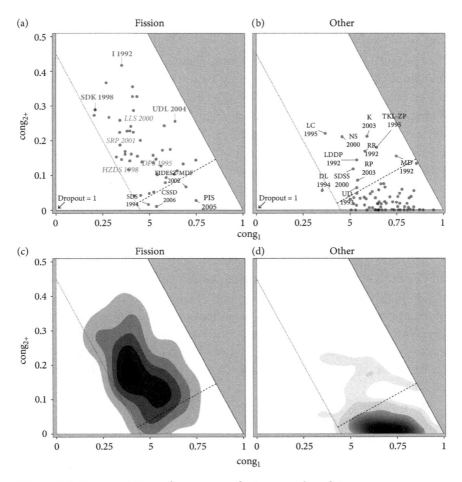

Figure 7.6 Fragmentation of successors: fissions vs other slates

Notes: Slates with $v \geq 10\%$. All observations must be inside the white triangles as $cong_1 \geq 0$, $cong_{2+} \geq 0$, $cong_1 + cong_{2+} \leq 1$. Novelty decreases from bottom left to top right. Years refer to the election contested by the joint slate.

equally congruent to its principal heirs, the Democratic and Christian Union (SDKÚ) and the Christian Democratic Movement (KDH), but also rather high levels of candidate dropout as it largely disintegrated into its constituent parties. SDK shows how fuzzy the line between parties and coalitions can be: it was registered as a party to circumvent a ban on electoral coalitions but was de facto an electoral coalition. The Lithuanian Social Democrats dominated the 2004 electoral coalition Working for Lithuania (UdL) and had a higher congruence after its dissolution than the New Union, the junior coalition partner (0.64 and 0.17, respectively). In contrast to SDK, UdL experienced very low candidate dropout, possibly because being in the coalition had a less transformative effect than the establishment of SDK as a party.

Four of the RI fissions landed, unexpectedly, near the bottom in Figure 7.6a. Three of them demonstrate that formal fissions may fail to alter party systems meaningfully. In 2009, former Prime Minister Miloš Zeman left the Czech Social Democratic Party (ČSSD 2006) and set up the Party of Civic Rights (Zemanites). However, the splinter failed to attract high-ranking ČSSD candidates and won only 1.5% of votes in 2010. Even more drastically, the Bulgarian Radical Democratic Party/Free Radical Democratic Party, a splinter from the Union of Democratic Forces (SDS) after 1994, ceased to exist altogether before the following election. Finally, the Polish Law and Justice (PiS 2005) experienced fission when the former Sejm Marshall Marek Jurek and others set up the Right Wing of the Republic (PR). In the following Sejm elections, it joined two other parties in an electoral coalition with marginal congruence with PiS. Most of PR's leaders ran for the Senate but not under the party label, and its candidates failed to win seats in either chamber.[7] While technically and legally fissions, such non-viable splinters carry little significance for their party system and are a distant cry from other, transformative party splits. Conversely, some more important fissions may slip under the radar when viewed from an organizational perspective, such as some that occurred in the development of the Estonian Pro Patria coalition (I 1992) discussed above.[8]

In contrast to the three inconsequential party splits, FIDESZ–MDF lies closer to the fission territory. Still, the coalition formed in 2002 and disbanded before the 2006 election was highly uneven. Fidesz's strongly dominant position was reflected in its higher congruence (0.69 compared to MDF's 0.04) but also in the MDF's small vote share following the break-up: 5% compared to Fidesz's 42%. As both parties maintained distinct identities, the candidate dropout following the break-up of the rather impromptu coalition was very low.

Thus, almost all of the fissions identified in RI had multiple successors. Identifying all the splits (and mergers) in CEE based on fragments of evidence from sundry sources requires colossal effort; our candidate-based approach greatly

---

[7] As explained in Chapter 3, we do not analyse upper chamber elections considering different electoral systems and slates (e.g. different coalition combinations). PR remains a rare case where the upper chamber candidates could have increased its congruence with PiS and might have lifted it to the fission territory in Figure 7.6a.

[8] When researching for this chapter, we came across several splits not captured by RI data that are more significant than some of those included. For example, the 2002 split of the Latvian Social Democratic Party from the Social Democratic Workers' Party was more significant than the splinters from ČSSD and ODS discussed above.

facilitates the analysis by flagging up potential cases. We found signs of fission and fissionary tendencies among electoral slates that were not involved in formal splits or coalition break-ups. We reclassified as fissions four clear splits that were not identified in RI—probably because both parent parties and splinters changed names before the next election—that we unearthed during extensive background research into the outliers (labelled in italics in Figure 7.6a). First, the Lithuanian Liberal Democratic Party (LDP; Order and Justice, UTT, from 2006) split from the Lithuanian Liberal Union (LLS 2000) in 2002 and was led by former Prime Minister Rolandas Paksas after he was replaced as party leader. Here, only the splinter (UTT) proved viable while the parent (LLS) floundered. Second, the Movement for Democracy (HZD) split from the Movement for a Democratic Slovakia (HZDS 1998) in July 2002 after the former speaker of parliament (and later president) Ivan Gašparovič left the party. HZD unsuccessfully contested parliamentary elections between 2002 and 2006. Third, the Latvian Democratic Party Saimnieks (DPS 1995) fell from being the biggest party to near-obscurity and gave rise to a splinter (Labour Party, DP) that contested the 1998 elections in an unsuccessful electoral coalition (DP+KDS+LZP). Finally, the Polish Samoobrana (SRP 2001) experienced two splits during the parliamentary term, but neither of the splinters survived till the next election; the high $cong_{2+}$ results from the scattering of SRP's candidates among fifteen slates in 2005.

7.2.2 Candidate movement in non-fissions

Turning to the slates that did not experience fission, 86% of them landed in the expected territory in Figure 7.6b while only ten had high candidate congruence with multiple successors. In seven cases, significant candidates drifted away without formal splits. Sometimes offshoots complemented fusions: for example, the candidates of the Lithuanian New Union-Social Liberals (NS 2000), instead of jointly following their party into a coalition (Working for Lithuania, UdL), joined no fewer than eleven different slates. The Estonian Res Publica (RP 2003) was also involved in a fusion when it merged with Pro Patria; it was strongly congruent with the merged party, but some prominent candidates defected to the Reform Party. Defections can also accompany deteriorating electoral prospects. The People's Movement for Latvia (TKL-ZP 1995), the Lithuanian Democratic Labour Party (LDDP 1992), Latvia's Way (LC 1998) and the Estonian Moderates (MD 1999) lost between 50 and 90% of their votes. Of the seven examples of uncoordinated party switching, the

Social Democratic Party of Slovenia (SDSS 2000) was the only one to almost double its popularity.[9]

In contrast to these cases of uncoordinated switching, the Estonian Centre Party (K 2003) experienced a major collective defection when eight of its prominent MPs (mostly former ministers) formed an informal Social Liberal group in 2004. Due to the strict rules on party switching, they never registered as a party and nearly all of them later joined other parties, mostly the Social Democrats (SDE). Such informal groupings are often an important intermediate step before defectors find themselves a new political home. However, it is very difficult to operationalize levels of coordination among defectors or ascertain whether any interim grouping was established or not; moreover, we suspect that in the 1990s proper interim parties might have been established by various defectors throughout CEE even where available records remain silent.

The remaining two outliers experienced complicated series of defections and cooperations. First, the Polish Democratic Union (UD 1993) merged with the extra-parliamentary Liberal Democratic Congress to form the Freedom Union (UW), to which it was most congruent in the 1997 election. However, several candidates left UW for the newly formed Conservative People's Party (SKL), that joined the coalition Solidarity Electoral Action (AWS), also mildly congruent to UD. Second, the Estonian Popular Front (RR 1992) was a coalition of the eponymous mass social movement, the Centre Party (K), and two civic organizations.[10] Many candidates returned with K in 1995 but several joined the Reform Party (ER) and the Coalition Party and Country People's Union (KMÜ). RR gradually disintegrated and supplied politicians to proper parties. However, it is impossible to trace its organizational development in the politically hectic early 1990s as the original affiliations of its candidates are unknown, and there are no records of any intermediate parties being formed.

The left-wing coalition led by the Bulgarian Socialist Party (Democratic Left, DL) experienced a partial breakdown. In 1994, it won 43.5% of the votes and the majority of seats in the parliament but its government subsequently faced a rollercoaster of hyperinflation, mass unemployment, bread shortages, a surge in crime, and pervasive clashes with the country's president and within the party. Consequently, the successor coalition was unable to attract any new members (Spirova 2007: 90), and lost half of the candidates and votes

---

[9] We make no assumptions about the direction of causality: defections may be triggered by anticipated electoral losses or, equally plausibly, the departure of popular candidates can weaken parties. The question of which direction prevails departs from the main thrust of the book.
[10] RR did not qualify as a coalition break-up according to our criteria as only K continued to contest elections under a slightly changed name and RR was not included in RI coalition data set.

in 1997. DL was strongly self-congruent and congruence with other slates was negligible.

As we have seen, electoral slates can be congruent with several successors but not formally qualify as fissions. In some cases, the defecting candidates formed groupings or proto-parties extremely similar to 'proper' parties. In others, few prominent defectors amounted to a 'mini-fission'. Collective and high-profile defections may be qualitatively different from 'institutional' splits but they require attention for understanding party system change, in addition to the more 'individualistic' analysis of legislative party switching (e.g. Heller & Mershon 2009; Kemahlıoğlu & Sayarı 2017; Klein 2018; Mershon & Shvetsova 2013; O'Brien & Shomer 2013; Thames 2007; Volpi 2019). Defections play an important role in party system evolution but sit uneasily with the established notions of formal splits and mergers. Our approach not only highlights some easily overlooked cases of formal splits, but also opens up a wider vista of related developments. In the next section, we show how candidate movements can reveal cases of fissions in waters uncharted by existing data sets.

7.2.3 Detecting fissions based on candidate movement

We have shown that fissions and non-fissions, as defined in RI and by our criteria for coalition break-ups, are clearly distinct in terms of their candidate destinations. Candidates from electoral slates that do not split mostly end up in one slate in the following election; slates that do split provide candidates for several successors. Most of the exceptions were cases of insubstantial parties splitting away from their parents, prominent defections, or complicated fissions missing from RI data.

Candidate movement data can also be used to detect fission for elections not covered by authoritative data sets. Nine out of the forty-four slates ($v \geq 10\%$) from elections beyond the scope of RI data landed in the fissions territory in Figure 7.7. Almost all of them experienced either coordinated defections or splits of new political organizations (including some parties). Three slates fall in the party disintegration territory: although they were congruent with several successors, their candidate dropout was very high. The most notable of these was the disintegration of the Czech Public Affairs (VV), a successful genuinely new party in 2010 that rapidly lost popularity and experienced extreme candidate dropout. In May 2012, the Liberal Democrats (LIDEM) split from VV, yet neither the splinter nor the parent contested the 2013 elections. Most

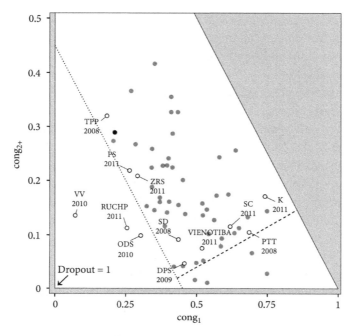

Figure 7.7 Fission detected based on candidate movement
Note: Non-RI elections; light grey markers for fissions in RI data set.

LIDEM MPs unsuccessfully ran on the list of the Freeholder Party (SsČR); while some VV candidates joined the list of the radical right Dawn (ÚSVIT), most dropped out and VV was eventually dissolved in 2015. Former VV candidates joined no fewer than thirteen slates in 2013 but only ÚSVIT recorded substantial congruence with VV (0.14).

The Polish Palikot's Movement (RUCHP) and the Czech Civic Democratic Party experienced more limited breakdowns, both landing close to the threshold in Figure 7.7. RUCHP (2011), set up by Civic Platform MP Janusz Palikot, came third in the 2011 parliamentary election but lost support and many candidates after that. During the parliamentary term, it transformed into Your Movement (TR), attracting new members from other parties but also alienating most of its own deputies. Among the 2015 slates, RUCHP was most congruent with the United Left coalition (ZL), which included TR, but also with the Polish People's Party (PSL) that absorbed several parliamentary groupings (proto-parties) formed by RUCHP MPs. In contrast, the Czech ODS managed to stay in parliament despite suffering a loss of popularity between 2010 and 2013. While most ODS candidates left politics, several MPs formed the Head-Up (HV) Electoral Bloc, which—despite an endorsement from former president Václav Klaus—completely flopped, winning only 0.43% of the vote. In summary, all three party downfalls were characterized both by candidate dropout and significant defections, although only VV experienced a clear formal split.

The remaining nine cases in the fission territory in Figure 7.7 show a wide variety of party changes. Two of them experienced *formal splits* and while five did not, some still spawned proto-parties. Among the three formal splits, Positive Slovenia (PS 2011) was the most clear-cut case. Shortly before the 2014 election, the Alliance of Alenka Bratušek (ZAAB) split from PS and the splinter was even more congruent to PS in 2011 than PS itself (0.26 and 0.22, respectively). Both did poorly and only ZAAB entered parliament with 4.4% of votes (compared to 28.5% for PS in 2011). The Lithuanian National Resurrection Party (TPP 2008) experienced both a split and a merger. TPP, a genuinely new party led by a popular TV host and brimming with celebrity power, began to disintegrate soon after its breakthrough. Most of the defectors joined the Christian Party (KP) but joined other parties at the next election. The TPP itself merged with the Liberal and Centre Union (LICS) but only half of its former candidates followed suit and others ran on several other slates in 2014. Finally, the Bulgarian Movement for Rights and Freedoms (DPS) after 2009 was highly self-congruent but also mildly congruent to Center, a coalition that included a splinter (Freedom and Dignity, NPSD) formed by MPs expelled from DPS.

Two collective defections fell just short of a formal split. The Estonian Centre Party (K) suffered a major defection after 2011, which mostly benefited the Social Democrats (SDE, $cong_2$ = 0.09) and the Reform Party (ER, $cong_3$ = 0.05). The defectors included more than a quarter of K's MPs, most of whom formed Democrats, a prominent but short-lived proto-party in 2012. The Latvian Zatlers's Reform Party (ZRS) disappeared after only one election but left too many candidates behind to be classified as a complete collapse. After winning 20.8% of the vote in 2011, ZRS began to disintegrate just weeks later when six MPs left the party to form the Free Democrats political association. The association never became a party and most of the defectors joined Unity (Vienotība, the leading party of government), followed by eight other ZRS MPs. In the 2014 elections, six ZRS MPs ran with the Latvian Association of Regions (LRA) as the rump ZRS ran on Unity's slate which eventually absorbed it.

Two fissions involved defections shortly before an election. The Latvian Unity (Vienotība, 2011) was mildly congruent with the National Alliance (NA) as a handful of MPs left shortly before the 2014 election, citing tensions between liberal and nationalist tendencies in the new party based on a 2011 electoral coalition. The Slovenian Social Democrats (SD) showed high self-congruence between 2008 and 2011, but due to the defection of several MPs shortly before the election, it was also mildly congruent to other slates, e.g. Positive Slovenia (PS) and the Democratic Party of Pensioners (DeSUS).

The two remaining cases show that even minor defections can add up to a significant $cong_{2+}$ without any formal F&F events. The Latvian Harmony Centre (SC) retained a large number of candidates between 2011 and 2014 but also contributed candidates to others, notably the new For Latvia from the Heart (NSL) and the Russian Union (LKRS). The Lithuanian Order and Justice (UTT 2008) also had strong self-congruence, but also lost candidates to nine other slates.

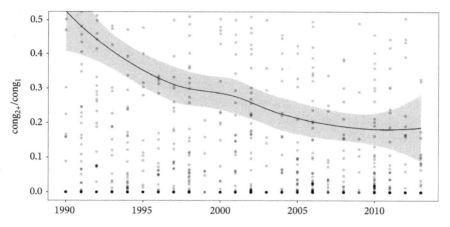

Figure 7.8 Successor fragmentation over time

Note: The trend line is weighted by slate vote share. Slates with $cong_{2+}/cong_1 > 0.5$ not displayed

Many more slates from the period covered by the RI data set landed in the fission territory than in the more recent elections (cf. Figures 7.6a and 7.7). This suggests that the fission of large slates has become less common. Figure 7.8 shows the overall successor fragmentation regardless of whether slates are classified as fissions or not. The average $cong_{2+}/cong_1$ ratio more than halved between the early 1990s and the mid-2010s. While the CEE party systems show few signs of overall stabilization, instability seems to be driven more by the emergence of new parties and increasingly less by the break-up of parties and electoral coalitions, lending credence to Haughton and Deegan-Krause's suggestion that new parties in CEE constitute a somewhat separate party 'subsystem' (2015). We do not wish to dismiss the importance of qualitative evidence or country expertise (on which we rely heavily here); however, this chapter demonstrates that general trends in fissions can be gleaned from party congruence scores, without painstakingly cataloguing cases of fissions.

7.3 Fusion

Parties often join forces in the hope of boosting their electoral fortunes or avoiding annihilation. The variety of party fusions is kaleidoscopic: mergers can involve two equal-sized parties or create lopsided unions of three or more parties. For ECCEE elections, the RI data set lists forty-three party mergers, 86% of which involved two parties while some had many more components, such as the Bulgarian Union of Democratic Forces in 1994 (11). Most of the mergers were based on an earlier electoral coalition. In addition to mergers, ECCEE elections involved sixty-one electoral coalitions, i.e. more than one coalition per election.[11] Their average support was high (15%) and nine of the coalitions won more than 30% of the vote. Our criteria classified twenty-nine electoral coalitions as fused, i.e. newly established; their average electoral support was similar to other coalitions.

Some fused coalitions were amalgams of equals, such as the Czech Christian and Democratic Union (KDU–ČSL) in 2002, bringing together the eponymous KDU–ČSL (9% of votes in the previous election) and the Freedom Union (US, 8.6%). Other fusions amalgamated parties of unequal electoral strength, such as the 2001 Democratic Left Alliance–Labour Union (SLD–UP) in Poland, composed of SLD (27%) and UP (4.7%). However, the electoral support of components was often unavailable as parties had changed their names or moved from one coalition into another. For example, one of the most successful coalitions, the 1997 Bulgarian United Democratic Forces (ODS) included the Union of Democratic Forces (SDS) and three other parties. However, only SDS had previously run on its own and one of the others had run in a different coalition.

What happens to candidates when electoral slates fuse? Figure 7.9 summarizes the distribution of four indicators among fused (filled areas) and other slates (empty areas); the dashed lines show distributions of non-fusions excluding highly novel slates. As expected, the congruence of the main predecessor ($cong_1$) was much lower for fused slates than all others (median 0.40 vs 0.58, respectively). Congruence with any single predecessor seldom exceeded two-thirds for fused slates, while this was common for other slates.

---

[11] This excludes twenty-seven coalitions that ran in the first ECCEE election (where we could not link candidates to past slates) or where RI only listed a single constituent party.

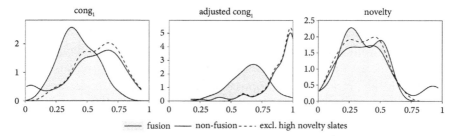

Figure 7.9 Distribution of component congruence and novelty: fusions and non-fusions

Note: $v \geq 10\%$.

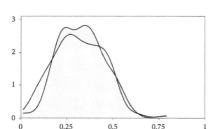

Figure 7.10 Candidate dropout: pre-fusion slates and other slates

Notes: High dropout (> 0.75) slates excluded. $v \geq 10\%$.

The difference is particularly pronounced for adjusted congruence which excludes new candidates (see explanation under fission). Congruence with the main predecessor was almost always above 0.80 for non-fusions, while this was rare for fusions: candidate background was much more diverse among fused slates than others. However, this difference is not reflected in the levels of candidate novelty, the medians of which are virtually identical for fusions and other slates (0.35 vs 0.37, respectively).[12] The levels of candidate dropout are also very similar between slates that enter fusions and those that do not (Figure 7.10). This contrasts our initial expectation and our earlier finding that *fissions* affect candidate turnover in both directions: splits increase candidate dropout but splinters also recruit more new candidates.

7.3.1 Candidate movement in fusions

Figure 7.11 contrasts predecessor fragmentation between fused and non-fused slates, showing the congruence with the most similar slate ($cong_1$) and with

---

[12] Excluding slates with extreme novelty (> 0.8, dashed lines on Figure 7.9), the difference in the medians would disappear entirely.

all other slates in the previous election ($cong_{2+}$). As expected, most non-fused slates have one dominant predecessor and occupy the lower right-hand corner of the graph while some are in the lower left-hand corner, indicating genuine newness. The upper half, where almost all the fused slates are located, is almost empty. The contrast between fusions and non-fusions is even clearer in the overall distribution of slates (Figure 7.11, c and d). The location of the darkest area suggests that fusions often have a relatively high parity of components and more new candidates than non-fusions. The overlap in the distribution areas would increase only slightly and differences would remain clear even if we included smaller slates.

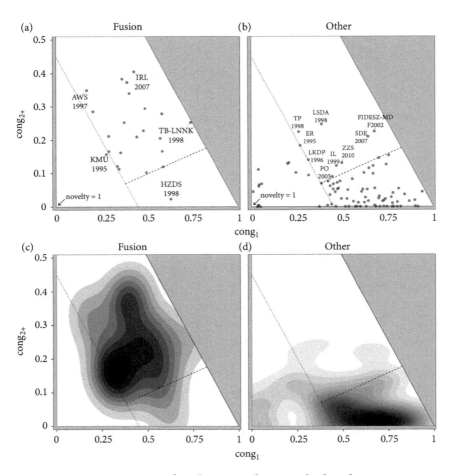

Figure 7.11 Fragmentation of predecessors: fusion and other slates
Notes: See Figure 7.6.

Overall, candidate data places 85% of the fusions from the RI data set where we expect them to be; the unusual case of HZDS (1998) will be discussed below. Candidate data suggests a fusion for eleven additional slates, most of which involved collective defections, a phenomenon that has received little attention in the literature (Kemahlıoğlu & Sayarı 2017 is a rare exception). Collective defections are arguably different from fusions, and they can either be conceptualized as (1) a hybrid of F&F because they involve a group of politicians leaving a party and entering another, or (2) a phenomenon halfway between an individual defection and F&F. However, the line between collective defections and 'proper' splits followed by a merger can be very thin. Oftentimes, defectors form temporary political organizations that fail to develop into formal parties because of uncertain electoral prospects, the attractiveness of joining existing parties, or party regulations that complicate the establishment of new parties (possibly all three).

The fused slates were diverse in terms of the fragmentation of their predecessors and their candidate novelty. The Estonian Pro Patria and Res Publica Union (IRL) in 2007 was an archetypal merger of two equals (see Sikk & Köker 2019). The Polish Solidarity Electoral Action (AWS 1997) was an electoral coalition of nine fairly equally sized parties ($cong > 0.05$ with seven slates from 1993) which also had high candidate novelty. In contrast, the Latvian For Fatherland and Freedom/LNNK (TB–LNNK 1998) was a moderately equal merger of TUB and LNNK–LZP with virtually no candidate novelty. Finally, the Estonian Coalition Party and Country People's Union (KMÜ 1995) was a borderline genuinely new slate, but most of the continuing candidates came from the Safe Home electoral coalition (KK), which included two member parties of KMÜ. The background of the rest of its candidates was diverse and the individual congruences very low, despite a medium $cong_{2+}$.

Only one fusion identified by RI appears to have had a dominant predecessor. The Movement for a Democratic Slovakia (HZDS) in 1998 was a highly unequal merger between the HZDS and the Party of Entrepreneurs and Businessmen (SPŽSR). Previously, the SPŽSR had formed a coalition with the small Democratic Party (DS), which only contributed two low-ranking candidates to the HZDS. The HZDS had very high self-congruence but also attracted defectors from other parties, one of which had a higher level of congruence than the SPŽSR. Although technically a merger, it had no discernible impact on national party politics, unlike the cases discussed above and many other 'true fusions' in Figure 7.11a; this demonstrates how candidate data helps us to distinguish between meaningful and less meaningful fusions.

7.3.2 Candidate movement in non-fused slates

The vast majority of non-fused slates dominated by a single predecessor hover at the bottom of Figure 7.11b but nine slates with no history of a formal merger were diverse in terms of their candidate background and are located in the F&F range. Two highly successful *partially new parties* attracted significant candidates from several parties. First, the Latvian People's Party (TP 1998) was founded by Andris Šķēle, a former non-partisan prime minister. Šķēle himself had never stood for election before but in addition to prominent newcomers, the TP drew candidates from the coalition of the Farmers' Union, the Christian Democrat Union and the Latgale Democratic Party (LZS–LKDS–LDP), and Latvia's Way (LC): out of its thirty most prominent candidates five had previously stood for LZS–LKDS–LDP and six for other parties. Second, the Estonian Reform Party (ER), a new party founded by the incumbent governor of the central bank, Siim Kallas, shortly before the 1995 elections, absorbed the older Liberal Democrats (LD, part of the Pro Patria coalition in 1992) but also attracted prominent candidates from other parties. The ER was effectively a merger between a genuinely new and a parliamentary party: possibly the fastest in history as it took place within hours of ER's creation (Muuli 2013: 146–7).

The Estonian Social Democratic Party (SDE 2007) illustrates the fine line between formal mergers and collective defections. The party was strongly self-congruent but also attracted high-profile candidates, including some former ministers, from the Centre Party (K), who collectively defected without forming a separate party in the interim.[13] This important form of party change is not captured by the literature on fusions because it does not involve a formal merger and both parent parties survive. However, prominent MPs switching parties is very likely to change the nature (e.g. policies) of the parties, possibly more so than some very unequal mergers or tiny splinters.

Several other continuous formations attracted candidates from a range of predecessors, for example, Pro Patria (IL 1999, Estonia) or the Latvian Green and Farmers' Union (ZZS 2010). IL, a merged party based on a 1995 electoral coalition, drew candidates from eight other slates and ZZS recruited prominent candidates from four other parties. These are examples of high $cong_{2+}$ (0.12 and 0.13, respectively) despite relatively low $cong_2$ (0.07 and 0.06). In contrast, the Polish Civic Platform (PO 2005) was highly self-congruent

---

[13] In Estonia, parliamentary groups must be based on parties that contested elections, the defectors formed an informal Social Liberal grouping with other defectors from K with whom they later parted ways.

with considerable candidate novelty. Although it took candidates from several other parties the overall congruence with other slates was limited. Coordination between defectors was rudimentary but the limited fusion amounted to some change in the PO. Such collective defections, whether coordinated and institutionalized or even chaotic, amount to more significant external party change than some smaller party mergers such as the HZDS and SPŽSR merger discussed above.

Finally, the Fidesz–Hungarian Democratic Forum alliance (FIDESZ–MDF 2002) was a curious repeat coalition. In 1998, they had fielded common candidates in one-third of the single-mandate districts while running separately in the proportional part of the mixed system.[14] In 2002, the coalition was extended to the proportional part and was highly congruent with Fidesz and slightly congruent to MDF. Here, the candidate data highlights the deepening of cooperation between the parties which would be missed by data that simply record existing coalitions.

7.3.3 Detecting fusions based on candidate movement

Candidate congruence data also allows us to identify cases of fusion in elections beyond the RI data set. Figure 7.12 shows slates with a significant share of the vote ($v \geq 10\%$), two of which clearly experienced a fusion: the Lithuanian Labour Party (DP 2012), the Slovak Ordinary People and Independent Personalities (OĽaNO 2016), and the Latvian Unity (Vienotība 2014). DP was a clear case of party merger, having swallowed up the ailing New Union (NS). OĽaNO was a continuing party with high novelty and low self-congruence, most likely because the party's move to the right alienated more liberal candidates; it also formed a new coalition with New Majority, an outfit based on defectors from several parties. Finally, Unity was a de facto new coalition with the ailing Zatlers's Reform Party (ZRS) whose leader ran on the Unity's ticket. In addition, some ZRS MPs left the party soon after the 2011 elections to form an interim proto-party, the Free Democrats, some of whom also ended up in Unity.

Figure 7.12 also highlights two cases of collective defection involving the Estonian Social Democrats (SDE). First, its 2011 list included many former candidates from the People's Union (RL)—including five ministers and

---

[14] Twenty-six MDF candidates (derived from the ordering of party labels, see Nikolenyi, 2004: 1046) and MDF won a total of seventeen seats, against Fidesz's ninety.

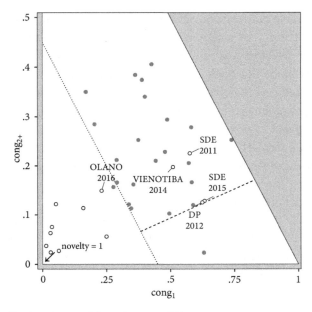

Figure 7.12 Fusion detected based on candidate movement
Note: Hollow markers: predicted fusions in non-RI elections (45 other slates outside of the fusion area not shown); grey markers for fusions in the RI data set. $v \geq 10\%$

a former party leader—who left RL after a narrowly failed merger attempt. When RL eventually dissolved in 2012, the radical-right Conservative People's Party (EKRE) picked up the pieces. Interestingly, a proper merger between RL and SDE could have had a similar effect on the Estonian party system because EKRE could have absorbed those alienated by the merger. Second, SDE again attracted various defectors in 2015, mostly from the Centre Party (K). Although it also formally merged with the tiny Russian Party (VE) around the same time, SDE's congruence with K was much higher. Here, a formal merger had a negligible impact on the party system compared to the collective defection without a formal merger.

Although the last two cases involved a significant formal merger, they are indistinguishable from 'proper' mergers. Starting a new party is costly for splinter groups, especially so in Estonia where parliamentary defectors cannot form parliamentary groups, a rule that is supposed to prevent splits and stabilize the party system. Collective defections show that this does not prevent all fusionary tendencies: MPs still leave their parties but may be tempted to join established parties rather than found new ones. Formal F&F could have been conceivable under different rules, which would have made it easier to form new parties.

Earlier, we noted that successor fragmentation of electoral slates has declined since the 1990s (Figure 7.8). The pattern in the average fragmentation of predecessors is less clear, but fusions have still seen some gradual decline (Figure 7.13). While the success rates of genuinely new parties and electoral volatility have not decreased (see Chapters 5 and 6), party politics in CEE has experienced some stabilization as established actors recombine and break up less frequently than before.

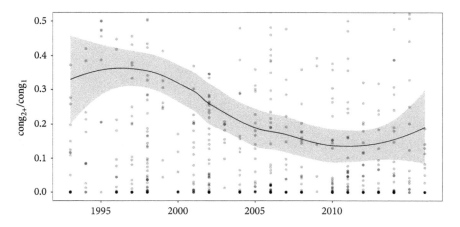

Figure 7.13 Predecessor fragmentation over time

Note: Slates weighted by vote share. Slates with novelty > .8 excluded and slates with $cong_{2+}/cong_1$ > .5 not displayed.

Our candidate-based analysis showcases the diversity among fusions and collective defections and helps to flag inconsequential ones that involve minor parties. We even spotted one 'fake fusion': the coalition between the Hungarian Christian Democratic People's Party and Fidesz (FIDESZ–KDNP 2006), was technically a new coalition because the KDNP had run in a coalition with CENTRUM in 2002. Remarkably, none of its candidates returned with FIDESZ–KDNP in 2006 because KDNP 2002 was very different from the KDNP in 2006. The party experienced a bitter split in 1997 after which many MPs joined Fidesz for the 1998 and 2002 elections. Following a court decision, the 'original' KDNP was restored in 2002 by those who had been 'exiled' in Fidesz. Thus, on paper, FIDESZ–KDNP looked like a new coalition but candidate data correctly emphasizes a high degree of continuity in the arrangement.

Hence, candidate data separates the wheat from the chaff among F&Fs. The Latvian Green and Farmers' Union (ZZS in 2010) and the Czech Christian and Democratic Union (KDU–ČSL in 2002) may look superficially like similarly expanded coalitions, but candidate data highlights that ZZS was only expanded by a tiny Liepaja Party while KDU–ČSL was a new coalition between existing parties of equal strength. Also, we saw that candidate data can identify fusions not covered by dedicated data sets and signal the significance or insignificance of formal mergers for party system development: contrast the equal merger of major parliamentary parties Res Publica and Pro Patria, and the absorption of the minuscule Russian Party by the Social Democrats (both in Estonia).

7.4 Conclusion

Party splits, mergers, and electoral coalitions have been very common in CEE and a proper understanding of them is crucial for a meaningful analysis of party system developments in the region. The patterns of candidate movement largely confirm the cases of F&F recorded in Raimondas Ibenskas's extensive data sets. Fissions, as defined in RI, are much less likely to be dominated by a single successor than non-fissions; this also applies to fusions and their predecessors. In contrast, it is rare for electoral slates unaffected by organizational change to record significant congruence with more than one slate. This may sound unsurprising as fusions are the successors of several parties and fissions by definition have several successors, but it does validate the use of candidate data as a tool for detecting and understanding such party changes. If the reader finds these results trivial, then they are prepared to accept candidate congruence as a useful tool for understanding party change.

The use of candidate data goes beyond the validation of existing data sets. It can improve existing data sets by highlighting spurious, insignificant, and omitted cases of F&F. It also helps to identify parties with fissionary and fusionary tendencies in elections not covered by existing data sets. Furthermore, candidate data reveals the innate diversity in external party change and allow us to distinguish between equal and unequal F&Fs. By focusing on electoral slates, we also eliminate the often blurred distinction between parties and electoral coalitions. Moreover, this chapter has shown once again that a party with the same name in two consecutive elections is not necessarily the 'same' party. Nor is everything that looks or sounds like a 'party' necessarily a party; something that sounds like a coalition, or a movement may, in fact, be a registered party. Sometimes parties can even merge into 'mock parties'—such as the Slovak SDK discussed above—and fairly institutionalized political groups may fail to register as parties if they are discouraged from doing so by provisions in electoral rules.

This chapter has shown that significant fissionary and fusionary tendencies can and do exist in the absence of formal mergers, splits, or the making and breaking of coalitions. We cannot claim to have discovered the phenomenon of collective defection, or that individual defections can substantially alter party systems. What our candidate data does is reveal similarities between 'real' F&Fs and defections, a rather neglected topic in the literature on party systems (although party switching has been studied from the perspective of individual politicians, e.g. Mershon & Shvetsova 2013). It also provides a platform for analysing all fissionary and fusionary phenomena together. Informal developments may be more relevant than formal ones—even compared to those happening at the same time in the same parties—as in the example of the Estonian Social Democrats in 2015 mentioned above, which benefited from an important collective defection and an insignificant merger.

We take the idea of fissionary and fusionary tendencies even further by arguing that they are almost always present in parties, to varying degrees. Candidate movement data allows us to study the *phenomenon* without explicit reference to defined cases of splits, mergers, and electoral coalitions. Finally, we also offer something for agnostics who may not yet fully agree with our approach. At the very least, data on candidate movements are extremely useful in highlighting potential cases of F&F for further scrutiny. Therefore, for the benefit of accepters and doubting Thomases alike, the full data on pairwise party congruence is available online (https://osf.io/nm5ek/).

8
Leadership change

Change in leadership is one of the most visible changes in the life of a political party. Whereas other changes to candidates' political 'survival machines' can easily be overlooked, a change in the person behind the steering wheel is a definite marker of change. Leadership and its change are especially relevant in the modern era where—due to the changing nature of media, campaigning, and party organizational models—political parties have become increasingly 'presidentialized' and 'personalized' (Blondel & Thiébault 2009; Longley & Hazan 1999; Musella 2015, 2017; Passarelli 2015; Rahaț & Kenig 2018; Sandri et al. 2016; Schumacher & Giger 2018; Webb et al. 2012). If leaders are as important as these studies imply, then their change must be one of the most fundamental aspects of party change and should herald or follow shifts in party strategy, policy, or organization. Likewise, the relative importance of predecessors should be reflected in the leadership of electoral alliances or merged parties, and the leadership of splinters should indicate their significance for the party of origin.

A wealth of studies on party leaders has focused on the methods of their selection (Aylott & Bolin 2017; Kenig et al. 2015; Marino 2021; Musella 2017; Pilet & Cross 2014; Quinn 2012; Sandri et al. 2016a), individual traits of leaders (Bittner 2011; Gherghina 2020), leadership survival (Cross & Blais 2012; Cross & Pilet 2015), and public appeals and electoral impact (Aarts et al. 2011; Bittner 2011; Fernandez-Vazquez & Somer-Topcu 2019; Garzia 2012; Somer-Topcu 2016). In contrast, the impact of leaders and their turnover on their parties has received more limited attention but has yielded promising insights. Alexiadou and O'Malley (2022) show that dominant leaders influence the institutional, policy, and electoral 'faces' of parties, and can leave their parties worse off when they exit; similarly, Schumacher and Giger find that parties with dominant leadership have more fluid programmes (2018). Gherghina (2020), on the other hand, highlights that change in leaders' personal traits during their time in office can affect their parties' electoral performance and organization (i.e. membership or intra-party cohesion).

To our knowledge, no studies have hitherto linked leadership change to candidate turnover. Gouglas et al. (2020) come closest by examining eight West

European democracies between 1945 and 2015 and finding that a change in leadership increases MP turnover. In a similar vein, Barnfield and Bale (2022) argue that leadership change can trigger an exodus of members. These examples underscore that leadership change has consequences not only for party programmes, organization, and electoral performance but also for party people; furthermore, leadership change is perhaps even more likely than poor electoral performance to lead to other changes among political parties (Harmel et al. 1995). Hence, this chapter considers to what extent leadership turnover impacts parties themselves by focusing on its relationship to candidate change.

We begin by conceptualizing the notion of party leaders. While most political parties have a clearly identifiable head of the organization, they are often not the de facto leaders or 'public face' of the party. The latter does not necessarily coincide with holding or running for key executive roles, most notably the office of the prime minister. We suggest that a flexible, qualitatively informed approach is needed for identifying leaders or groups of leaders of slates—to use our joint term for parties—electoral coalitions, etc. in a given election. We propose a semi-quantitative scale of leadership novelty that emphasizes visibly party-political roles over ceremonial or technocratic ones and ranges from 0 (no change) to 1 (new leaders with no previous experience in party politics). For our quantitative analysis, we qualitatively code leadership novelty for all 169 slates in our data set that won at least 10% of the vote. We find that moderate to high levels of leadership novelty are associated with higher candidate novelty not only compared to leadership continuity but also in contrast to new leaders with limited novelty, i.e. former deputy leaders or other heirs apparent. The results are robust to controlling for the impact of levels of electoral support, one of the essential determinants of candidate turnover identified in previous chapters. The final section of the chapter considers leadership in slates following fission or fusion. We analyse the relationship between candidate congruence and leadership congruence among fissions and fusions involving eighty-two slates. We find that in a clear majority of cases, the successors and predecessors with a more congruent leader are also more congruent to the joint slate (after a fusion or before the fission) in terms of their candidates.

8.1 Who is a party leader?

The definition of 'party leader' is remarkably seldom problematized in the vast emerging literature on party leadership. This is mostly because the position of a party leader has been unambiguous in nearly all parties in Western Europe. The oddity of collective leadership—introduced first by the German

Greens and later adopted in other parties such as the Alternative for Germany and the Italian Five Star Movement (Campus et al. 2021)—presents a rare exception. However, things are often more complicated than formal organizational arrangements may suggest, and formal leaders are not always the most prominent people in the party. Many parties, including several large ones, have picked a different person as their prime ministerial candidates not only in CEE but also in many West European countries.

The Political Party Database (Poguntke et al. 2020) contains information about no fewer than four different kinds of leaders: (1) the leader of the parliamentary party, (2) the de facto leader of the national extra-legislative party organization, (3) the designated top candidate at the next election, and (4) the most important political leader of the national party. These often coincide, but not always: e.g. in both the 2009 and 2013 German federal elections, the Social Democrats' chancellor candidate was not the party leader, and the party leader at the time was neither the leader of the parliamentary party. Among the 207 data points (a party in a given year) in the Political Party Database for which any of the four leaders are reported, just forty listed the same person for all four positions. The top candidate was the political leader in 144 cases, the parliamentary group leader in 100 cases, and the leader of the party organization in 112 cases. Furthermore, the formal leaders of party organizations can be fairly minor figures (e.g. in the UK, Netherlands, Australia, or Canada) while in other cases the party group in the parliament is not led by the de facto leader of a party: e.g. all large Polish party groups in 2012, bar the Democratic Left Alliance (SLD) and Palikot's Movement (RUCHP).

The lack of correspondence between the party leader and the top candidate is sometimes understandable. For example, in 2011, Silvio Berlusconi was the presumptive top candidate for the 2013 election of not one but two Italian parties: the People of Freedom (led by Berlusconi) and Lega Nord, its coalition partner. However, parties often nominate someone who is not the party leader (in any of the four senses) as the prime minister or a prime ministerial candidate (Baylis 2007). For example, both Jiří Paroubek and Péter Medgyessy became prime ministers of the Czech Republic and Hungary, respectively, without leading or having led their parties (Enyedi & Tóka 2007; Samuels & Shugart 2010). Also in Hungary, Ferenc Gyurcsány ascended to the office of the prime minister from medium ranks of the Hungarian Socialist Party (MSZP) and only later formally took over party leadership; similarly, when Viktor Orbán relinquished the leadership of Fidesz in the run-up to the 2002 parliamentary elections while staying on as the prime minister, this was a purely strategic move and not a sign of weakened authority (Enyedi & Tóka

2007: 158). A more recent but odd case was the premiership of Beata Szydło in Poland (2015–17), who always remained in the shadow of Jarosław Kaczyński, the de facto leader of the country and leader of Law and Justice (PiS) (Stanley 2020; Zuba 2020).

The lack of clarity over who is the 'real' leader of a political party complicates our task of analysing the relationship between leadership and candidate change. A purely organizational focus on formal party leaders will inevitably overlook important changes among more visible leaders such as prime ministerial candidates. Furthermore, leaders of fused slates, such as electoral coalitions, are not always leaders of any of the constituent units and are sometimes difficult to determine as the role may not at all be formally defined. Instead of restricting our attention to any particular position, we are considering, based on extensive qualitative research, *the most important person or people in the party*. In some cases, these are formal leaders, and in other cases prime ministerial candidates; sometimes, when neither dominates, we consider both in terms of their novelty and congruence with leaders from the previous election. In that, we follow the general thrust of our approach outlined in Chapter 2: not to focus strictly and exclusively on formal organizations, but on the party people who can actually drive change. Following the emphasis on executive leadership in party presidentialization and centralization literature, we argue that even though formal party leaders may be easy to identify, the prominence of prime ministers and prime ministerial candidates requires due attention, and their novelty needs to be considered when assessing leadership novelty.

8.2 Measuring leadership novelty

The literature on party leadership and leadership selection may be thriving yet scholarship on leadership change or renewal is scant, not to mention the lack of research seeking to measure change beyond dichotomous indicators.[1] Importantly, we believe that a qualitative distinction can be drawn between new leaders with limited political experience and 'heirs apparent', e.g. deputy leaders or favoured successors. We propose a new scale of leadership novelty that distinguishes between five main levels of leadership change but also allows for intermediate placements in difficult cases (Table 8.1).

---

[1] Changes in leaders' characteristics have been extensively studied by Gherghina (2020) but his approach is very different from ours as leaders' characteristics can change even when the leaders remain the same, or characteristics remain the same when the leaders change.

The scale mirrors previous attempts to categorize party leaders yet broadens and extends their application. Such previous efforts include Musella (2015), who provides descriptive data on the pre-leadership background of 460 party leaders (mostly in old democracies), implicitly using similar categories to ours but stopping short of providing a scale of leadership novelty.[2] Sandri et al (2016) propose a four-point scale of leaders' political experience ranging from (1) no experience, through (2) only local level experience, and (3) only national level experience to (4) both local and national level experience.[3] Our scale is similar, but we distinguish between national offices of different importance and do not require local experience for the top score as even highly seasoned leaders may only have experience in national politics. Vice versa, local prominence can trump national experience: e.g. the mayor of the capital city can be politically more prominent than a junior cabinet minister, let alone a rank-and-file MP (see Colomer et al 2020).

At the extremes of our five-point scale of leadership novelty we have (a) leaders who were leading the party or a linked party already at the time of the previous election and (b) new leaders lacking any previous political experience. The former is very common: more than half of the leaders in our analysis had carried over from the previous election. However, quite a few party leaders have had no previous political experience: most notably, Simeon Saxe-Coburg-Gotha (better known as Simeon II, the leader of his eponymous party, NDSV, Bulgaria), Miro Cerar (eponymous party, SMC, Slovenia), Juhan Parts (Res Publica, RP, Estonia), and Einars Repše (New Era, Latvia). None of them had been involved in party politics yet led their newly founded parties to electoral victories and instantly landed the post of prime minister.[4]

---

[2] Musella's (2015) data also lists the political position immediately before becoming a leader; for contrasting candidate and leadership novelty, we consider the position at the time of the previous election.

[3] Sandri et al. (2016) simply omit cases of collective leadership, including among electoral coalitions or the divided positions between a party leader and prime ministerial nominee. These are, however, some of the most intriguing cases in our analysis.

[4] We also identified the following genuinely novel leaders: Artūras Paulauskas (Lithuania, the founding leader of New Union, NS), Andrej Babiš (Czech Republic, ANO), Radek John (the official leader of the Czech Public Affairs, VV) or Vít Bárta (the widely recognized de facto leader of VV), Arūnas Valinskas (Lithuania, National Resurrection Party, TPP), Siim Kallas (Estonia, Reform Party, ER). Most of them had held a senior non-political role, such as the president of the national bank (Repše, Kallas), prosecutor general (Paulauskas, also an independent runner-up in direct presidential elections), auditor general (Parts), or a monarch under regency (Simeon II).

Table 8.1 The scale of slate leadership novelty

Leader novelty	Description
0.0	Leader at the time of the previous election
0.25	(a) De facto deputy leader or heir apparent before the election as a leader,[a] (b) Holder of a major party-political office or (c) A former party leader
0.5	(a) Party[a] member in a minor office; (b) Non-partisan prime minister
0.75	(a) As an independent, either held a major political office (e.g. mayor) or a minor political office (e.g. a minister) (b) Rank-and-file MP
1.0	No previous party-political experience

[a] the same party or a strongly linked slate

Between the two extremes, we find various degrees of novelty. Heirs apparent and previous deputy leaders (formally or de facto)[5] possess the least novelty, as do those who had held a major party-political office (e.g. senior cabinet members) either for the same party or a clearly linked slate. More genuine *party*-political leadership novelty can be found among those who ascended to party leadership after serving as non-partisan mayor of the capital city, e.g. Boyko Borisov (the mayor of Sofia before setting up GERB) or Zoran Janković (Positive Slovenia, PS, Ljubljana). Finally, some of the most complicated and idiosyncratic cases can be found in the middle (score of 0.5). For instance, Andris Šķēle was an independent prime minister in Latvia but, in contrast to directly elected mayors, the office is within the gift of parliamentary parties; hence he was a more party-political figure when founding the People's Party (TP) in 1998. In Estonia, Taavi Rõivas replaced Andrus Ansip as the leader of the Estonian Reform Party (ER) and prime minister in 2014; while he was clearly a member of the party's elite, he was no heir apparent. Having served as a relatively low-profile Minister of Social Affairs for less than two years, he was dubbed as a 'dark horse' by the media when he took over as the prime minister, following a competitive and narrow vote at the party board (ERR 2014).

---

[5] We only consider deputy leaders immediately before their ascension to leadership. Deputy leaders from the more distant past can be more akin to outsiders. Their scoring depends on the time elapsed between their holding of the office and whether they became the leader of the party in which they held the deputy chair or a different party. For example, Robert Fico was a prominent member and once a deputy leader of the Slovak Party of the Democratic Left (SDĽ) before he established Smer and became its leader (novelty score 0.5).

We can use the sliding scale of leadership novelty for measuring change or continuity in continuing parties but also in new and seemingly new parties, in which leaders can be political novices or experienced politicians (even previous leaders of connected parties). Notably, our scale focuses on leadership novelty, rather than leader dropout or exit because leader 'dropout' is more difficult to conceptualize and measure. Leaders often leave office because of other forms of party change (in particular, poor electoral results) or conflict within the party, but may cite health or family concerns to veil the actual circumstances of their exit. While we have data on candidate dropout, the impact of leader exit on candidates depends on a host of contextual variables that may be difficult to assess, at least without laborious qualitative research.

For the quantitative analysis of the relationship between leadership and candidate novelty, we analyse all 168 slates with $v \geq 10\%$ in our data set. We obtained data on leadership and leadership changes from various online sources: usually starting with Wikipedia in various languages, followed by the Nexis media database and other online resources. Even with some complicated cases, the five-point scale suits most of the leaders in our analysis. A small group of leaders (6.5%) do not neatly fit under any of the categories and their novelty is most appropriately coded with values between those listed in Table 8.1.

We assigned an intermediate score of 0.875 to Valdis Zatlers (the leader of the eponymous ZRS in 2011), a former ceremonial and non-partisan president of Latvia, and to Richard Sulík, a senior but non-partisan Slovak government adviser (leader of Freedom and Solidarity, SaS, since 2009). An intermediate score (0.675) was also assigned to Viktor Uspaskich, who had been an independent MP before founding the Lithuanian Labour Party (DP) in 2003, and to Janusz Palikot, the leader of Palikot's Movement in 2011 (Poland). Palikot had been one of the eight deputy leaders of the Citizen's Platform (PO) parliamentary group, a position somewhere between a junior minister and a rank-and-file MP.

Lower intermediate novelty scores (0.375) were overall more common and usually derived from unusual leadership configurations and leader backgrounds. For instance, this applied to Maciej Płażyński, the first formal leader of the Polish Citizen's Platform (PO) who had served in the semi-ceremonial post of the Marshal of the *Sejm* before becoming the PO's formal leader. Nevertheless, PO had initially had a de facto tripartite leadership also involving Donald Tusk and Andrzej Olechowski who had more novelty (especially Olechowski); hence, Płażyński was arguably more novel than other cases of deputy leaders or holders of major offices (that we coded as 0.25). Other cases coded as 0.375 include Jiří Paroubek (Czech Social Democrats, ČSSD) and

Andrejs Panteļējevs (Latvian Way, LC) who had both served in a variety of political positions before the 2006 and 1998 elections, respectively; however, their prominence was below the level required by the descriptors for 0.25, considering that their parties had ample opportunities to appoint them into prominent positions while in government.

The leadership novelty of a few slates was also set at 0.375 because when the roles of the formal party leader and the prime minister or prime ministerial candidate were split. The Hungarian Socialist Party (MSZP) has regularly split these roles. In 2002, Péter Medgyessy, the Minister of Finance until 1998 who then moved away from politics, was the prime ministerial candidate while László Kovács, a former Foreign Minister, and then party group leader, served as the formal party leader. In 2006, the party was led by István Hiller, previously a deputy leader, while Ferenc Gyurcsány, previously a relatively junior figure in the party, had become the prime minister, partly because he was acceptable to MSZP's coalition partner. By the time of the 2010 election, Ildikó Lendvai, the parliamentary group leader since 2002, had become the party leader while Attila Mesterházy had been chosen as the party's prime ministerial candidate; he was previously the parliamentary group leader and MSZP vice president.[6] In Latvia, prime minister Laimdota Straujuma and the top candidate of 'Unity' (Vienotība) at the time of the Latvian 2014 parliamentary election had served earlier as an independent Minister of Agriculture and only joined the party upon becoming the prime minister. However, Solvita Āboltiņa continued as the leader of the party from the previous (2011) election. In the Polish Democratic Left Alliance (SLD) in 2005 these roles were somewhat reversed. Wojciech Olejniczak, the new leader of the party had only held a relatively junior post of an agriculture minister and his election as party leader was seen as a 'face lift' for the party (Polish News Bulletin 2005). In contrast, Prime Minister Marek Belka was not only a long-term party member but had also assumed his position following two spells as the finance minister and deputy prime minister (1997 and 2001–2).

Finally, mergers and new electoral coalitions also posed some challenges for leadership novelty scoring. After competing as an electoral coalition in 2010, the National Alliance 'All for Latvia!'/ For Fatherland and Freedom/LNNK (PVL-TB-LNNK) had merged into a party for the 2011 Latvian snap election. The party was led jointly by the leader of PVL (Raivis Dzintars, novelty 0)

---

[6] The Hungarian Democratic Forum (MDF) in 1994 is another example of split roles of prime minister and party leader. Péter Boross became the prime minister upon József Antall's death and had already been the party's second in command; Lajos Für who previously held several senior roles for the party and was its presidential candidate in 1989, replaced Antall as the party leader. Because of Boross's and Für's previous experiences, MDF's leadership novelty (0.25) was lower than for the MSZP cases.

and a former Minister of Justice from TB–LNNK (Gaidis Bērziņš, novelty 0.25), resulting in an aggregate leadership novelty of 0.125. The 2000 Social-Democratic Coalition of Algirdas Brazauskas (BSDA) in Lithuania was more complicated still. The coalition consisted of the Democratic Labour Party (LDDP) led by Algirdas Brazauskas, the Social Democratic Party (LSDP) led by Vytenis Andriukaitis and two smaller coalition partners. Brazauksas, the titular leader of the coalition, had been elected the president of the country when he was the leader of LDDP in 1993; he resigned from the party only because of incompatibility and assumed a more party-political role immediately upon the end of his tenure. Andriukaitis was a new leader of LSDP but a former presidential candidate for the party; the leaders of junior coalition partners had even more limited novelty. In the aggregate, this roughly approximates leadership by heirs apparent (novelty = 0.25), especially considering that Brazauskas became the leader of a merged party based on the electoral coalition half a year after the election.

Our scale of leadership novelty as well as our codings are not absolute and must be used with caution—like many other measures in political science (e.g. party policy positions; see Chapter 9). Yet, we believe that the scale and coding provide a valid approximation of leadership novelty within our multi-dimensional understanding of party change. This is backed up by the next two sections which demonstrate a clear relationship between leadership novelty and candidate novelty as well as between candidate congruence and leadership congruence under fission and fusion.

8.3 Leadership novelty and candidate novelty

As we have argued throughout the book, change is perpetual in political parties yet change among their leaders—the pinnacle of the party people pyramid—is infrequent. In our data set, more than half of the slates had continuing leaders, i.e. they also led the predecessor slate in the previous election, and fewer than 20% exhibited leadership novelty of 0.5 or greater (Figure 8.1a). Separating continuing and new parties as defined in the ParlGov data set (Döring et al. 2022), we can see that continuing parties also tended to have continuing leaders (62%, Figure 8.1b), with a further 26% showing low levels of leadership novelty (up to 0.25). Just two (1.5%) leaders of continuing parties had leadership novelty above 0.5, albeit with very different profiles. In Poland, Leszek Balcerowicz—widely associated with the economic shock therapy introduced during his tenure as non-partisan finance minister in 1989/1990—surprisingly beat the former Prime Minister Tadeusz Mazowiecki for the leadership of the

Freedom Union (UW) in 1995. In contrast, although the Slovak diplomat Jozef Migaš was one of the founders of the Party of the Democratic Left (SDĽ), he was generally little-known before leading the party in the 1998 elections.

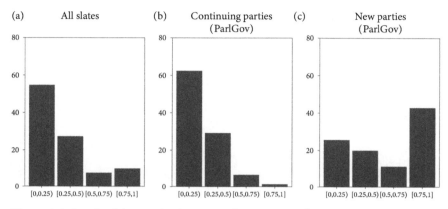

Figure 8.1 Leadership novelty in new and continuing slates

Notes: All slates in our data set with $v = 10\%$, N = 168. Continuing and new parties according to ParlGov (Döring et al. 2022)

Unsurprisingly, many of the parties classified as 'new' by ParlGov also had genuinely new leaders (Figure 8.1c). Yet, leadership novelty varied noticeably: less than half (46%) of parties classified as new had a leadership novelty over 0.5, indicating partially or seemingly new slates based on their leadership. Remarkably, the leaders of nine slates (26%) classified as new had led slates in the previous election. Hence, leadership novelty tends to be low among continuing parties, but leadership novelty varies greatly in parties conventionally classified as 'new', echoing our finding on candidate novelty (see Chapter 5).

Leadership continuity and novelty are not only associated with the newness of parties and electoral coalitions but also with candidate novelty. Figure 8.2 shows a strong linear fit between leadership novelty and candidate novelty ($r = 0.63$, dashed line). Most importantly, hardly any slates with low-novelty leaders have high candidate novelty (upper left quadrant), and the electoral slates of almost all slates with leadership novelty above 0.5 were highly novel (upper right quadrant). Looking at general measures of association, it would be easy to be content with the basic bivariate fit as the levels of statistical significance and the overall model fit are impressive (model 1 in Table 8.2). However, at low levels, leadership novelty does not seem to increase candidate novelty, as shown by a local polynomial fit (thin solid line in Figure 8.2). A linear fit would also underestimate candidate novelty among slates with genuine political novices for leaders (the right end of the graph). While these slates may

190 PARTY PEOPLE

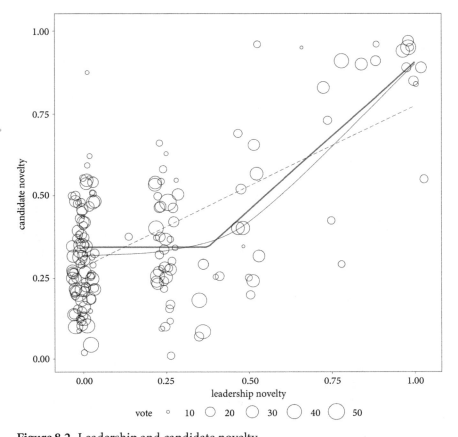

Figure 8.2 Leadership and candidate novelty

Notes: Slates with $v \geq 10\%$. Jitter added to avoid excessive overlapping. Dashed line: linear fit, thin solid line: smooth fit, thick solid line: predictions from the regression model (for median vote share).

be expected to field some continuing candidates, we would generally expect candidate novelty to be above 0.75.

In our regression analysis, we apply a floor for the leadership novelty score to account for the limited trend in candidate novelty at low levels of leadership novelty. We recode novelty scores to a minimum of 0.375, resulting in a 'deflected' linear fit (thick solid line in Figure 8.2; model 2 in Table 8.2). A model with floored leadership novelty improves the model fit and results in more meaningful expectations across the scale of leadership novelty.[7] This is an important finding as it suggests that for overall party change, a leadership

---

[7] Other floors (0.25, 0.4) lead to very similar results. Models with a quadratic term instead of the floor had similar results but sacrifice degrees of freedom, suffer from multicollinearity, and diverge from the data pattern.

'handover' to an heir apparent is more akin to leadership continuity than the selection of a political novice or someone from the sidelines.

Table 8.2 Candidate novelty and leadership novelty

	Model 1	Model 2	Model 3	Model 4
Leadership novelty (raw)	0.49*** (0.05)			
lnov: Leadership novelty (floor = 0.375)		0.90*** (0.07)		0.58*** (0.16)
$\log_{10} v$			−0.10 (0.10)	
$(1-\text{lnov})^*\log_{10} v$				−0.25* (0.11)
Constant	0.28*** (0.02)	0.01 (0.03)	0.52*** (0.13)	0.33* (0.15)
N	168	168	168	168
R^2	0.394	0.477	0.007	0.491

Notes: * $p<0.05$ ** $p<0.01$ *** $p<0.001$. Standard errors in parentheses.

We have argued previously in this book that party size should affect levels of candidate turnover. Therefore, we also test for the combined effect of leadership novelty and party size. While we found a relationship between a slate's vote share and its weighted candidate novelty in Chapter 4, we fail to detect any such association in the bivariate model here (model 3 in Table 8.2). This is likely because of the more limited sample size and, more importantly, left censoring of the data set: given the great difficulty in coding leadership change for smaller slates, our data only includes those that won at least 10% of the vote. For this reason, we cannot meaningfully include the variable of party support change (in contrast to our models in Chapter 4) as the set of cases is biased in favour of parties increasing their vote share: all that drop below 10% are excluded.

Nevertheless, when controlling for leadership novelty, slate size does have a statistically significant coefficient in the expected direction: larger slates have a lower weighted candidate novelty than smaller ones (model 4 in Table 8.2). The coefficient for leadership novelty remains very similar (when considered in conjunction with the intercept) and the overall model fit is somewhat improved. We expect slates led by political newcomers to have high levels of candidate novelty regardless of their electoral performance and, therefore, discount party size by leadership novelty, interacting the logged vote share with the inverse of the leadership novelty score. In other words, we predict higher levels of candidate novelty for smaller parties when leadership novelty is low or moderate, but the difference diminishes and eventually disappears as leaders become more novel (see Figure 8.3 for predictions for slates with 10, 30, and 50% of vote share). The results remain robust; although, expectedly, the coefficient for leadership novelty is reduced, as some of the variance is now explained by slate size.

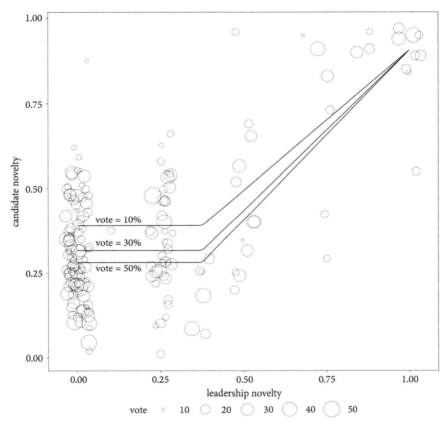

Figure 8.3 Leadership and candidate novelty: the effect of slates' vote share

8.4 Leadership continuity under fission and fusion

We can measure the importance of participants involved in fission and fusion by candidate congruence between the joint slates (i.e. before fission or after fusion) and their successors or predecessors (see Chapter 7). When parties split or merge or electoral coalitions are created or dissolved, candidates must decide whether to part ways with their erstwhile running mates or join forces with new party people. But what happens to the leaders of the affected slates? Like calculating candidate congruence between slates across elections, we can estimate leadership congruence between successor and predecessor slates based on the leaders' political biographies. Leadership congruence is essentially the reverse of leadership novelty, and we follow a similar scale as presented above, albeit with one key difference: we consider congruence specifically vis-à-vis the pertinent slate. Hence, if the leader of a slate happened to be a leader of a slate that was *not* involved in the fission/fusion, the congruence is zero. If candidate change and leadership change are linked, leadership congruences should reflect candidate congruences. To test that, we analyse leadership congruence among slates that experienced fission or fusion and: (a) were large ($v \geq 10\%$) and (b) where candidate congruence between the second most congruent slate and the predecessor/successor was above 0.15. In other words, we exclude cases of minor splinters and very unequal mergers.

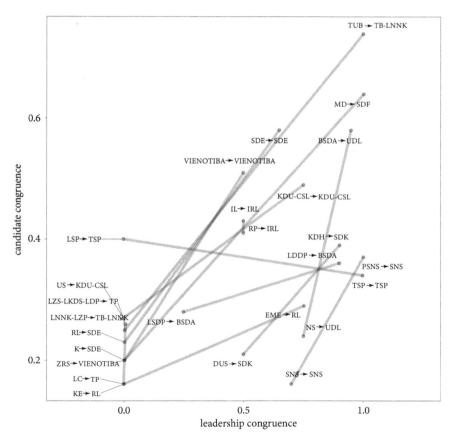

Figure 8.4 Fusion: candidate and leadership congruence
Note: lines connect predecessor slates.

The relationship between candidate and leadership congruence among *fusions* is clear: the slate with higher candidate congruence with the successor slate nearly always also exhibited higher leadership congruence. This is suggested by the upward-sloping lines in Figure 8.4. Out of thirteen major fusions involving twenty-six predecessors, there was only one instance where the more congruent slate had lower leadership congruence. In 1998, Jānis Jurkāns continued as the leader of the Latvian National Harmony Party (TSP) after the merger with the Latvian Socialist Party (LSP); however, the two predecessors were still very similar in terms of their candidate congruence with TSP, hence the only mildly downward sloping line in Figure 8.4. Two fusions had equal leadership congruences to their predecessors despite very small differences in candidate congruence. The Latvian People's Party (TP, bottom left in Figure 8.4) had zero leadership congruence with both predecessors (the Farmers' Union, Christian Democrats and the Latgale Democratic Party, LZS–LKDS–LDP, and the Latvian Way, LC) as it was a partially new party set up by non-partisan prime minister Andris Šķēle (also discussed above). Šķēle might be seen as marginally congruent to the predecessors in the governing coalition that he led; however, TP's candidate congruence with both was rather low. In Estonia, the merger of Res Publica (RP) and Pro Patria (IL) into Pro Patria and Res Publica Union (IRL) was fairly equal in terms of both candidate and leader congruences as the merged party was initially led by the former leaders of its predecessors (centre of Figure 8.4).

For *fission*, we analysed fourteen slates that split into twenty nine slates in the following election. All of them had two significant successors, except for the Estonian Pro Patria Union (I, 1992) which had high congruence with three successors (Pro Patria–National Independence Party, I–ERSP; the Right Wingers, PP; and the Reform Party, ER in 1995, circled markers in Figure 8.5). In a large majority of cases, higher candidate congruence between the successor and a predecessor coincided with higher leadership congruence between the successor and predecessor slates. Figure 8.5 is dominated by upward-sloping lines, i.e. a positive correlation between candidate and leadership congruence among slates involved in fission.

In some cases, the leader of the most congruent successor had been the leader of the predecessor (the right end of Figure 8.5).[8] In many cases, the second most congruent slate—most often the 'splinter'—also showed considerable leadership congruence with the predecessor slate. Notably, these cases frequently involved a (former) prime minister or the speaker of the parliament

---

[8] Interestingly, (near-)perfect leadership congruence is more common after fusion than fission (compare Figures 8.4 and 8.5).

LEADERSHIP CHANGE 195

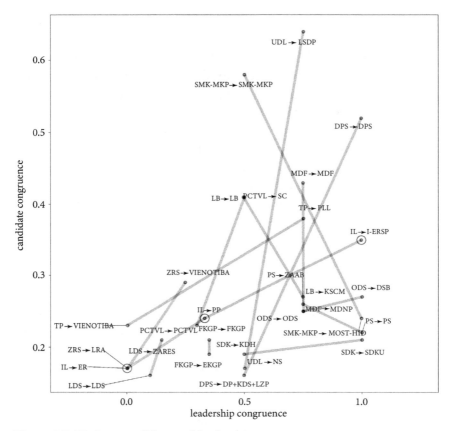

Figure 8.5 Fission: candidate and leadership congruence
Note: lines connect successor slates; Pro Patria Union (IL) with three successors highlighted.

leading one of the slates. For instance, when Saimnieks (DPS), the winner of the 1995 election in Latvia, faltered and disintegrated, Ziedonis Čevers continued to lead the severely weakened party. Nevertheless, some of its candidates defected to a motley electoral coalition (DP+KDS+LZP) that included the Labour Party (DP) led by Ilga Kreituse, who had previously served as the speaker of the Saeima for DPS. Somewhat similarly, the 2005 elections in Bulgaria saw the emergence of the Democrats for a Strong Bulgaria (DSB) headed by former Prime Minister Ivan Kostov, who had already led the United Democratic Forces (ODS) in the 2001 elections. Even though ODS also contested the 2005 election with Nadezhda Nikolova Mihaylova as its leader—likewise an already senior figure in ODS—the candidate congruence of DSB was higher.

The two 2002 slates with the highest candidate congruence with the Slovak Democratic Coalition (SDK) also exhibited high levels of leadership congruence. The SDK's former leader and Prime Minister Mikuláš Dzurinda now led the Slovak Democratic and Christian Union (SDKÚ), while the Christian Democratic Movement (KDH) contested the election under the leadership of Pavol Hrušovský, a deputy speaker of parliament and a deputy leader of KDH, a junior partner in SDK. In contrast, the successors to the Pro Patria Electoral Coalition (I) in Estonia had very different leadership congruences. Mart Laar, the former prime minister and leading figure of the Pro Patria–National Independence Party (I–ERSP) coalition in 1995 had been the leader of IL, one of its constituent parts, in 1992. However, the Liberal Democrats (part of IL in 1992) merged with the newly founded Reform Party (ER) led by Siim Kallas, the former president of the central bank and a political novice.[9]

Often, the most congruent successor slate was not headed by a leader of a predecessor party but by another senior figure. For example, in 2008, the Lithuanian Social Democratic Party (LSDP), a constituent party of the 2004 electoral coalition 'Working for Lithuania' (UdL), was led by Gediminas Kirkilas, a seasoned LSDP politician, who had succeeded Algirdas Brazauskas as the prime minister. The New Union (NS), a junior partner in UdL continued under the leadership of Artūras Paulauskas yet LSDP's leadership congruence was arguably higher as LSDP was the dominant force in UdL. The Latvian People's Party (TP) had notable candidate congruences to both 'For a Good Latvia!' (PLL) and 'Unity' (Vienotība) in the 2010 parliamentary elections. While Vienotība inherited some of TP's candidates, it was organizationally unrelated and was led by Valdis Dombrovskis who had no links to TP; hence, there was no formal fission involved. PLL was a coalition of TP and Latvia's First Party/Latvia's Way (LPP/LC) and had a considerable candidate and leadership congruence as to TP: while Andris Šķēle was not a leader of TP in 2006, he was the founder and long-term leader of the party.

Sometimes, two successor slates show equal leadership congruence with the predecessor. For example, two Hungarian fissions from the early 1990s produced slates headed by politicians who were equally close to their parent slates. In 1994, both the Independent Smallholders (FKGP) and United Smallholders (EKGP) were led by politicians closely linked to the original FKGP (József Torgyán and János Szabó, respectively); it also had very similar candidate congruence with both successors. In the 1998 elections, the Hungarian

---

[9] The leader of the Right Wingers (PP)—the third slate with significant congruence with IL—was difficult to pin down. Ülo Nugis, the speaker of parliament, was one of the party's most recognizable figures while Karin Jaani, a relatively junior politician, was the formal leader. Hence, its leadership congruence was somewhere between that of I–ERSP and ER.

Democratic People's Party (MDNP) had split from the Democratic Forum (MDF), but the leaders of both slates had firm roots in MDF: MDNP was led by Sándor Lezsák, a founding member of MDF, and MDF by Iván Szabó, a former interim leader of MDF and the leader of its parliamentary group.

Leadership and candidate congruences point in the opposite direction only in three cases marked by downward-sloping lines in Figure 8.5. The Slovak Party of the Hungarian Community (SMK–MKP) was one such case. Before the 2010 election, 'Bridge' (Most–Híd) was set up by members of SMK–MKP dissatisfied with the increasingly nationalist line of the party. The party was headed by Béla Bugár, the former leader of SMK–MKP who had narrowly lost a leadership election to Pál Csáky three years earlier. This is a rare instance of a party leader defecting and *not* taking most candidates with them. The complex fission of the Czech communists after the 1992 elections presents another exceptional case. In 1992, the Communist Party of Bohemia and Moravia (KSČM) had been the leading party in an electoral coalition called 'Left Bloc' (LB). In the 1996 elections, the KSČM ran on its own, yet an offshoot from the coalition—confusingly named Left Bloc—also contested the election and had a higher candidate congruence with LB than KSČM. However, leadership congruence was reversed as the leader of the KSČM, Miroslav Grebeníček, was more congruent to the original LB than the leader of the new LB, Jaroslav Ortman. Finally, the 2014 elections in Slovenia saw Positive Slovenia (PS) return under its old name and founding leader Zoran Janković. Nevertheless, the List of Alenka Bratušek (ZAAB) had a slightly higher candidate congruence with PS of 2010 (top-left corner of Figure 8.5). Bratušek had been the leader of PS and the prime minister nominated by the party between the two elections. Hence, leadership congruence of PS was only marginally lower to ZAAB than to continuity PS. Apart from these three and somewhat idiosyncratic exceptions, leadership congruence shows a remarkably clear association with candidate congruence under fission.

8.5 Conclusion

Party leaders are the most visible stratum of party people. Existing scholarship has highlighted leaders' increased relevance amidst the personalization of politics and presidentialization of political parties as well as their ability to influence party programmes and electoral performance. However, few scholars have engaged with the question of who counts as a party leader. This is surprising as formal leadership of party organizations does not always coincide with other equally or more important positions, such as the (candidate for) prime minister or the leader of the parliamentary party; depending on the context, formal leaders may have limited prominence. In assessing leadership change, we considered these different faces at the helm of the party rather than strictly focusing on one of the roles. In our analysis, we also went beyond a simple dichotomous differentiation between new and continuing leaders. We presented a quasi-quantitative approach to measuring leadership novelty that considers the leader's erstwhile role within the party or related parties where fission or fusion had occurred. Analysing the 168 largest slates from our data set, we showed that among continuing parties a clear relationship exists between leadership novelty and candidate novelty. Furthermore, our empirical analysis revealed that for overall party change, leaders who had previously held prominent party positions (with a novelty score of up to 0.25) are more akin to continuing leaders than new leaders with higher degrees of novelty. Finally, we also found a high correspondence between candidate and leadership congruence among the eighty-two slates involved in fission and fusion. Especially among fusions the leadership congruence scores reflect candidate congruences between slates.

Overall, these results underscore that different aspects of party change often go hand in hand and lend credibility to our suggestion to use candidate change as an indicator of overall party change. In addition, they highlight further avenues of research on party leadership and potential challenges to the organizational paradigm of party research. Most prominently, while in formal terms the election of an heir apparent is equivalent to the election of a novice outsider, in terms of evolutionary-electoral change, such handovers hardly appear to matter. The fact that slates with high leadership congruence only rarely exhibit high levels of candidate novelty raises the question of how much change continuing leaders can—and want to—initiate within their parties. Likewise, slates with novel leaders seldom retained significant numbers of 'old' candidates: while this lends credence to the argument that leadership change can trigger an exodus of members, it also calls for further research on the role of leadership in the process of slate-making.

9
Programmatic change

Party policies are central to our understanding of party politics and electoral competition. Formulating and implementing policies is one of the core functions of political parties and the prospect of shaping these processes is an important motivation for people to enter politics. Furthermore, parties use their policy platforms—either expressed in public debates or electoral manifestos—to attract voters as well as candidates. Even though parties usually sustain their general ideological orientation over time (occasional leapfrogging aside), their policy outlooks are subject to regular and sometimes considerable shifts. Such changes can happen for a myriad of reasons, such as in response to economic crises, changing electoral fortunes, or the entry of a new challenger that pushes parties to new programmatic pastures (for an overview, see Fagerholm 2016). Nevertheless, none of this happens spontaneously: policies are formulated and altered by party personnel, while changes in programmatic direction carry the dual potential to attract new people and alienate others.

In this chapter, we study the relationship between candidate turnover and programmatic change. The set of people running in national elections often considerably overlaps with the circles that formulate policies. Even where candidates themselves are not involved in the drafting, debating, or adopting of programmes and policy proposals, parties and proto-slates (i.e. electoral lists in the making, see Chapter 2) must consider the impact of such changes on their electoral candidates. Significant changes can breathe new life into the candidate pool—either by recruiting new people or promoting existing ones—but also carry the potential to alienate others who can leave to join other formations or exit the electoral scene altogether. Conversely, the influx of new party people can tip the balance in internal disputes, shifting priorities or putting new issues on the agenda. For these reasons, we expect party programmatic change to be related to change among candidates.

The aim of this chapter is twofold. First, by examining the link between candidate turnover and policy change we add to the growing number of studies that have sought to identify determinants of programmatic shifts but have yet to consider the impact of people beyond leaders and elite factions, i.e. those at the very top of the pyramid of party people (Harmel & Tan 2003; Meyer 2013; Somer-Topcu 2009). Second, this chapter makes a methodological contribution. Scholars have repeatedly cautioned against the use of ready-made left–right indices in the context of Central and East European (CEE) party systems and, as we will see below, measuring change based on such aggregates is highly problematic. Therefore, we propose a new measure of programmatic similarity that accounts for changes in a spectrum of specific policies. We calculate indices based on data from two authoritative data sets with time-series data on party policies: the Manifesto Research on Political Representation (MARPOR, Volkens et al. 2020) and the Chapel Hill Expert Survey (CHES, Jolly et al. 2022). In our analysis of 223 slates (parties, coalitions, and other formations in a single election) covered by MARPOR and sixty-five slates covered by CHES we find statistically significant links between policy change and candidate novelty and dropout. This contrasts with the lack of any relationship between candidate turnover and change in parties' left–right placement, regardless of whether we look at the change in the unidimensional, economic, or social left–right position (respectively, GAL–TAN in CHES). This lends credibility to the indices of policy change that we develop, although the relationship between policy change and other dimensions of party change is unlikely to be perfect, as demonstrated by the Hungarian Fidesz party, which underwent a complete metamorphosis from a liberal to a populist conservative party (Enyedi & Linek 2008), all while maintaining a fairly stable cadre. This suggests significant ideological or programmatic flexibility among at least some CEE parties, while our analysis also shows that the overall magnitude of policy changes has decreased over time since the 1990s.

9.1 Measuring programmatic change

Of the various approaches to measuring party policy positions, MARPOR and CHES are the most frequently used in comparative studies. Both have their strong proponents and critics on various methodological grounds but, ultimately, they reach a degree of consensus, for example, in the placement of political parties on the classic left–right scale (top row of Figure 9.1).[1] This is despite the very different ways in which these scores are obtained: in CHES, the scores are provided by country experts while in MARPOR, the RILE

---

[1] In our analysis, we interpolated CHES right–left scores for election years as these may not coincide with the waves of CHES surveys. For example, if a party scores 6 on the general left–right scale in 2010 and 5 in 2014, the interpolated score for 2012 is 5.5.

(right–left) indicator is derived from identifying policy categories relevant to the scale and deducting the sum of 'right' categories from the sum of 'left' categories.[2] The indices are correlated but only mildly, with a weaker agreement in CEE (r = 0.48) compared to Western Europe (r = 0.61, see Bakker et al. 2015 and the top row in Figure 9.1). However, the two data sources show no agreement regarding *changes* in left–right positions between pairs of elections (bottom half of Figure 9.1). The left–right position change is very weakly correlated in Western Europe and even points in the wrong direction in CEE (r = 0.08 and r = –0.07, respectively, the bottom row in Figure 9.1). Hence, while MARPOR and CHES are both excellent, their ready-made aggregate indices are more appropriate for measuring party policy positions rather than their change (see Adams et al. 2019).

Even more fundamental questions have been raised over the usefulness of the aggregated left–right scales for studying parties and their change, especially in CEE. First, parties simply do not change their left–right orientation much over time (Dalton & McAllister 2015). Second, while the traditional left–right scale has long been a standard way to measure party policy positions, it has been deemed less useful in CEE where parties often combine various policy positions in inventive ways and some traditionally leftist positions can be systematically related to some right-wing positions (Aspelund et al. 2013; Mölder 2016; Tavits & Letki 2013). CHES explicitly distinguishes between two key dimensions of left–right positions: the economic and the social GAL-TAN ('green–alternative–libertarian'–'traditional–authoritarian–nationalist') dimension. Methods of extracting economic and cultural dimensions from MARPOR data have also been proposed (e.g. Bakker & Hobolt 2013, for an alternative approach to RILE, see Prosser 2014). However, studying change by looking only at either the cultural or economic dimension would overlook any changes in the other dimension that may, indeed, cancel each other out (see Schumacher & Giger 2018) and would thus not appropriately represent party policy change in many circumstances.

The Polish Civic Platform (PO) between 2006 and 2010 illustrates the problem of aggregation and cancelling out, especially for the measurement of policy change. According to CHES, it started out as a very liberal party both

---

[2] Other approaches have been proposed, some involving (logged) ratios or factor analysis (see Budge et al. 2010 for an overview). Still, they always aggregate, in one way or another, the original MARPOR quasi-sentences. Alternative approaches for extracting left–right positions from the MARPOR data (e.g. Bakker & Hobolt 2013; Benoit & Däubler 2014; Prosser 2014) are unlikely to offer better insights into policy change because reducing information to a single or limited number of scales always leads to loss of information—some of which may signal important policy shifts.

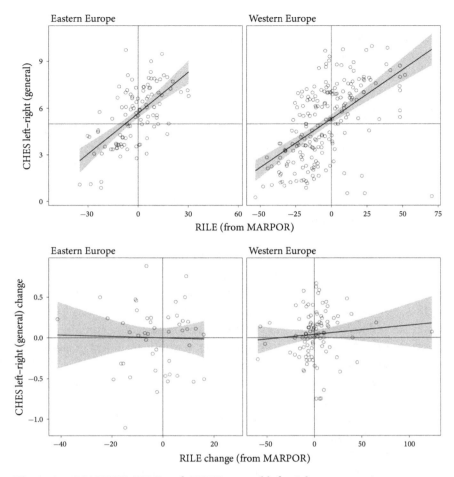

Figure 9.1 MARPOR RILE and CHES general left–right
Note: CHES left–right placements interpolated for election years.

economically and socially; yet, after entering the government in 2007, it moved considerably towards the centre on both dimensions (Table 9.1). However, this entailed a move to the left economically and to the right socially; its general left–right placement changed little, poorly reflecting the magnitude of its programmatic change. Summing up the change across dimensions would yield a more meaningful yardstick of programmatic change for PO: 2.3 + |−1.5| = 3.8. However, these two dimensions may still fail to capture programmatic change well, as they involve a degree of aggregation themselves (especially GAL–TAN). Several parties show poor correspondence between the change in the three aggregates and the change in individual policy dimensions assessed in CHES: these include, for example, the Hungarian Fidesz-KDNP (2006–10) and the Latvian New Era (2006–10). Both experienced significant programmatic changes in individual policy domains but recorded only modest changes in the aggregate dimensions, with absolute values around the lowest quartile of all East European cases for general left–right and GAL–TAN, and below the median for the economic left–right. According to our measure that reflects programmatic changes across all policy domains (MCPP, introduced below), the two parties experienced some of the biggest programmatic changes (see Table 9.3).

Table 9.1 Aggregate programmatic change: Polish Civic Platform 2006–10 in CHES

Dimension/year	2006	2010	Change
Left–right general	5.3	6.0	0.7
Left–right economic	8.2	6.7	−1.5
GAL–TAN	2.7	5.0	2.3

Instead of employing ready-made aggregate indices, we propose new measures that account for changes in a spectrum of specific policies. Fortunately, both MARPOR and CHES allow for a significantly more nuanced and meaningful measurement of changes than can be obtained from single- or two-dimensional scales as we can dig deeper into the change in particular policy dimensions. In MARPOR, this can be done by exploiting 110 topic categories based on manifesto quasi-sentences.[3] In CHES, country experts locate parties on a variety of policy scales, of which we use the fourteen core items that have appeared in all relevant surveys.[4]

For our indices of programmatic change, we draw on Franzmann's (2013) index of programmatic similarity (Ü) originally devised for analysing similarities between different parties, that can also be used for analysing similarities or differences between the same party over consecutive elections. When used

---

[3] We concur with Meyer (2013) that whatever its other shortcomings, MARPOR is at least useful for analysing change in party policy positions.

[4] We use the positions on improving public services vs. reducing taxes, deregulation of markets, redistribution of wealth from the rich to the poor, civil liberties vs. law and order, social lifestyle, role of religious principles in politics, immigration policy, integration of immigrants and asylum seekers, urban vs. rural interests, environmental sustainability, political decentralization to regions/localities, international security and peacekeeping missions, ethnic minorities.

with MARPOR data, the index adds up the changes in all quasi-sentence categories, very much like the index of disproportionality between parties' vote and seat shares or electoral volatility:

$$\ddot{U} = 1 - \frac{1}{2}\sum |s_a - s_b| \qquad (9.1)$$

where s_a and s_b are shares of quasi-sentence categories mentioned in the manifestos of parties a and b over all MARPOR categories; for measuring similarity between a party's manifesto in two elections in t and $t-1$, these can be replaced by s_t and s_{t-1}. As we are interested in measuring change (rather than similarity or lack of change), we omit '1' and the negative sign:

$$\ddot{U} = \frac{1}{2}\sum |s_t - s_{t-1}| \qquad (9.2)$$

A similar approach can be used with CHES data by finding the mean change in party positions (MCPP) across all policy domains covered by the survey. A party can conceivably experience a significant change on a single issue, leaving the rest of its policy profile broadly intact, as happened with several European parties when the 2015 refugee crisis became politicized. One potential problem with MCPP is that great fluctuations can occur on dimensions where there is considerable uncertainty among experts on whose assessment the CHES scores are based. However, we expect that if uncertain, country experts tend to locate parties in the middle of the scale, limiting the potential for fluctuations; if the experts disagree, the averages will regress towards the mean.[5]

Finally, two particular issues regarding the nature of CHES data and CEE party politics need to be addressed. First, while the MARPOR data is based on party manifestos and thus coincides with elections, the CHES survey is conducted in waves that do not usually coincide with electoral cycles. Therefore, we interpolate scores between CHES waves to match them to election years. While this makes the implicit assumption that party positions change linearly between the survey years, alternatives to interpolation are worse: for example, using the survey closest to an election would result in zero change if two elections are closest to the same CHES survey. Second, we can only measure party policy change if a party contests two consecutive elections. As we have seen in previous chapters, clear party continuities are far less common in CEE than in Western European party systems. Parties frequently undergo fissions and fusions and are involved in coalition-making and coalition-breaking that are

---

[5] Schumacher and Giger (2018) use a similar approach but count the number of substantial changes in CHES positions and nineteen aggregated dimensions in MARPOR.

often very complex (see Ibenskas & Sikk 2017; Marinova 2015). For identifying continuing parties, we rely on party codes in MARPOR and CHES and complement them by coding pairs of slates in consecutive elections with high congruence (see Chapter 3) as continuing parties.[6]

9.2 Programmatic change and candidate change

Party programmes are an essential part of party identity and usually define the ideological stance on key issues that its representatives vow to follow once elected. Parties regularly revisit and revise their positions and formulate short-term goals in advance of elections. Although a change in short-term goals is more frequent, even long-held views can be abandoned or de-emphasized. The potential triggers for these changes are manifold, including shifts in patterns of party competition and changing socio-economic circumstances (see, e.g. Abou-Chadi 2016; Borbáth & Borbáth 2020; Han 2015; Ibenskas & Polk 2022; Koedam 2021; Krause & Giebler 2020; Pytlas 2015). Yet, as any changes must ultimately be enacted by party elites, major shifts are very unlikely and almost inconceivable without change in candidates and other party people. Although not all candidates are directly involved in the drafting of party manifestos, we can still expect a relationship between candidate turnover and programmatic change. Shared programmatic goals serve as a foundation for like-minded candidates during slate formation and a reference point for would-be candidates considering entry into politics (see Chapter 2). Any change in party programmes holds the potential to attract new candidates—either former candidates of other parties or those who have never run for office—but can also alienate previous candidates as some may join other 'survival machines' or leave politics altogether (cf. Barnfield & Bale 2022; Kölln & Polk 2016; Thomsen 2017). Programmatic shifts can also lead to the promotion of rank and file to plum spots on electoral lists and the demotion of erstwhile draught horses. Finally, a successful recruitment drive of new candidates and/or exit of the old guard is likely to reshuffle the deck in internal disputes. Similarly to the relationship between candidate change and organizational and leadership change, it is not only difficult to determine the primary causal direction of effects, but it is also beyond the scope of this book and the data at our disposal. Hence, for the sake of simplicity, we once again use candidate change as a dependent variable below or make no specific assumption about directionality.

---

[6] We coded slates with $v \geq 1\%$ and congruence ≥ 0.3 as continuing parties; in cases with several high congruences, priority was given to the slate with the highest congruence. The German minority party in Poland was excluded because big fluctuations in its list length affected its candidate turnover.

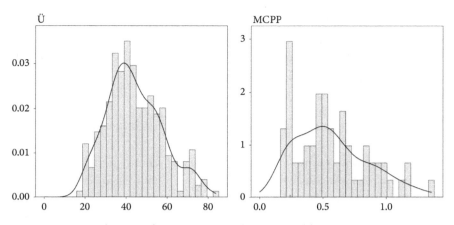

Figure 9.2 Distribution of programmatic change variables

Figure 9.2 shows the distribution of our programmatic change indicators among the parties covered by our data as well as MARPOR (N = 223) and CHES (N = 65) or, more precisely, pairs of slates analysed. Both indicators are positively skewed, meaning that parties with more limited policy change are more common than those with higher levels of change. To account for this skewness, the indices are logged in our subsequent analysis.

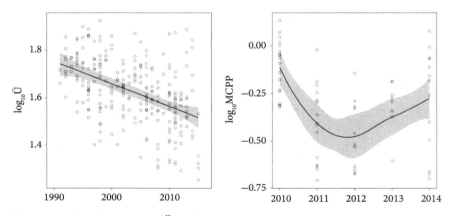

Figure 9.3 Development of Ü and MCPP over time

Remarkably, the average Ü has consistently declined from typically above 50 ($\log_{10} 50 = 1.7$) until the mid-1990s to below 40 ($\log_{10} 40 = 1.6$) since the mid-2000s (Figure 9.3). The trend in MCPP is less pronounced, mostly because of the narrow period for which data is available. The falling Ü suggests that continuing parties have become more stable in the language of their manifestos over time. However, this should not be interpreted as a sign of increasing party system stability or institutionalization of party competition: change remains ubiquitous in CEE party systems and neither the success of new parties or electoral volatility has decreased overall (Chapters 5 and 6). Hence, it appears that policy profiles of continuing parties, rather than the party system overall, have become more 'institutionalized'. Decreasing Ü also concurs with arguments of partial consolidation in CEE party politics, at least when it comes to the 'established party subsystem' (Haughton & Deegan-Krause 2020). Notably, the changes between elections in the left–right positions or its economic and social components show no such trend towards stability, highlighting that stabilization may have occurred under the radar of conventional aggregates or the aggregates have limited value in CEE—or, very possibly, both.

Table 9.2 Parties with highest and lowest Ü

Electoral cycle	Party	Ü	Weighted candidate novelty Overall	Weighted candidate novelty Including arrivals from other parties	Weighted candidate dropout Overall	Weighted candidate dropout Including departures to other parties
HU1994–8	FKGP	83.8	0.44	0.50	0.30	0.50
BU2009–13	ATAKA	76.8	0.27	0.40	0.45	0.40
LV2010–1	SC	74.6	0.18	0.22	0.26	0.22
SI2000–4	SNS	74.0	0.36	0.43	0.34	0.43
LV2006–10	LLP-LC → PLL	73.5	0.45	0.48	0.12	0.48
CZ1992–6	SPR-RSČ	72.7	0.77	0.80	0.60	0.80
LT1992–6	SK → TS	71.7	0.55	0.55	0.32	0.55
HU1994–8	SZDSZ	71.7	0.14	0.18	0.14	0.18
HU1990–4	SZDSZ	70.5	0.33	0.43	0.43	0.43
HU2010–14	FIDESZ-KDNP	69.5	0.04	0.18	0.30	0.18
Mean:		73.9	0.35	0.42	0.33	0.42
EE2011–15	SDE	17.8	0.15	0.23	0.10	0.23
SK2010–12	SMER-SD	19.6	0.04	0.07	0.02	0.07
LT2004–8	LICS	20.0	0.16	0.36	0.14	0.36
EE2011–15	ER	20.0	0.30	0.33	0.23	0.33
SI2004–	SDS	20.5	0.32	0.31	0.31	0.31
EE2007–11	ER	20.8	0.22	0.23	0.17	0.23
EE2011–5	K	21.0	0.05	0.19	0.09	0.19
CZ2006–10	KDU-ČSL	21.1	0.51	0.56	0.35	0.56
EE2007–11	SDE	21.2	0.20	0.38	0.28	0.38
LT2004–8	UTT → PTT	21.7	0.24	0.46	0.41	0.46
Mean:		20.4	0.22	0.31	0.21	0.31

Table 9.3 Parties with highest and lowest MCPP

Electoral cycle	Party	MCPP	Weighted candidate novelty Overall	Weighted candidate novelty Including arrivals from other parties	Weighted candidate dropout Overall	Weighted candidate dropout Including departures to other parties
LV2006–10	JL → VIENOTIBA	1.36	0.54	0.54	0.41	0.54
HU2010–14	FIDESZ–KDNP	1.19	0.04	0.18	0.30	0.18
LV2006–10	SC	1.18	0.45	0.47	0.38	0.47
SK2006–10	SDKU–DS	1.11	0.25	0.30	0.29	0.30
CZ2006–10	SZ	1.05	0.54	0.57	0.54	0.57
HU2006–10	FIDESZ–KDNP	1.00	0.21	0.23	0.21	0.23
SI2011–4	SDS	0.98	0.30	0.30	0.29	0.30
PL2007–11	PO	0.95	0.22	0.26	0.28	0.26
CZ2006–10	ODS	0.93	0.46	0.48	0.43	0.48
HU2006–10	MSZP	0.90	0.07	0.18	0.25	0.18
Mean:		1.06	0.31	0.35	0.34	0.35
LV2010–1	SC	0.19	0.18	0.22	0.26	0.22
BU2013–4	GERB	0.20	0.19	0.19	0.17	0.19
BU2013–4	ATAKA	0.21	0.05	0.12	0.09	0.12
SK2010–2	MOST–HID	0.21	0.09	0.13	0.02	0.13
SK2010–2	SAS	0.21	0.07	0.21	0.12	0.21
BU2013–4	DPS	0.22	0.20	0.26	0.29	0.26
SK2010–12	SMK–MKP	0.22	0.31	0.31	0.29	0.31
SI2008–11	SD	0.22	0.48	0.52	0.47	0.52
SI2010–2	KDH	0.23	0.15	0.17	0.26	0.17
LV2010–1	ZZS	0.23	0.02	0.18	0.25	0.18
Mean:		0.22	0.17	0.23	0.22	0.23

Tables 9.2 and 9.3 list parties with the highest and lowest values for Ü and MCPP. As party programmatic shifts between elections have not been studied comparatively and systematically we lack firm expectations of which parties should score high or low, but some of the parties listed certainly did experience substantial programmatic shifts. The high placement of several Hungarian parties is unsurprising. The conservative and staunchly anti-communist Smallholders' Party (FKGP) moved to the right and became a personal vehicle for its leader József Torgyán (Political Risk Services 2000) after leaving the government in 1993. In the early 1990s, the Alliance of Free Democrats (SZDSZ) gradually moved from the liberal centre to the left of the political scale: from a 'virulently and radically anti-communist' party in the early 1990s (Kovács 1996: 514) to rapprochement with the Socialists (MSZP) in opposition and

eventually joining them in government after the 1994 election (Oltay 1995; Wittenberg 2006: 61–2). Fidesz boasted high levels of programmatic change in 2014 according to both Ü and MCPP. It had won the 2010 parliamentary election in a landslide and during its first term in office since 2002 introduced many controversial changes such as passing a new constitution and reducing the number of seats in the legislature by half. Having implemented its manifesto, Fidesz not only increasingly turned its ire on the European Union (Csehi & Zgut 2021) and immigration (Korkut 2014) but also the welfare state (aiming to replace it by a 'work-based society', Vidra 2018). The Hungarian Socialist Party (MSZP, with a high MCPP value for 2006–10) suffered from the political fallout from the leaked Őszöd speech where Prime Minister Gyurcsány admitted to repeated lying during the 2006 electoral campaign (Körösényi et al. 2017). Amidst the turmoil, the party moved left—at least according to CHES country experts—in various aspects, abandoning its neo-liberal economic stance, embracing alternative social lifestyles and civil liberties over law and order, etc., hence distinguishing itself from the surging and increasingly illiberal Fidesz.

A closer look at some parties from other countries in Tables 9.2 and 9.3 also reveals evidence of significant policy shifts. In the run-up to the Bulgarian 2013 election, the far-right Ataka upped its xenophobic rhetoric but had, at the same time, outlined a rather comprehensive economic programme (Kostadinova & Popova 2014), potentially to signal its potential for becoming a governing coalition member (it had supported the GERB government briefly in 2009). As already discussed above, the Polish Civic Platform (PO) exhibited high MCPP despite a limited change in the generic CHES left–right placement due to aggregation of diverging trends (as discussed above, see Table 9.1). The Latvian Harmony Centre (SC) appears near the top of the list at different periods for Ü and MCPP.[7] The party was certainly in flux between 2006 and 2011: it sought the ideological mainstream by (not entirely successfully) tempering its pro-Russian image (Ikstens 2011) and later came to the cusp of joining the governing coalition despite harsh anti-austerity rhetoric (Ikstens 2012). Its high MCPP (2006–10) could also be linked to its metamorphosis from an electoral coalition of four parties into a political party.

---

[7] SC experienced significant change in its average placement across policy domains between the CHES waves of 2010 and 2014. Much of it probably happened before the 2011 election but MCPP is here interpolated for the very short inter-electoral period. This highlights an issue with MCPP: if we adjust the value by the time between elections, change can be overestimated for parties that experienced gradual incremental change between the CHES waves.

Some of the slate dyads with high Ü or MCPP experienced organizational changes, i.e. the transformation of electoral coalitions into parties or the formation of electoral alliances. In Lithuania, most of the Sąjūdis Coalition (SK) in 1992 was transformed into Homeland Union (TS, established as a party in 1993). The Latvian Unity (Vienotība) electoral alliance in 2010 experienced the highest MCPP in our sample: when contrasted with New Era (JL), its largest constituent party, in 2006. It had moved to a much more centrist position on several policy dimensions while the changes in general and economic left–right position and GAL–TAN had been very modest. Vienotība had been a staunch critic of oligarchs' influence in Latvian politics but presided over the governing coalition during the economic crisis that somewhat softened its anti-oligarch message but also its neo-liberal image when it had to combine austerity with increased state intervention. It was also subject to contradictory pressures from junior partners of the electoral coalition (the conservative Civic Union and the social-liberal Society for Political Change), all while Vienotība was also becoming more accepting of SC, an erstwhile pariah in Latvian politics mostly supported by Russian speakers, as a potential governing partner. Organizational changes appeared among other parties with a high Ü: for example, the alliance of the Latvia First Party and Latvia's Way (LLP–LC in 2006) formed a party in 2007 and, in turn, entered an electoral alliance called For a Good Latvia (PLL) with the People's Party (TP) in 2010.

Several of the parties that scored low on either Ü or MCPP have been very stable in other respects. For instance, Smer-SD dominated Slovak party politics for nearly two decades: led by Robert Fico since its foundation in 1999, it came first in every election between 2006 and 2016. Likewise, the Slovak Christian Democratic Movement (KDH) was continuously represented in parliament since 1990 and took part in several governments until dropping out of parliament in 2016. The Reform Party (ER) became a core staple of Estonian politics upon its inception in 1995 and emerged as the largest party in all elections between 2007 and 2019; likewise, the Estonian Social Democratic Party (SDE) settled down programmatically after nailing its colours to the mast by dropping the ambiguous 'Moderates' label in 2004.

Even though the overlap between the tables on Ü and MCPP is limited—partly due to differences in coverage, albeit the measures may also pick up different signals of programmatic change—some general patterns emerge. The average measures of candidate turnover are higher for parties with high programmatic change than for those with more limited programmatic change, even if some parties with high candidate turnover have been programmatically stable and vice versa. Figure 9.4 plots the bivariate relationship between

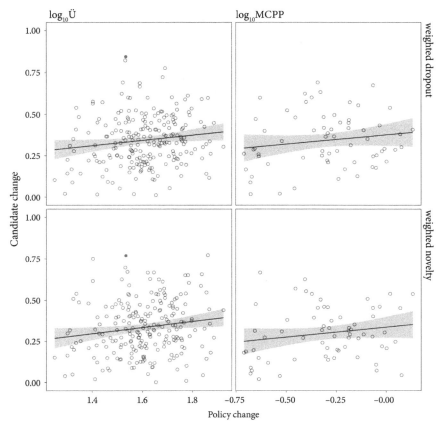

Figure 9.4 Programmatic change and weighted candidate novelty and dropout
Note: Slovenian LDS 2008–11 highlighted (see discussion in the text).

Ü, MCPP and weighted candidate turnover for all continuing parties (i.e. slate dyads) in the data set. The simple bivariate correlations run in the expected direction but are not particularly strong. In the rest of the book, we have emphasized complex continuities between slates and have been primarily focused on candidates that enter or exit from the electoral scene altogether. This chapter focuses exclusively on continuing parties as programmatic change is not defined for entering and exiting parties. That also allows us to draw a line between a party and all other parties. Hence, we can also look at candidate novelty or dropout vis-à-vis others: candidates that enter the slate but used to run for other parties and candidates that only exit their party, not only the electoral scene, in other words, 'party hoppers'. Tables 9.2 and 9.3 suggest a relationship similar to that between programmatic change and candidate turnover: increased novelty and dropout thus defined tend to coincide with programmatic change. When we consider all parties in our data set (Figure 9.5) the relationship between programmatic change and candidate turnover including inter-party movements is stronger than that with the overall novelty and dropout; the statistical significance of the relationship between all indicators of programmatic change and candidate turnover increases, especially for Ü.

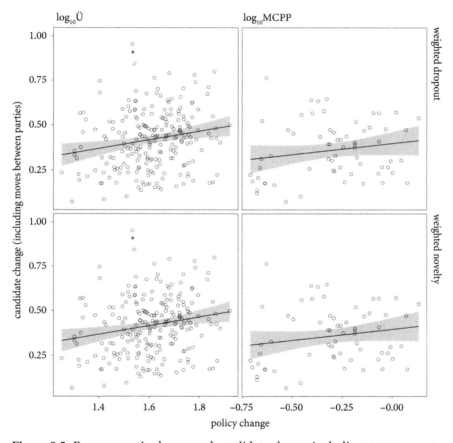

Figure 9.5 Programmatic change and candidate change including moves between parties
Note: see Figure 9.4.

As suggested by our preliminary models in Chapter 4, we need to control for factors such as party size and change in vote share. This becomes clear when looking at some of the outliers in Figures 9.4 and 9.5 as these parties often either saw their voter base disappear or, vice versa, experienced high and stable electoral support. For instance, between 2008 and 2011, the Slovenian Liberal Democratic Party (LDS, highlighted in the scatterplots) registered only medium policy change according to Ü but very high levels of candidate novelty and dropout. This was likely due to its continuously decreasing electoral fortunes: it had fallen from the top-ranking party in 2000 to the smallest parliamentary party in 2008, before dropping out of parliament altogether in 2011, reducing the incentives for its candidates to run again.

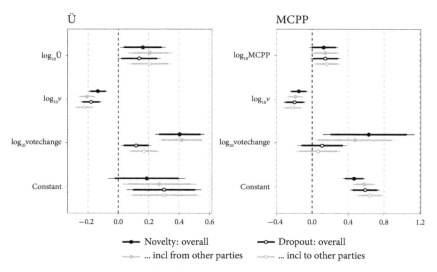

Figure 9.6 Regression models for candidate turnover: policy change and control variables

Notes: Thin lines: 95% confidence intervals, thick lines: 90% confidence intervals. Full models (including those with country dummies) are available in online supplementary materials (https://osf.io/nm5ek/). See this chapter and Chapter 4 for explanations of the functional form of the vote change variable.

Figure 9.6 summarizes the results of regression models for weighted novelty and dropout controlling for other factors. First, we control for party size (its vote share) which we found to be a major predictor of candidate turnover in Chapter 4: the candidate slates of larger parties are more stable than those of smaller parties. Second, we control for changes in parties' electoral support. For that, we use the functional forms suggested by the bivariate analysis in Chapter 4. For weighted novelty and dropout alike, we are looking at the logged ratio v_t/v_{t-1} so that proportionally equal vote losses or gains result in a value of the same magnitude but different signs. Hence, a party that increases its vote share from 20 to 30% would have a logged ratio of 0.18 and a party that goes from 30 to 20% would have a logged ratio of −0.18. As our earlier analysis suggests, the direction of party support change does not matter for weighted dropout: candidate loss is increasingly likely when party support changes, regardless of the direction. Therefore, we used the absolute value of logged vote change in models for candidate dropout. For candidate novelty, we found that only vote gains increased turnover: losses did not increase turnover compared to stable electoral support. Hence, in the novelty models, we are using the logged vote change ratio floored at zero, i.e. all decreasing vote shares are recoded as 0.[8]

The effect of Ü suggested by bivariate correlations is confirmed both for novelty and dropout (left panel in Figure 9.6). The models suggest that *ceteris paribus* a tenfold increase in Ü increases candidate novelty by 16% and dropout by 14%; this corresponds to a smaller but still considerable increase of about 10% within the actual range of Ü (83.8/17.8 = 4.7). The impact on the share of candidates moving between parties is stronger at 14% within the actual range of Ü. The effect of CHES-based MCPP is only very mildly statistically significant. Nevertheless, the effect is clearer for the candidate change variable that also accounts for moves between parties (grey in Figure 9.6) even given the much more limited sample size as MCPP is only available from 2009 onwards. Strikingly, in contrast to our measures of programmatic shifts, the change in parties' left–right placement either in MARPOR or CHES data does not correlate with any of the measures of candidate change (available in online supplementary materials, https://osf.io/nm5ek/).

The party vote share remains statistically significant across all models in Figure 9.6. The same applies to the vote change variables except for the two versions of candidate dropout in MCPP models. Also, the effect magnitudes remain very close to the ones discovered in Chapter 4 and are even more pronounced as the magnitude increases for both novelty and dropout when controlling for programmatic change, especially for candidate novelty (−0.08 to −0.14). Similarly, vote change (with appropriate functional forms as explained above) still tends to increase turnover, with an effect size similar to that in the more basic models in Chapter 4.

---

[8] We also tested models with country-fixed effects to capture variation in a cocktail of unmeasured variables such as electoral system, party regulation, traditions. The resulting models (shown in Figure 9.6) are similar to those presented here but, understandably, explain more of the variance in candidate turnover. Hungary (as well as Latvia and Lithuania, to a lesser extent) stands out with a more limited candidate turnover overall.

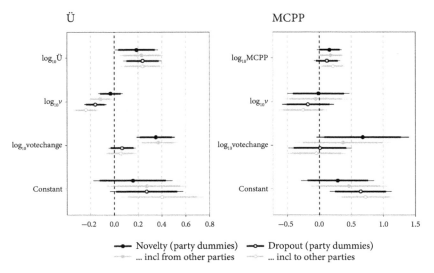

Figure 9.7 Regression models for candidate turnover: policy change and control variables (individual continuing parties)
Notes: see Figure 9.6.

To control for party-specific factors that we are not able to measure such as traditions or internal rules that may affect levels of candidate turnover, we also ran models with dummies for continuous parties, i.e. where we could detect continuity over two electoral cycles. The programmatic change coefficients retained the predicted direction and were in some cases statistically more significant than in the pooled models, even though party dummies had ample opportunity to 'soak up' variation in candidate change scores as they, indeed, did regarding the party size and vote change variables (see Figure 9.7).[9]

9.3 Programmatic change after fission and fusion

When parties split or merge, or under fission and fusion, to use our preferred terms (see Chapter 7), some successor slates are more congruent in terms of their candidates to their predecessors than others. Likewise, we can measure

---

[9] We also tested models with modified dependent variables (turnover indicators divided by the continuing party mean), independent variables (programmatic change variables divided by their party means), and multilevel models with the continuing party as the grouping variable. The results suggested the same direction for Ü with statistically significant coefficients.

congruence between their manifestoes by calculating Ü for the two largest successors/predecessors instead of just one as we have done so far. To exclude successors/predecessors with trivial linkages, we adopt a congruence threshold of 0.15. Unfortunately, this does not allow us to systematically analyse the relationship based on MCPP as, due to the more limited timespan of the data, we would be left with only two cases of fission and fusion each.

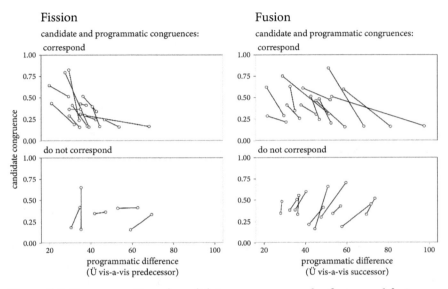

Figure 9.8 Programmatic and candidate congruence under fission and fusion
Note: congruence threshold 0.15.

The picture for fissions shows that successor slates that are more congruent to the predecessor in terms of their programmatic profiles (i.e. their programmatic difference is smaller), also exhibit higher candidate congruence. Downward sloping lines dominate Figure 9.8 (left panel) as in thirteen out of the eighteen (72%) pairs of slates with fissionary tendencies, higher candidate congruence is associated with smaller programmatic differences. Only two cases in the 'fission group' point in the opposite direction but even there the differences are moderate in both candidate and manifesto congruences compared to many in the correct direction. The mean difference in Üs is negative (–4.6) and the differences in the correct direction are larger (–8.7) than in the incorrect direction (5.9). The picture is less clear for fusion as just over half (57%) of the lines tilt in the expected direction (Figure 9.8, right panel).

However, the differences in Üs in the expected direction are on average considerably larger (−13.6) than in the opposite direction (5.7).[10] In other words, the successors emerging from fusions are programmatically more similar to their predecessors when candidate congruence is high, while lower candidate congruence between successors and predecessors is associated with lower programmatic similarity. Where candidate and programmatic congruences point in the same direction, the predecessor that offers fewer candidates tends to be programmatically much more distant.

This again suggests that candidate and programmatic congruences—as measured in this book—are in step with each other. The differences in Figure 9.8 are also intriguing for understanding fission and fusion. They suggest that following a split the main successor usually adapts the manifesto (or programmatic profile more in general) of the parent and the minor successor needs to distinguish itself programmatically. While after fusion the programmatic profile of the main predecessor often dominates and the minor partners often adjust considerably, it is also common for the merged parties to lean towards the less congruent predecessor or find a middle ground by making roughly equal adjustments, shown by near-vertical lines in the bottom right panel of Figure 9.8. Alternatively, one could argue that following a split, a smaller splinter has more freedom to adjust its programmatic profile than the main successor who may, nevertheless, also feel liberated from the shackles of an internal fraction or a tricky coalition partner. In contrast, fusion requires parties to find common ground: indeed, Ü tends to be higher for slates undergoing fusion than those experiencing fission.

9.4 Conclusion

In previous chapters, we established relationships between candidate change and electoral support (Chapter 4), party entry and exit (Chapter 5), fission and fusion (Chapter 7), and leadership change (Chapter 8). This chapter analysed the link between candidate turnover and party policy change which is another important dimension of party change. We pick up clear signals about a relationship between the two in models with various specifications. The models

---

[10] As noted earlier, we cannot systematically analyse MCPP due to data limitations. However, if we adopted a very low candidate congruence threshold of 0.05, four out of five cases of fission and eight out of nine cases of fusion would point in the correct direction; the two exceptions where the candidate and programmatic congruence point in opposite directions had very minor differences in MCPP between the two successors/predecessors.

certainly contain noise; after all, one should not expect a perfect relationship between candidate change and programmatic change. We know that parties can be programmatically flexible even with a similar set of people, as testified by the well-known programmatic somersaults of the Hungarian Fidesz. Yet, our analysis shows that change in party policies and people often does correlate; we believe that the relationship could appear even stronger with further refinements of the measures used here.

Our results suggest that our proposed measure of Ü—that instead of relying on ready-made aggregate indices considers changes in all different policy dimensions in MARPOR—is linked to weighted candidate novelty and dropout. Controlling for party-specific factors in parties with continued presence over several electoral cycles, we still detected a clear relationship between programmatic and candidate change. Our analysis of fission and fusion lends further credibility to the reliability of our proposed measures of organizational change based on candidate congruences and programmatic change. The predecessors with greater programmatic similarity to the merged slate exhibited higher candidate congruence; the relationship between programmatic and candidate congruence was even stronger and clearer for slates following fission.

The relationships were more evasive when using MCPP, a measure of mean change in policy positions in the CHES data set. While we cannot overstate the usefulness and validity of the CHES data set, its coverage and structure pose challenges for building an indicator of policy change between elections. First, the time span and hence the number of continuing parties covered by MCPP is more limited compared to Ü. Even more importantly, the CHES waves do not correspond to electoral cycles. Not to make unwarranted assumptions regarding the rate of policy change, we employed a linear interpolation of scores for years between waves. However, party policy change may not happen at a constant rate throughout the electoral term but may be more likely shortly before or after an election. However, even if the results for MCPP were mild, it outclassed all ready-made left–right indices that showed no relationship to candidate turnover.

Even though Ü and MCPP perform better than the generic aggregate indicators, they are themselves uncorrelated. We believe that the indicators of programmatic change (especially MCPP) can be improved in future studies. The fact that the left–right scales of MARPOR and CHES *are* correlated suggests that a carefully constructed and interpolated programmatic change variable based on CHES could produce clearer results. Not only is the more the merrier, but we remain strongly convinced about the complementary merits of CHES and MARPOR and the opportunities they offer for measuring different types of change. What our results do show is that considering changes across many specific policy dimensions can yield important new insights on party change.

10
Conclusion

10.1 Summary: candidate change and party evolution

Modern representative democracy is almost unthinkable without political parties: they aggregate and articulate political interests, they mobilize voters, recruit and train political personnel, and they structure political competition and decision-making processes. To perform all these functions, parties need people such as leaders, activists, members, and voters; crucially, they need candidates to represent them in elections. However, candidate and their parties are not in wedlock as candidates can leave politics, switch parties, forge new alliances, and move along or stay behind as parties split or merge. As candidates change, so do parties. Even in outwardly stable formations, candidate change happens below the surface, ultimately changing what the parties stand for.

In this book, we have proposed a 'genetic' or 'electoral' approach to understanding political parties and party change. In contrast to the 'organizational paradigm' that has dominated party research, and which ascribes to parties a certain nature and legal status, we propose a shift of focus to the people who make up party organizations. Inspired by evolutionary biology, we argue in Chapter 1 that parties can be conceptualized as 'survival machines', for people who are involved in politics and compete in elections. Just as genes help to shape the characteristics of organisms and drive their evolutionary adaptation, changing sets of candidates shape and transform various aspects of their parties. In fact, the metaphor of 'survival machines' fits electoral candidates much better than genes. Unlike genes, party people possess agency and they guide party evolution consciously, even if not always rationally because of limited human faculties. Although many parties, especially in Western democracies, have been remarkably stable over long periods of time, the 'survival machines' are not necessarily timeless—they can fail or may not even be meant to last. Once parties have served their people's purpose, they can be dismantled while their candidates' political journeys continue in new or reconfigured organizations. In our view, party change is a perpetual process that varies in pace and scope. It is also multidimensional, affecting different aspects of parties—such as programmatic profiles, leadership, and personnel—some possibly more than others. For the party people, the durability of institutions is not an end in itself; such structures are only worth preserving if they continue to serve their purposes—which they often but not always do.

Our approach focuses on elections, and we use the term 'slate' to refer to parties, electoral coalitions, and any other formations that present candidates in a single election. While many slates are similar (or 'congruent') to those in a previous or subsequent election, this is far from a given. We consider connections not only between handpicked slates (i.e. stable parties or known splits and mergers) but between all pairs of slates in subsequent elections, often revealing intricate patterns of continuity and change. While not without its limitations, the term 'slate' captures the essence of what a 'party' is as it focuses on one of the key functions of parties, namely the presentation of candidates in elections. The definition is highly parsimonious and tangible; it saves us from making exceptions for a myriad of quasi-parties that the political science literature tends to regard as an aberration—even though they have always existed and are, if anything, becoming more common.

Throughout this book, we have shown how candidate change can be used both as an indicator of party change and to refine existing measures of party system change. We do so by using our original Electoral Candidates in Central and Eastern Europe (ECCEE) data set which includes over 200,000 candidates in sixty elections across nine Central and East European (CEE) democracies from 1990 to 2016. This data set is introduced in more detail in Chapter 3, along with explanations of our candidate weighting scheme and key terms (candidate novelty, dropout, congruence).

Using the ECCEE data set, our book has produced six main findings and contributions. First, and most importantly, we have shown that candidate change—the movement of candidates within and between parties, and into and out of politics—is a valid and reliable indicator of overall party change. As we show in Chapter 5, a continuous variable of candidate change gives us a nuanced picture of changes within parties. The many examples of parties that are neither 'old' nor 'new' but partially new which we identify throughout the book underline that party novelty and change is not a dichotomous choice, but a matter of degree. Apparently new parties often have low levels of candidate novelty, and parties that no longer appear in election results see most of their candidates return.

Second, electoral volatility has been a workhorse in quantitative studies on party system stability; yet, even renowned experts in the field have relied on widely varying values of volatility for the same sets of elections. We believe that a key reason for this is that existing approaches to volatility have required scholars to make less-than-perfect coding decisions and to discount important links between parties. Our measure of candidate congruence—the overlap between candidate lists—allows us to develop a new approach to volatility that explicitly allows for multiple links between parties in successive elections. Using our congruence-based volatility scores, we show in Chapter 6 that economic growth affects party system stability in CEE—a relationship that has been found in other parts of the world but has not previously been confirmed for CEE.

Third, our candidate-based approach allows for a more nuanced approach to party fission and fusion, which we offer in Chapter 7. We also develop a common framework for analysing party splits and mergers, as well as electoral coalition formation and dissolution. Candidate movements offer several new insights into fission and fusion: not only can we distinguish between equal and unequal splits and mergers, but we also highlight the widespread phenomenon of collective defections, which cannot be adequately analysed within the 'organizational paradigm' because it does not involve any changes in formal–legal organizations.

Fourth, candidate change is clearly associated with significant change in perhaps the most visible of party people—the party leaders. While previous studies have largely treated leadership change as a dichotomous event, in Chapter 8 we propose a quasi-quantitative measure of leadership change/novelty. We find that novel leaders are associated with greater candidate novelty, while greater candidate congruence between slates in fissions and fusions is also associated with greater leader congruence. Fifth, changes in party programmes are associated with changes in people, and vice versa. Ready-made indicators—especially those based on the classic but problematic unidimensional left–right scale—and existing measures do not fully capture programmatic change among parties. In Chapter 9, we propose an indicator that takes into account a full range of changes in party manifestos beyond any predefined scales (e.g. left–right) and demonstrate a clear relationship between party policy change and candidate turnover. We also find that after fissions the slates that are more congruent with their predecessors in terms of candidates are also more similar to them programmatically; similarly, slates stemming from a merger are most similar programmatically to their most congruent predecessors.

Finally, we show throughout the book that candidate turnover is clearly related to party size and change in party popularity, as expected based on our theoretical models developed in Chapter 2 and tested at the beginning of Chapter 4. The effect persists when we examine the relationship between candidate change and other dimensions of party change (Chapters 7–9) and when we consider the impact of societal factors such as varying levels of corruption perception and socio-economic change (Chapter 4). Thus, our candidate-based view of party evolution has considerable potential to improve our understanding of the determinants of broader political and social changes.

10.2 Beyond institutionalization: embracing the soggy world

What are the implications of these findings, and more fundamentally the notion of perpetual party change, for the study of electoral and party system change? In this section, we briefly discuss the implications for the notions of new and continuing parties, for measures of party system stability such as electoral volatility, and for the study of party and party system (and 'subsystem') institutionalization. In particular, we encourage researchers to acknowledge and engage with the complexity of party novelty and continuity by moving beyond ever-imperfect thresholds and adopting a more critical approach to the notion of party system institutionalization.

Several researchers before us have pointed out that party novelty varies in degree (e.g. Barnea & Rahat 2011; Haughton & Deegan-Krause 2020). The discussion of electoral volatility and the related issue of new party success has so far focused on finding thresholds for classifying parties as new that take into account, in the words of Tim Haughton and Kevin Deegan-Krause, the 'soggy world' of party novelty and continuity (2020: 32). However, the electoral reality in CEE is consistently so complex that it may be necessary to abandon blunt dichotomies altogether and instead embrace the 'soggy world' fully. In this book, we propose tools for doing just that. While our recipes for dealing with complexity and avoiding dichotomies may be more demanding than existing approaches, they avoid many cumbersome choices and sometimes near-arbitrary thresholds for classifying new parties. As we show in Chapters 5 and 6, a failure to embrace the 'soggy world' can force researchers to make decisions that are not only difficult but downright impossible.

Central to our proposed toolkit is the empirically well-supported premise that parties never remain exactly the same between elections. While parties can experience change at any point in time, existing research on parties, and in particular on party change (electoral volatility, new parties, party support patterns, and manifestos) tends to focus on elections more than any other point in time. This is when many changes manifest themselves most clearly, and elections provide meaningful, convenient, and standardized snapshots of party life. We do not dismiss important developments between elections or those not fully captured by the snapshots—these deserve proper academic scrutiny—but we do show that using electoral slates as the unit of analysis provides rich new insights into the evolution of parties and party systems.

The most basic and widely used measure of electoral and party system change is the index of electoral volatility—the aggregate fluctuation in party vote shares between a pair of elections. Electoral volatility alone is an incomplete measure of party system change—patterns of party interaction in government/opposition and their institutionalization are also important (Casal Bértoa & Enyedi 2021). However, for analysing volatility and more profound aspects of party systems alike, we need a clear view of the parties involved. The calculation of volatility relies on establishing clear links between parties in successive elections and these decisions have 'an extremely strong impact' on volatility scores (Casal Bértoa et al. 2017: 148). The rules for determining continuity vary widely between authors, which has led to low correlations between volatility scores (145). While party continuity is not the only culprit—the threshold for excluding smaller parties is another—it plays a dominant role. Some studies have usefully distinguished between intra-system and extra-system volatility. The latter has dominated over intra-system volatility in CEE (Powell & Tucker 2014) and can be interpreted as a measure of (the lack of) party system institutionalization (Mainwaring et al. 2009). However, extra-system volatility builds directly on the categorization of parties as new or continuing. While major party entries and exits are undoubtedly more common in CEE than in older democracies, the difference may be exaggerated by better information on West European parties and better identification of links between parties that, for example, undergo minor name changes. For example, few would argue that the various incarnations of the French centre-right, from de Gaulle's Rally of the French People to Les Républicains, were completely new parties, despite significant changes in names and appearances. The high level of extra-system volatility in CEE underlines the importance of establishing meaningful linkages and thresholds for party novelty. If one were to adopt very strict continuity criteria—that only fully intact parties qualify as continuations—almost all volatility would become extra-systemic, as parties that undergo any change would be considered 'new'.

Although this book focuses on parties in elections, we embrace the view that 'party systems' are more than just a set of electoral slates. To fully understand how the systems work, we need to observe their interactions, such as patterns of governing coalitions and the entry of new parties into executive positions, i.e. the degree of 'party system closure' (Casal Bértoa & Enyedi 2016 2021; Mair 1996). Party systems conceptualized in this way can change without the rise of new parties or the decline of old ones, without significant candidate turnover, and even without significant electoral volatility, for example when a coalition government brings together new bedfellows. However, to analyse party interactions and party system closure, it is necessary to pinpoint the parties that interact, the ones that are excluded, and the ones that do the excluding. Therefore, our perspective on political parties as continuously evolving organizations carries important implications for the literature on party system institutionalization.

The institutionalization of party systems (and parties) is an important topic although we cannot address it in much substantial detail here not least because scholarly consensus on the notion of institutionalization is far from established (Casal Bértoa 2018). At a fundamental level, institutionalization refers to electoral predictability (Mainwaring & Torcal 2006) even if de-institutionalization can occur (Chiaramonte & Emanuele 2017). Claims of party system institutionalization in one country or another suggest, at least implicitly, a somewhat stable equilibrium by projecting stability in the past and the present into the future. We argue that the evolution of party politics is ultimately messy and party system institutionalization can be illusory or fleeting, for example, because existing forces of instability may not have had their moment of opportunity. The CEE experience suggests that de-institutionalization may not be a rare aberration after all, as the region offers several examples where rumours of party system institutionalization turned out to be exaggerated or premature, such as Slovenia and the Czech Republic (O'Dwyer 2014) or Lithuania (Krupavičius 1998; Žeruolis 1998). While the Lithuanian party system certainly seemed institutionalized in the late 1990s and the Czech and Slovenian party systems in the early twenty-first century, they subsequently experienced considerable instability; in other words, the relative stability of the past did not make their party systems predictable. Moreover, even well-institutionalized party systems may not be completely frozen and deinstitutionalization can occur suddenly and unpredictably, as the examples of some West European countries such as France or Italy suggest (Emanuele & Chiaramonte 2018).

Thus, seemingly institutionalized parties and party systems may simply be undergoing a phase of limited change that is, at least potentially, always transient. Established actors in a stable system tend to preserve the institutions that allowed them to flourish, and parties in government and parliament have the means to preserve existing structures, as the famous cartelization argument highlights (Katz & Mair 1995). However, a party system or a political system itself has no preferences or agency and thus cannot 'seek' institutionalization. Moreover, actors who do have agency, such as party people, may sometimes prefer 'creative destruction' to the status quo. Even voters, who ultimately mould party systems in democracies, are often collective agents of change when they elect political newcomers.

This book focuses on party evolution as a perpetual process of change and adaptation rather than a march towards some finite state or stable equilibrium. We welcome Haughton & Deegan-Krause's (2020) suggestions that parties in a party system can be heterogeneous, meaning that a party system can accommodate different 'subsystems' and be stable and unstable at the same time. Interestingly, in this book, we spotted many genuinely new parties throughout the time period covered but also a decline in candidate turnover among continuing parties since the early 1990s. This suggests that stability and instability can indeed go hand in hand: a 'subsystem' of new party breakthroughs can be balanced by an increasingly stable establishment. However, because political parties come in more flavours than simply 'new' and 'old', real-world party systems sometimes defy neat categorization into distinct quarters of stability and instability. Moreover, stability and change can coexist not only in the same country but even within individual parties.

For example, the boundaries between stability and change can be blurred when well-established parties merge with political newcomers. In 2006, the Estonian Pro Patria (IL), a party rooted in the early 1990s merged with the four-year-old Res Publica (RP) to form Pro Patria and Res Publica Union (IRL) which combined traits of both parents. Therefore, it was difficult to determine the age of the merged party and, thus, whether it belonged to the stable or unstable subsystem. To complete the circle, in 2018, IRL readopted Pro Patria's original name from the early 1990s (Isamaa) while still maintaining clear ties to RP and IL, and giving rise to some offshoots. The emergence of the Civic Coalition (KO) in Poland in 2018 was similarly ambiguous. Its main component, former Prime Minister Donald Tusk's Civic Platform (PO), was formed in 2001 by merging splinters from the disintegrating Solidarity Electoral Action (AWS) and the Freedom Union (UW). The other founding member, Modern (N), was a genuinely new party from 2015. KO was later joined by the Greens (Z) which—despite being founded in 2004—had no parliamentary representation before running with KO in 2019. Finally, the Polish Initiative (IPL)—a merger of a PO offshoot and splinters from two centre-left parties—also joined KO for the 2019 elections. In Slovenia, the Freedom Movement (GS) won the 2022 elections just three months after its founding congress and soon absorbed two parties of former Prime Ministers—the

Party of Alenka Bratušek (SAB; in office 2013–14) and the List of Marjan Šarec (LMŠ; in office 2018–20)—which were themselves new formations of yesteryear that quickly fell out of favour with voters. While the twists and turns of these parties' life histories would make for a passable thriller, more importantly, they highlight the blending of the new and the old within parties and electoral coalitions, and the fluidity between the institutionalized and non-institutionalized subsystems.

10.3 The road ahead

This book has proposed a candidate-centred approach to party evolution and applied our ideas empirically to a number of CEE countries. While it has been useful to test the approach in a region with constantly changing parties, we believe that the candidate-centred approach to party change will also be illuminating for the study of parties in other parts of the world. As in CEE, it could reveal hidden patterns of party continuity and change in other newer, unstable democracies. In more stable environments, such as Western Europe, studying party change through the lens of candidates can reveal the extent of subterranean change that is otherwise hidden from view. However, even West European party systems are showing signs of 'unfreezing' and are to some extent converging towards levels of instability more familiar from CEE (Emanuele, Chiaramonte, & Soare 2020). We expect that applications in other parts of the world will reveal ways in which our approach can be further refined. Nevertheless, we believe that less 'developed' parts of the democratic world provide appropriate starting points for general theories or approaches to political parties. Political science has largely built upon the rich experience of Western (European) democracies—countries that were lucky enough to be democratic when CEE was under the yoke of communism and other parts of the world were busy throwing off the shackles of colonialism. Some of the most important theories in other disciplines have been influenced and inspired by 'obscure' corners of the world. Charles Darwin's theory of evolution drew more on his travels to remote places like the Galápagos Islands than on his strolls in rural Kent. Our book uses CEE as an inspiration and testing ground for a general approach, albeit a far narrower and less ambitious one than the origins of life.

More generally, we want to emphasize the importance of bringing (party) people back in, and putting their motivations at the centre of the analyses of political parties and party systems. The 'genetic turn' we propose could also be useful in other areas of political or social research that sometimes inadvertently ascribe human-like agency to institutions such as countries, governments, bureaucracies, or international organizations. Of course, all of them occasionally behave as if they had agency and preferences, even for extended periods, but this should not be taken for granted, since changes in the behaviour of such non-human entities must ultimately arise from changes in humans or their preferences.

We believe that the development of these and many other institutions can be studied using the techniques introduced in this book. We show that much can be learned from 'big but thin' data consisting of a limited number of variables: essentially ordered lists of names with additional information on electoral districts, with a generous dash of critical regional and case expertise. It would have been possible to collect slightly more detailed data (e.g. dates of birth) for some of the countries covered, but exploiting these would have made the approach much less easily extendable to the study of party evolution in other parts of the world, in the more distant past, or at other levels (e.g. regional or local). In an ideal world, we would like to have more detail on all candidates; other researchers, too, are often keen for more data on the object of their study. In this book, we show how to make effective use of limited data. With the right tools, big but thin data is not only a valuable source on its own but can be linked to other data sets to produce even more valuable insights.

In the future, our ECCEE data set could be used, for example, to augment data on legislative switching, political careers, and electoral reform. However, our approach could also be useful beyond the realm of (party) politics, e.g. in the analysis of demographic data consisting of names accompanied by limited additional variables (public electoral rolls, telephone directories, business and court records, historical records of life events, etc.). These and other sources of big but thin data are often hidden in plain sight, treasuring far more information than is apparent at first glance. Less is not always more—but sometimes you can do more with limited data than you might think.

Bibliography

Aarts, Kees, André Blais, and Hermann Schmitt (eds). 2011. *Political Leaders and Democratic Elections*. Oxford: Oxford University Press.

Abou-Chadi, Tarik. 2016. 'Niche Party Success and Mainstream Party Policy Shifts—How Green and Radical Right Parties Differ in Their Impact'. *British Journal of Political Science* 46 (2): pp. 417–36.

Adams, James, Luca Bernardi, Lawrence Ezrow, Oakley B. Gordon, Tzu-Ping Liu, and Christine Phillips. 2019. 'A Problem with Empirical Studies of Party Policy Shifts: Alternative Measures of Party Shifts Are Uncorrelated'. *European Journal of Political Research* 58 (4): pp. 1234–44.

Aldrich, John H., and William T. Bianco. 1992. 'A Game-Theoretic Model of Party Affiliation of Candidates and Office Holders'. *Mathematical and Computer Modelling* 16 (8): pp. 103–16.

Aldrich, Andrea S., and William T. Daniel. 2020. 'The Consequences of Quotas: Assessing the Effect of Varied Gender Quotas on Legislator Experience in the European Parliament'. *Politics and Gender* 16 (3): pp. 738–67.

Alexiadou, Despina, and Eoin O'Malley. 2022. 'The Leadership Dilemma: Examining the Impact of Strong Leaders on Parties'. *European Journal of Political Research* 61 (3): pp. 783–806.

Allern, Elin H., and Karina Pedersen. 2007. 'The Impact of Party Organisational Changes on Democracy'. *West European Politics* 30 (1): pp. 68–92.

Altman, David, and Daniel Chasquetti. 2011. 'Re-election and Political Career Paths in the Uruguayan Congress, 1985–99'. *Journal of Legislative Studies* 11 (2): pp. 235–53.

Anderson, Christopher J. 2000. 'Economic Voting and Political Context: A Comparative Perspective'. *Electoral Studies* 19 (2–3): pp. 151–70.

André, Audrey, Sam Depauw, and Shane Martin. 2015. 'Electoral Systems and Legislators' Constituency Effort: The Mediating Effect of Electoral Vulnerability'. *Comparative Political Studies* 48 (4): pp. 464–96.

Ansolabehere, Stephen, and James M. Snyder Jr. 2004. 'Using Term Limits to Estimate Incumbency Advantages When Officeholders Retire Strategically'. *Legislative Studies Quarterly* 29 (4): pp. 487–515.

Armingeon, Klaus, Virginia Wenger, Fiona Wiedemeier, Christian Isler, Laura Knöpfel, David Weisstanner, and Sarah Engler. 2021. *Comparative Political Data Set 1960–2019*. Zürich: Department of Political Science, University of Zürich. www.cpds-data.org/.

Aspelund, Anna, Marjaana Lindeman, and Markku Verkasalo. 2013. 'Political Conservatism and Left–Right Orientation in 28 Eastern and Western European Countries'. *Political Psychology* 34 (3): pp. 409–17.

Asquer, Raffaele. 2014. 'Corruption Charges and Renomination Chances: Evidence from the 1994 Italian Parliamentary Election'. Paper presented at the APSA Annual Meeting, Washington, DC, August 28–31.

Asquer, Raffaele. 2015. 'Media Coverage of Corruption and Renomination: Evidence from Italian Parliamentary Elections'. Doctoral dissertation, University of California, Los Angeles.
Aylott, Nicholas, and Niklas Bolin. 2017. 'Managed Intra-Party Democracy: Precursory Delegation and Party Leader Selection'. *Party Politics* 23 (1): pp. 55–65.
Bäckersten, Oskar H. 2022. 'May's Law May Prevail: Evidence from Sweden'. *Party Politics* 28 (4): pp. 680–90.
Bågenholm, Andreas. 2013a. 'The Electoral Fate and Policy Impact of "Anti-Corruption Parties" in Central and Eastern Europe'. *Human Affairs* 23 (2): pp. 174–95.
Bågenholm, Andreas. 2013b. 'Throwing the Rascals Out? The Electoral Effects of Corruption Allegations and Corruption Scandals in Europe 1981–2011'. *Crime, Law and Social Change* 60 (5): pp. 595–609.
Bågenholm, Andreas, and Nicholas Charron. 2014. 'Do Politics in Europe Benefit from Politicising Corruption?' *West European Politics* 37 (5): pp. 903–31.
Bågenholm, Andreas, and Nicholas Charron. 2015. 'Anti-Corruption Parties and Good Government'. In *Elites, Institutions and the Quality of Government*, edited by Carl Dahlström and Lena Wängnerud, pp. 263–82. London: Palgrave Macmillan.
Bågenholm, Andreas, and Nicholas Charron. 2020. 'Accountable or Untouchable? Electoral Accountability in Romanian Local Elections'. *Electoral Studies* 66: 102183.
Bakke, Elisabeth, and Nick Sitter. 2005. 'Patterns of Stability: Party Competition and Strategy in Central Europe since 1989'. *Party Politics* 11 (2): pp. 243–63.
Bakker, Ryan, and Sara Hobolt. 2013. 'Measuring Party Positions'. In *Political Choice Matters: Explaining the Strength of Class and Religious Cleavages in Cross-National Perspective*, edited by Geoffrey Evans and Nan Dirk de Graaf, pp. 27–45. Oxford: Oxford University Press.
Bakker, Ryan, Catherine de Vries, Erica Edwards, Liesbet Hooghe, Seth Jolly, et al. 2015. 'Measuring Party Positions in Europe: The Chapel Hill Expert Survey Trend File, 1999–2010'. *Party Politics* 21 (1): pp. 143–52.
Bale, Tim. 2012. *The Conservatives since 1945: The Drivers of Party Change*. Oxford: Oxford University Press.
Banducci, Susan A., and Jeffrey A. Karp. 1994. 'Electoral Consequences of Scandal and Reapportionment in the 1992 House Elections'. *American Politics Research* 22 (1): pp. 3–26.
Bardi, Luciano, Stefano Bartolini, and Alexander Trechsel. 2014. 'Party Adaptation and Change and the Crisis of Democracy'. *Party Politics* 20 (2): pp. 151–9.
Barnea, Shlomit, and Gideon Rahat. 2011. '"Out with the Old, in with the 'New'": What Constitutes a New Party?' *Party Politics* 17 (3): pp. 303–20.
Barnfield, Matthew, and Tim Bale. 2022. '"Leaving the Red Tories": Ideology, Leaders, and Why Party Members Quit'. *Party Politics* 28 (1): pp. 3–9.
Bartolini, Stefano, and Peter Mair. 1990. *Identity, Competition, and Electoral Availability: The Stabilisation of European Electorates 1885–1985*. Cambridge: Cambridge University Press.
Basinger, Scott J. 2013. 'Scandals and Congressional Elections in the Post-Watergate Era'. *Political Research Quarterly* 66 (2): pp. 385–98.
Baylis, Thomas A. 2007. 'Embattled Executives: Prime Ministerial Weakness in East Central Europe'. *Communist and Post-Communist Studies* 40 (1): pp. 81–106.
Benoit, Kenneth, and Thomas Däubler. 2014. 'Putting Text in Context: How to Estimate Better Left–Right Positions by Scaling Party Manifesto Data using Item Response'. Paper presented at the Mapping Policy Preferences from Texts Conference, Berlin, 15–16 May.

Benoit, Kenneth, and Michael Laver. 2007. 'Benchmarks for Text Analysis: A Response to Budge and Pennings' *Electoral Studies* 26 (1): pp. 130–5.
Beyens, Stefanie, Kris Deschouwer, Emilie van Haute, and Tom Verthé. 2017. 'Born Again, or Born Anew: Assessing the Newness of the Belgian New–Flemish Alliance (N–VA)' *Party Politics* 23 (4): pp. 389–99.
Beyens, Stefanie, Paul Lucardie, and Kris Deschouwer. 2016. 'The Life and Death of New Political Parties in the Low Countries'. *West European Politics* 39 (2): pp. 257–77.
Bielasiak, Jack. 2002. 'The Institutionalization of Electoral and Party Systems in Postcommunist States'. *Comparative Politics* 34 (2): pp. 189–210.
Bille, Lars. 2001. 'Democratizing a Democratic Procedure: Myth or Reality? Candidate Selection in Western European Parties, 1960–1990'. *Party Politics* 7 (3): pp. 363–80.
Birch, Sarah. 2003. *Electoral Systems and Political Transformation in Post-Communist Europe*. New York: Palgrave Macmillan.
Bittner, Amanda. 2011. *Platform or Personality? The Role of Party Leaders in Elections*. Oxford: Oxford University Press.
Blondel, Jean, and Ferdinand Müller-Rommel. 2001. *Cabinets in Eastern Europe*. London: Palgrave Macmillan.
Blondel, Jean, and Jean-Louis Thiébault (eds). 2009. *Political Leadership, Parties and Citizens: The Personalisation of Leadership*. London: Routledge.
Bochsler, Daniel, and Miriam Hänni. 2022. 'Who Benefits from the Retrospective Vote? Bringing in New Parties'. *West European Politics*. Online First.
Bolleyer, Nicole. 2013. *New Parties in Old Party Systems: Persistence and Decline in Seventeen Democracies*. Oxford: Oxford University Press.
Bolleyer, Nicole, and Evelyn Bytzek. 2013. 'Origins of Party Formation and New Party Success in Advanced Democracies'. *European Journal of Political Research* 52 (6): pp. 773–96.
Bolleyer, Nicole, Patricia Correa, and Gabriel Katz. 2019a. 'Political Party Mortality in Established Party Systems: A Hierarchical Competing Risks Approach'. *Comparative Political Studies* 52 (1): pp. 36–68.
Bolleyer, Nicole, Raimondas Ibenskas, and Carina Bischoff. 2019b. 'Perspectives on Political Party Death: Theorizing and Testing Downsian and Sociological Rationales'. *European Political Science Review* 11 (1): pp. 19–35.
Borbáth, Endre 2020. 'Two Faces of Party System Stability: Programmatic Change and Party Replacement'. *Party Politics* 27 (5): pp. 996–1008.
Bosco, Anna. 2000. *Comunisti: trasformazioni di partito in Italia, Spagna e Portogallo*. Bologna: Il Mulino.
Bosco, Anna, and Leonardo Morlino. 2007. *Party Change in Southern Europe*. London: Routledge.
Bridgewater, Jack. 2021. 'Leader Change, Time in Office and the Determinants of Voter Perceptions'. *Parliamentary Affairs* 76 (1): pp. 146–61.
Budge, Ian, Lawrence Ezrow, and Michael D. McDonald. 2010. 'Ideology, Party Factionalism and Policy Change: An Integrated Dynamic Theory'. *British Journal of Political Science* 40 (4): pp. 781–804.
Budge, Ian, and Paul Pennings. 2007. 'Missing the Message and Shooting the Messenger: Benoit and Laver's "Response"'. *Electoral Studies* 26 (1): pp. 136–41.
Bustikova, Lenka, and Elizabeth Zechmeister. 2017. 'Voting in New(er) Democracies'. In *The SAGE Handbook of Electoral Behaviour: Volume 2*, edited by Jocelyn Evans, Kai Arzheimer, and Michael S. Lewis-Beck, pp. 92–133. Singapore: Sage.

Bynander, Fredrik, and Paul 't Hart. 2008. 'The Art of Handing Over: (Mis)Managing Party Leadership Successions'. *Government and Opposition* 43 (3): pp. 385–404.
Campbell, Rosie, and Jennifer van Heerde-Hudson. 2018. *The Representative Audit of Britain*. https://gtr.ukri.org/projects?ref=ES%2FL016508%2F1.
Campus, Donatella, Niko Switek, and Marco Valbruzzi. 2021. *Collective Leadership and Divided Power in West European Parties*. Cham: Palgrave Macmillan.
Casal Bértoa, Fernando. 2014. 'Party Systems and Cleavage Structures Revisited: A Sociological Explanation of Party System Institutionalization in East Central Europe'. *Party Politics* 20 (1): pp. 16–36.
Casal Bértoa, Fernando. 2017. 'Political Parties or Party Systems? Assessing the "Myth" of Institutionalisation and Democracy.' *West European Politics* 40 (2): pp. 402–29.
Casal Bértoa, Fernando. 2018. 'The Three Waves of Party System Institutionalisation Studies: A Multi- or Uni-Dimensional Concept?' *Political Studies Review* 16 (1): pp. 60–72.
Casal Bértoa, Fernando, Kevin Deegan-Krause, and Tim Haughton. 2017. 'The Volatility of Volatility: Measuring Change in Party Vote Shares'. *Electoral Studies* 50: pp. 142–56.
Casal Bértoa, Fernando, and Zsolt Enyedi. 2016. 'Party System Closure and Openness: Conceptualization, Operationalization and Validation'. *Party Politics* 22 (3): pp. 265–77.
Casal Bértoa, Fernando, and Zsolt Enyedi. 2021. *Party System Closure: Party Alliances, Government Alternatives, and Democracy in Europe*. Oxford: Oxford University Press.
Ceron, Andrea. 2015. 'The Politics of Fission: An Analysis of Faction Breakaways among Italian Parties (1946–2011)'. *British Journal of Political Science* 45 (1): pp. 121–39.
Chang, Eric C. C., Miriam A. Golden, and Seth J. Hill. 2010. 'Legislative Malfeasance and Political Accountability'. *World Politics* 62 (2): pp. 177–220.
Charron, Nicholas, and Andreas Bågenholm. 2016. 'Ideology, Party Systems and Corruption Voting in European Democracies'. *Electoral Studies* 41: pp. 35–49.
Chiaramonte, Alessandro, and Vincenzo Emanuele. 2017. 'Party System Volatility, Regeneration and De-institutionalization in Western Europe (1945–2015)'. *Party Politics* 23 (4): pp. 376–88.
Ciccarelli, Francesca D., Tobias Doerks, Christian von Mering, Christopher J. Creevey, Bernd Sneland, and Peer Bork. 2006. 'Toward Automatic Reconstruction of a Highly Resolved Tree of Life'. *Science* 311 (5765): pp. 1283–7.
Close, Caroline, and Sergiu Gherghina. 2019. 'Rethinking Intra-Party Cohesion: Towards a Conceptual and Analytical Framework'. *Party Politics* 25 (5): pp. 652–63.
Colomer, Josep, Allan Sikk, and Rein Taagepera. 2020. 'Comparing the Importance of Political Offices: A Position Prominence Index'. Working Paper. http://dx.doi.org/10.13140/RG.2.2.11015.34722.
Coppedge, Michael. 1997. 'District Magnitude, Economic Performance, and Party-System Fragmentation in Five Latin American Countries'. *Comparative Political Studies* 30 (2): pp. 156–85.
Coppedge, Michael, John Gerring, Carl Henrik Knutsen, Staffan I. Lindberg, Jan Teorell, et al. 2022. 'V-dem [country–year/country–date] dataset v12'. Varieties of Democracy (V-Dem) Project. https://doi.org/10.23696/vdemds22.
Costas-Pérez, Elena, Albert Solé-Ollé, and Pilar Sorribas-Navarro. 2012. 'Corruption Scandals, Voter Information, and Accountability'. *European Journal of Political Economy* 28 (4): pp. 469–84.
Cross, William P., and André Blais. 2012. *Politics at the Centre: The Selection and Removal of Party Leaders in the Anglo Parliamentary Democracies*. Oxford: Oxford University Press.

Cross, William P., and Jean-Benoit Pilet (eds). 2015. *The Politics of Party Leadership: A Cross-national Perspective*. Oxford: Oxford University Press.
Cross, William, and Lisa Young. 2013. 'Candidate Recruitment in Canada'. In *Parties, Elections, and the Future of Canadian Politics*, edited by Amanda Bittner and Royce Koop, pp. 24–45. Vancouver: UBC Press.
Csehi, Robert, and Edit Zgut. 2021. '"We Won't Let Brussels Dictate Us": Eurosceptic Populism in Hungary and Poland'. *European Politics and Society* 22 (1): pp. 53–68.
Daalder, Hans, and Peter Mair. 1983. *Western European Party Systems: Continuity & Change*. Beverly Hills, CA: Sage.
Dalton, Russell J., and Ian McAllister. 2015. 'Random Walk or Planned Excursion? Continuity and Change in the Left–Right Positions of Political Parties'. *Comparative Political Studies* 48 (6): pp. 759–87.
Dassonneville, Ruth, and Marc Hooghe. 2011. 'Mapping Electoral Volatility in Europe: An analysis of trends in electoral volatility in European democracies since 1945'. Paper presented at the European Conference on Comparative Electoral Research, Sofia, 1–3 December.
Dawkins, Richard. 1976. *The Selfish Gene*. Oxford: Oxford University Press.
Dawkins, Richard. 1982. *The Extended Phenotype*. Oxford: Oxford University Press.
Dawkins, Richard. 2011. 'The Tyranny of the Discontinuous Mind'. 19 December. *New Statesman*. www.newstatesman.com/politics/2011/12/issue-essay-line-dawkins.
Deegan-Krause, Kevin, and Tim Haughton. 2018. 'Surviving the Storm: Factors Determining Party Survival in Central and Eastern Europe'. *East European Politics and Societies and Cultures* 32 (3): pp. 473–92.
Deegan-Krause, Kevin, Marko Klašnja, and Joshua Tucker. 2011. 'It's the Bribe, Stupid! Pocketbook vs. Sociotropic Corruption Voting'. Paper presented at the APSA Annual Meeting, Seattle, WA, 1–4 September.
Desposato, Scott W. 2006. 'Parties for Rent? Ambition, Ideology, and Party Switching in Brazil's Chamber of Deputies'. *American Journal of Political Science* 50 (1): pp. 62–80.
de Vries, Catherine E., and Sara B. Hobolt. 2020. *Political Entrepreneurs: The Rise of Challenger Parties in Europe*. Princeton, NJ: Princeton University Press.
Döring, Holger. 2016. 'Mapping Established Democracies: Integrated Data on Parties, Elections and Cabinets'. *Electoral Studies* 44: pp. 535–43.
Döring, Holger. 2018. 'The Origins of New Parties: Genuinely New or Party Fission?' Paper presented at the ECPR General Conference, Hamburg, 22–25 August.
Döring, Holger, Constantin Huber, and Philip Manow. 2022. Parliaments and governments database (ParlGov): Information on parties, elections and cabinets in established democracies. https://doi.org/10.7910/DVN/U
Dubrow, Joshua Kjerulf, and Nika Palaguta (eds). 2016. *Towards Electoral Control in Central and Eastern Europe*. Warsaw: IFiS PAN.
Ecker, Alejandro, Konstantin Glinitzer, and Thomas M. Meyer. 2016. 'Corruption Performance Voting and the Electoral Context'. *European Political Science Review* 8 (3): pp. 333–54.
Egerod, Benjamin C. K. 2021. 'The Lure of the Private Sector: Career Prospects Affect Selection out of Congress'. *Political Science Research and Methods* 10 (4): pp. 722–38.
Eggers, Andrew, and Alexander C. Fisher. 2011. 'Electoral Accountability and the UK Parliamentary Expenses Scandal: Did Voters Punish Corrupt MPs?' Working Paper. https://papers.ssrn.com/sol3/papers.cfm?abstract_id=1931868.

Emanuele, Vincenzo, and Alessandro Chiaramonte. 2018. 'A Growing Impact of New Parties: Myth or Reality? Party System Innovation in Western Europe after 1945'. *Party Politics* 24 (5): pp. 475–87.

Emanuele, Vincenzo, Alessandro Chiaramonte, and Sorina Soare. 2020. 'Does the Iron Curtain Still Exist? The Convergence in Electoral Volatility between Eastern and Western Europe'. *Government and Opposition* 55 (2): pp. 308–26.

Emanuele, Vincenzo, and Allan Sikk. 2021. 'Party Crashers? Modeling Genuinely New Party Development Paths in Western Europe'. *Party Politics* 27 (5): pp. 883–95.

Enamorado, Ted, Benjamin Fifield, and Kosuke Imai. 2019. 'Using a Probabilistic Model to Assist Merging of Large-Scale Administrative Records'. *American Political Science Review* 113 (2): pp. 353–71.

Engler, Sarah. 2016. 'Corruption and Electoral Support for New Political Parties in Central and Eastern Europe'. *West European Politics* 39 (2): pp. 278–304.

Engler, Sarah. 2020. '"Fighting Corruption" or "Fighting the Corrupt Elite"? Politicizing Corruption within and Beyond the Populist Divide'. *Democratization* 27 (4): pp. 643–61.

Engler, Sarah, Bartek Pytlas, and Kevin Deegan-Krause. 2019. 'Assessing the Diversity of Anti-Establishment and Populist Politics in Central and Eastern Europe'. *West European Politics* 42 (6): pp. 1310–36.

Enyedi, Zsolt, and Kevin Deegan-Krause. 2017. 'Voters and Parties in Eastern Europe'. In *The Routledge Handbook of East European Politics*, edited by Adam Fagan and Petr Kopecký, pp. 169–83. London: Taylor & Francis.

Enyedi, Zsolt, and Lukáš Linek. 2008. 'Searching for the Right Organization: Ideology and Party Structure in East-Central Europe'. *Party Politics* 14 (4): pp. 455–77.

Enyedi, Zsolt, and Gábor Tóka. 2007. 'The Only Game in Town: Party Politics in Hungary'. In *Party Politics in New Democracies*, edited by Paul Webb and Stephen White, pp. 147–78. Oxford: Oxford University Press.

Erk, Jan. 2005. 'From Vlaams Blok to Vlaams Belang: The Belgian Far-Right Renames Itself'. *West European Politics* 28 (3): pp. 493–502.

ERR. 2014. 'Reform Party Picks Dark Horse as New PM Candidate'. ERR. 12 March. https://news.err.ee/111903/reform-party-picks-dark-horse-as-new-pm-candidate.

Evans, Richard J. 1991. 'Candidates and Competition in Consular Elections at Rome between 218 and 49 BC'. *Acta Classica* 34 (1): pp. 111–36.

Fagerholm, Andreas. 2016. 'Why Do Political Parties Change Their Policy Positions? A Review'. *Political Studies Review* 14 (4): pp. 501–11.

Fernandez-Vazquez, Pablo, and Zeynep Somer-Topcu. 2019. 'The Informational Role of Party Leader Changes on Voter Perceptions of Party Positions'. *British Journal of Political Science* 49 (3): pp. 977–96.

Ferraz, Claudio, and Frederico Finan. 2008. 'Exposing Corrupt Politicians: The Effects of Brazil's Publicly Released Audits on Electoral Outcomes'. *Quarterly Journal of Economics* 123 (2): pp. 703–45.

Franzmann, Simon. 2013. 'From Data to Inference and Back Again: Perspectives from Content Analysis'. In *Mapping Policy Preferences from Texts Statistical Solutions for Manifesto Analysts*, edited by Andrea Volkens, Judith Bara, Ian Budge, Michael D. McDonald, and Hans-Dieter Klingemann, pp. 210–38. Oxford: Oxford University Press.

Gallagher, Michael, and Michael Marsh (eds). 1988. *Candidate Selection in Comparative Perspective: The Secret Garden of Politics*. London: Sage.

Garzia, Diego. 2012. 'Party and Leader Effects in Parliamentary Elections: Towards a Reassessment'. *Politics* 32 (3): pp. 175–85.

Gherghina, Sergiu. 2014. *Party Organization and Electoral Volatility in Central and Eastern Europe: Enhancing Voter Loyalty*. London: Routledge.

Gherghina, Sergiu. 2015. 'The MP Renomination Indicator: A Measure of Elite Continuity and Its Importance for Legislative Research'. *Parliamentary Affairs* 68 (2): pp. 393–400.

Gherghina, Sergiu. 2020. 'Party Leaders in Eastern Europe: Traits, Behaviors and Consequences'. In *Party Leaders in Eastern Europe*, edited by Sergiu Gherghina, pp. 1–15. Cham: Palgrave Macmillan.

Giannetti, Daniela, and Michael Laver. 2001. 'Party System Dynamics and the Making and Breaking of Italian Governments'. *Electoral Studies* 20 (4): pp. 529–53.

Golosov, Grigorii V. 2017. 'Legislative Turnover and Executive Control in Russia's Regions (2003–2014)'. *Europe-Asia Studies* 69 (4): pp. 553–70.

Gouglas, Athanassios, Gabriel Katz, Bart Maddens, and Marleen Brans. 2020. 'Transformational Party Events and Legislative Turnover in West European Democracies, 1945–2015'. *Party Politics* 27 (6): pp. 1211–22.

Graur, Dan. 2017. 'An Upper Limit on the Functional Fraction of the Human Genome'. *Genome Biology and Evolution* 9 (7): pp. 1880–5.

Grofman, Bernard, Evald Mikkel, and Rein Taagepera. 2000. 'Fission and Fusion of Parties in Estonia, 1987–1999'. *Journal of Baltic Studies* 31 (4): pp. 329–57.

Grzymała-Busse, Anna M. 2002. *Redeeming the Communist Past: The Regeneration of Communist Parties in East Central Europe*. Cambridge: Cambridge University Press.

Gwiazda, Anna. 2015. *Democracy in Poland: Representation, Participation, Competition and Accountability since 1989*. London: Routledge.

Gwiazda, Anna. 2017. 'Women in Parliament: Assessing the Effectiveness of Gender Quotas in Poland'. *Journal of Legislative Studies* 23 (3): pp. 326–47.

Haegel, Florence. 2004. 'The Transformation of the French Right: Institutional Imperatives and Organizational Changes'. *French Politics* 2 (2): pp. 185–202.

Han, Kyung Joon. 2015. 'The Impact of Radical Right-Wing Parties on the Positions of Mainstream Parties Regarding Multiculturalism'. *West European Politics* 38 (3): pp. 557–76.

Hanley, Seán. 2001. 'Are the Exceptions Really the Rule? Questioning the Application of "Electoral–Professional" Type Models of Party Organisation in East Central Europe'. *Perspectives on European Politics and Society* 2 (3): pp. 453–79.

Hanley, Seán, and Allan Sikk. 2016. 'Economy, Corruption or Floating Voters? Explaining the Breakthroughs of Anti-Establishment Reform Parties in Eastern Europe'. *Party Politics* 22 (4): pp. 522–33.

Harmel, Robert, Uk Heo, Alexander Tan, and Kenneth Janda. 1995. 'Performance, Leadership, Factions and Party Change: An Empirical Analysis'. *West European Politics* 18 (1): pp. 1–33.

Harmel, Robert, and Kenneth Janda. 1994. 'An Integrated Theory of Party Goals and Party Change'. *Journal of Theoretical Politics* 6 (3): pp. 259–87.

Harmel, Robert, and John D. Robertson. 1985. 'Formation and Success of New Parties: A Cross-National Analysis'. *International Political Science Review* 6 (4): pp. 501–23.

Harmel, Robert, and Alexander C. Tan. 2003. 'Party Actors and Party Change: Does Factional Dominance Matter?' *European Journal of Political Research* 42 (3): pp. 409–24.

Haughton, Tim, and Kevin Deegan-Krause. 2015. 'Hurricane Season: Systems of Instability in Central and East European Party Politics'. *East European Politics and Societies and Cultures* 29 (1): pp. 61–80.

Haughton, Tim, and Kevin Deegan-Krause. 2020. *The New Party Challenge: Changing Cycles of Party Birth and Death in Central Europe and Beyond*. Oxford: Oxford University Press.

Hauss, Charles, and David Rayside. 1978. 'The Development of New Parties in Western Democracies since 1945'. In *Political Parties: Development and Decay*, edited by Louis Maisel and Joseph Cooper, pp. 32–58. London: Sage.

Hazan, Reuven Y. 2014. 'Candidate Selection: Implications and Challenges for Legislative Behaviour'. In *The Oxford Handbook of Legislative Studies*, edited by Shane Martin, Thomas Saalfeld, and Kaare W. Strøm, pp. 213–30. Oxford: Oxford University Press.

Hazan, Reuven Y., and Gideon Rahat. 2010. *Democracy within Parties: Candidate Selection Methods and Their Political Consequences*. Oxford: Oxford University Press.

Heller, William B., and Carol Mershon. 2009. *Political Parties and Legislative Party Switching*. New York: Palgrave Macmillan.

Hernández, Enrique, and Hanspeter Kriesi. 2016. 'The Electoral Consequences of the Financial and Economic Crisis in Europe'. *European Journal of Political Research* 55 (2): pp. 203–24.

Herrick, Rebekah, and David L. Nixon. 1996. 'Is There Life after Congress? Patterns and Determinants of Post-Congressional Careers'. *Legislative Studies Quarterly* 21 (4): pp. 489–99.

Hino, Airo. 2013. 'Party System Dynamics in Japan: Measuring the Underlying Changes and Status-Quos'. Tokyo: Waseda University, Institute for Research in Contemporary Political and Economic Affairs, Working Paper No. E1310.

Hobolt, Sara B., James Tilley, and Susan Banducci. 2013. 'Clarity of Responsibility: How Government Cohesion Conditions Performance Voting'. *European Journal of Political Research* 52 (2): pp. 164–87.

Hopkin, Jonathan, and Caterina Paolucci. 1999. 'The Business Firm Model of Party Organisation: Cases from Spain and Italy'. *European Journal of Political Research* 35 (3): pp. 307–339.

Hug, Simon. 2001. *Altering Party Systems: Strategic Behavior and the Emergence of New Political Parties in Western Democracies*. Ann Arbor: University of Michigan Press.

Huo, Jingning. 2009. *Third Way Reforms: Social Democracy after the Golden Age*. Cambridge: Cambridge University Press.

Ibenskas, Raimondas. 2014. 'Activists or Money? Explaining the Electoral Success and Persistence of Political Parties in Lithuania'. *Party Politics* 20 (6): pp. 879–89.

Ibenskas, Raimondas. 2016a. 'Understanding Pre-Electoral Coalitions in Central and Eastern Europe'. *British Journal of Political Science* 46 (4): pp. 743–61.

Ibenskas, Raimondas. 2016b. 'Marriages of Convenience: Explaining Party Mergers in Europe'. *Journal of Politics* 78 (2): pp. 343–56.

Ibenskas, Raimondas. 2020. 'Electoral Competition After Party Splits'. *Political Science Research and Methods* 8 (1): pp. 45–59.

Ibenskas, Raimondas, and Jonathan Polk. 2022. 'Congruence and Party Responsiveness in Western Europe in the 21st Century'. *West European Politics* 45 (2): pp. 201–22.

Ibenskas, Raimondas, and Allan Sikk. 2017. 'Patterns of Party Change in Central and Eastern Europe, 1990–2015'. *Party Politics* 23 (1): pp. 43–54.

Ikstens, Jānis. 2011. 'Latvia'. *European Journal of Political Research* 50 (7–8): pp. 1035–44.

Ikstens, Jānis. 2012. 'Latvia'. *European Journal of Political Research Political Data Yearbook* 51 (1): pp. 175–86.

Ilonszki, Gabriella, and Michael Edinger. 2007. 'MPs in Post-Communist and Post-Soviet Nations: A Parliamentary Elite in the Making'. *The Journal of Legislative Studies* 13 (1): pp. 142–63.
Innes, Abby. 2002. 'Party Competition in Postcommunist Europe: The Great Electoral Lottery'. *Comparative Politics* 35 (1): pp. 85–104.
Ishiyama, John. 2000. 'Candidate Recruitment, Party Organisation and the Communist Successor Parties: The Cases of the MSzP, the KPRF and the LDDP'. *Europe-Asia Studies* 52 (5): pp. 875–96.
Ishiyama, John, and András Bozóki. 2010. 'Adaptation and Change: Characterizing the Survival Strategies of the Communist Successor Parties'. *The Journal of Communist Studies and Transition Politics* 17 (3): pp. 32–51.
Ismayr, Wolfgang (ed.). 2010. *Die politischen Systeme Osteuropas*, third updated and extended edition. Wiesbaden: VS Verlag für Sozialwissenschaften.
Janda, Kenneth. 1980. *Political Parties: A Cross-National Survey*. New York: Free Press.
Janda, Kenneth. 1983. 'Cross-National Measures of Party Organizations and Organizational Theory'. *European Journal of Political Research* 11 (3): pp. 319–32.
Jastramskis, Mažvydas, and Ainė Ramonaitė. 2015. 'Lithuania'. *European Journal of Political Research Political Data Yearbook* 54 (1): pp. 190–8.
Jolly, Seth, Ryan Bakker, Liesbet Hooghe, Gary Marks, Jonathan Polk, Jan Rovny, Marco Steenbergen, and Milada A. Vachudova. 2022. 'Chapel Hill Expert Survey Trend File, 1999–2019'. *Electoral Studies* 75: 102420.
Kalyvas, Stathis N. 1998. 'From Pulpit to Party: Party Formation and the Christian Democratic Phenomenon'. *Comparative Politics* 30 (3): pp. 293–312.
Karlsen, Rune, and Eli Skogerbø. 2013. 'Candidate Campaigning in Parliamentary Systems: Individualized vs. Localized Campaigning'. *Party Politics* 21 (3): pp. 428–39.
Katz, Richard S., and Peter Mair (eds). 1994. *How Parties Organize: Change and Adaptation in Party Organizations in Western Europe*. London: Sage.
Katz, Richard S., and Peter Mair. 1995. 'Changing Models of Party Organization and Party Democracy: The Emergence of the Cartel Party'. *Party Politics* 1 (1): pp. 5–28.
Kazee, Thomas A., and Mary C. Thornberry. 1990. 'Where's the Party? Congressional Candidate Recruitment and American Party Organizations'. *Western Political Quarterly* 43 (1): pp. 61–80.
Kemahlıoğlu, Özge, and Sabri Sayarı. 2017. 'Defecting Alone or Splitting Together? Individual and Collective Party Switching by Legislators'. *Public Choice* 171 (1–2): pp. 187–6.
Keman, Hans, and Ferdinand Müller-Rommel. 2012. 'The Life Cycle of Party Government across the New Europe'. In *Party Government in the New Europe*, edited by Hans Keman and Ferdinand Müller-Rommel, pp. 25–46. London: Routledge.
Kenig, Ofer, Gideon Rahat, and Or Tuttnauer. 2015. 'Competitiveness of Party Leadership Selection Processes'. In *The Politics of Party Leadership: A Cross-National Perspective*, edited by William Cross and Jean-Benoit Pilet, pp. 50–72. Oxford: Oxford University Press.
Kennedy, Fiachra, Pat Lyons, and Peter Fitzgerald. 2006. 'Pragmatists, Ideologues and the General Law of Curvilinear Disparity: The Case of the Irish Labour Party'. *Political Studies* 54 (4): pp. 786–805.
Kerby, Matthew, and Kelly Blidook. 2011. 'It's Not You, It's Me: Determinants of Voluntary Legislative Turnover in Canada'. *Legislative Studies Quarterly* 36 (4): pp. 621–43.
Key, V. O. 1964. *Politics, Parties and Pressure Groups*. New York: Crowell.

Kiewiet, D. Roderick, and Langche Zeng. 1993. 'An Analysis of Congressional Career Decisions, 1947–1986'. *American Political Science Review* 87 (4): pp. 928–41.

Kim, Mi Son, and Frederick Solt. 2015. 'The Dynamics of Party Relabeling: Why Do Parties Change Names?' *Party Politics* 23 (4): pp. 437–47.

Kitchin, Rob. 2013. 'Big Data and Human Geography: Opportunities, Challenges and Risks'. *Dialogues in Human Geography* 3 (3): pp. 262–7.

Kitschelt, Herbert. 1994. *The Transformation of European Social Democracy*. Cambridge: Cambridge University Press.

Kitschelt, Herbert P. 1988. 'Left-Libertarian Parties: Explaining Innovation in Competitive Party Systems'. *World Politics* 40 (2): pp. 194–234.

Klein, Elad. 2018. 'The Personal Vote and Legislative Party Switching'. *Party Politics* 24 (5): pp. 501–10.

Klein, Elad. 2021. 'Explaining Legislative Party Switching in Advanced and New Democracies'. *Party Politics* 27 (2): pp. 329–40.

Klingemann, Hans-Dieter, Andrea Volkens, Judith Bara, Ian Budge, and Michael D. McDonald. 2006. *Mapping Policy Preferences II: Estimates for Parties, Electors, and Governments in Eastern Europe, European Union, and OECD 1990–2003*. Oxford: Oxford University Press.

Koedam, Jelle. 2021. 'A Change of Heart? Analysing Stability and Change in European Party Positions'. *West European Politics* 45 (4): pp. 693–715.

Kölln, Ann-Kristin. 2015. 'The Effects of Membership Decline on Party Organisations in Europe'. *European Journal of Political Research* 54 (4): pp. 707–25.

Kölln, Ann-Kristin, and Jonathan Polk. 2016. 'Emancipated Party Members: Examining Ideological Incongruence within Political Parties'. *Party Politics* 23 (1): pp. 18–29.

Kopeček, Lubomír. 2016. '"I'm Paying, So I Decide": Czech ANO as an Extreme Form of a Business-Firm Party'. *East European Politics and Societies and Cultures* 30 (4): pp. 725–49.

Kopecký, Petr. 2006. 'Political Parties and the State in Post-Communist Europe: The Nature of Symbiosis'. *Journal of Communist Studies and Transition Politics* 22 (3): pp. 251–73.

Korkut, Umut. 2014. 'The Migration myth in the Absence of Immigrants: How Does the Conservative Right in Hungary and Turkey Grapple with Immigration?' *Comparative European Politics* 12 (6): pp. 620–36.

Körösényi, András, Péter Ondré, and András Hajdú. 2017. 'A "Meteoric" Career in Hungarian Politics'. In *The Leadership Capital Index. A New Perspective on Political Leadership*, edited by Mark Bennister, Ben Worthy, and Paul 't Hart, pp. 82–100. Oxford: Oxford University Press.

Kostadinova, Petia, and Maria Popova. 2014. 'The 2013 Parliamentary Elections in Bulgaria'. *Electoral Studies* 34: pp. 365–8.

Kostadinova, Tatiana. 2009. 'Abstain or Rebel: Corruption Perceptions and Voting in East European Elections'. *Politics and Policy* 37 (4): pp. 691–714.

Kovács, András. 1996. 'Did the Losers Really Win? An Analysis of Electoral Behavior in Hungary in 1994'. *Social Research* 63 (2): pp. 511–30.

Krause, Werner, and Heiko Giebler. 2020. 'Shifting Welfare Policy Positions: The Impact of Radical Right Populist Party Success beyond Migration Politics'. *Representation* 56 (3): pp. 331–48.

Krauss, Svenja, and Heike Kluever. 2022. 'Cabinet Formation and Coalition Governance: The Effect of Portfolio Allocation on Coalition Agreements'. *Government and Opposition*. Online First.

Kreuzer, Marcus, and Vello Pettai. 2003. 'Patterns of Political Instability: Affiliation Patterns of Politicians and Voters in Post-Communist Estonia, Latvia, and Lithuania'. *Studies in Comparative International Development* 38 (2): pp. 76–98.
Krook, Mona L. 2009. *Quotas for Women in Politics: Gender and Candidate Selection Reform Worldwide*. Oxford: Oxford University Press.
Krouwel, André. 2006. 'Party Models'. In *Handbook of Party Politics*, edited by Richard S. Katz and William J. Crotty, pp. 249–69. London: Sage.
Krouwel, André. 2012. *Party Transformations in European Democracies*. Albany, NY: State University of New York Press.
Krupavičius, Algis. 1998. 'The Post-Communist Transition and Institutionalization of Lithuania's Parties'. *Political Studies* 46 (3): pp. 465–91.
Kumar, Sudhir. 2005. 'Molecular Clocks: Four Decades of Evolution'. *Nature Reviews Genetics* 6 (8): pp. 654–62.
Lane, Jan-Erik, and Svante Ersson. 2007. 'Party System Instability in Europe: Persistent Differences in Volatility between West and East?' *Democratization* 14 (1): pp. 92–110.
Larcinese, Valentino, and Indraneel Sircar. 2017. 'Crime and Punishment the British Way: Accountability Channels Following the MPs' Expenses Scandal'. *European Journal of Political Economy* 47: pp. 75–99.
Lasswell, Harold D., and Abraham Kaplan. 1950. *Power and Society*. New Haven, CT: Yale University Press.
Laver, Michael (ed.). 2001. *Estimating the Policy Position of Political Actors*. London: Routledge.
Laver, Michael, and Kenneth Benoit. 2003. 'The Evolution of Party Systems between Elections'. *American Journal of Political Science* 47 (2): pp. 215–33.
Laver, Michael, and Junko Kato. 2001. 'Dynamic Approaches to Government Formation and the Generic Instability of Decisive Structures in Japan'. *Electoral Studies* 20 (4): pp. 509–27.
Lee, Don S., and Fernando Casal Bértoa. 2021. 'On the Causes of Electoral Volatility in Asia since 1948'. *Party Politics* 28 (6): pp. 1187–99.
Leoni, Eduardo, Carlos Pereira, and Lúcio Rennó. 2004. 'Political Survival Strategies: Political Career Decisions in the Brazilian Chamber of Deputies'. *Journal of Latin American Studies* 36 (1): pp. 109–30.
Lilliefeldt, Emelie. 2010. 'A Coalition of Coalitions: The 2010 Parliamentary Elections in Latvia'. BalticWorlds. 9 October.
Lipset, Seymour M., and Stein Rokkan. 1967. 'Cleavage Structures, Party Systems, and Voter Alignments: An Introduction'. In *Party Systems and Voter Alignments: Cross-National Perspectives*, edited by Seymour M. Lipset and Rokkan Stein, pp. 1–64. New York: Free Press.
Lisi, Marco. 2015. *Party Change, Recent Democracies, and Portugal: Comparative Perspectives*. Lanham, MD: Lexington Books.
Lisi, Marco (ed). 2019. *Party System Change, the European Crisis and the State of Democracy*. London: Routledge.
Litton, Krystyna. 2015. 'Party Novelty: Conceptualization and Measurement of Party Change'. *Party Politics* 21 (5): pp. 712–25.
Lloren, Anouk, and Jan Rosset. 2017. 'Gendered Policy Preferences? Candidates' Views on Political Issues in a Comparative Perspective'. *Comparative European Politics* 15 (6): pp. 944–68.

Longley, Lawrence D., and Reuven Y. Hazan. 1999. 'On the Uneasy, Delicate, Yet Necessary Relationships between Parliamentary Members and Leaders'. *Journal of Legislative Studies* 5 (3–4): pp. 1–22.

Lovenduski, Joni. 2016. 'The Supply and Demand Model of Candidate Selection: Some Reflections'. *Government and Opposition* 51 (3): pp. 513–28.

Lucardie, Paul. 2000. 'Prophets, Purifiers and Prolocutors: Towards a Theory on the Emergence of New Parties'. *Party Politics* 6 (2): pp. 175–85.

Lundell, Krister. 2004. 'Determinants of Candidate Selection: The Degree of Centralization in Comparative Perspective'. *Party Politics* 10 (1): pp. 25–47.

Lutz, Georg, Anke Tresch, Nicolas Pekari, Annika Lindholm, Lukas Lauener, et al. 2018. The Comparative Candidate Survey (CCS)—Cumulative Data Set (Wave I, 2005–2013; Wave II, 2013–2018). https://doi.org/10.23662/FORS-DS-886-3.

McDonald, Michael, and Ian Budge. 2005. *Elections, Parties, and Democracy: Conferring the Median Mandate*. Oxford: Oxford University Press.

Machin, Howard. 1989. 'Stages and Dynamics in the Evolution of the French Party System'. *West European Politics* 12 (4): pp. 59–81.

McMenamin, Iain, and Anna Gwiazda. 2011. 'Three Roads to Institutionalisation: Vote-, Office- and Policy-seeking Explanations of Party Switching in Poland'. *European Journal of Political Research* 50 (6): pp. 838–66.

Mainwaring, Scott, Annabella España, and Carlos Gervasoni. 2009. 'Extra System Electoral Volatility and the Vote Share of Young Parties'. Paper presented at the Annual Meeting of the Canadian Political Science Association, Ottawa, 27–29 May.

Mainwaring, Scott, Carlos Gervasoni, and Annabella España-Najera. 2016. 'Extra- and within-System Electoral Volatility'. *Party Politics* 23 (6): pp. 623–35.

Mainwaring, Scott, and Mariano Torcal. 2006. 'Party System Institutionalization and Party System Theory after the Third Wave of Democratization'. In *Handbook of Party Politics*, edited by Richard S Katz and William Crotty, pp. 204–27. London: Sage.

Mainwaring, Scott, and Yen-Pin Su. 2021. 'Electoral Volatility in Latin America, 1932–2018'. *Studies in Comparative International Development* 56 (3): pp. 271–96.

Mair, Peter. 1990. 'The Electoral Payoffs of Fission and Fusion'. *British Journal of Political Science* 20 (1): pp. 131–42.

Mair, Peter. 1996. 'Party Systems and Structures of Competition'. In *Comparing Democracies: Elections and Voting in Global Perspective*, edited by Lawrence LeDuc, Richard G. Niemi, and Pippa Norris, pp. 83–106. Thousand Oaks, CA: Sage.

Mair, Peter. 1997. *Party Systems Change: Approaches and Interpretations*. Oxford: Oxford University Press.

Mair, Peter, Wolfgang Muller, and Fritz Plasser. 2004. *Political Parties and Electoral Change: Party Responses to Electoral Markets*. London: Sage.

Manow, Philip. 2013. 'Mixed Rules, Different Roles? An Analysis of the Typical Pathways into the Bundestag and of MPs' Parliamentary Behaviour'. *Journal of Legislative Studies* 19 (3): pp. 287–308.

Manuel, Rob. 2015. 'What Do Political Party Logos Actually Mean?' *Mirror*. 5 May. www.mirror.co.uk/news/ampp3d/what-political-party-logos-actually-5604537.

Marino, Bruno. 2021. *Party Leaders and Their Selection Rules in Western Europe*. London: Routledge.

Marinova, Dani M. 2015. 'A New Approach to Estimating Electoral Instability in Parties'. *Political Science Research and Methods* 3 (2): pp. 265–80.

Marsh, Michael. 1993. 'Introduction: Selecting the Party Leader'. *European Journal of Political Research* 24 (3): pp. 229–31.

Matland, Richard E., and Donley T. Studlar. 2004. 'Determinants of Legislative Turnover: A Cross-National Analysis'. *British Journal of Political Science* 34 (1): pp. 87–108.
May, John D. 1973. 'Opinion Structure of Political Parties: The Special Law of Curvilinear Disparity'. *Political Studies* 21 (2): pp. 135–51.
Mazzoleni, Oscar, and Gerrit Voerman. 2017. 'Memberless Parties: Beyond the Business-Firm Party Model?' *Party Politics* 23 (6): pp. 783–92.
Meleshevich, Andrey A. 2007. *Party Systems in Post-Soviet Countries: A Comparative Study of Political Institutionalization in the Baltic States, Russia, and Ukraine.* New York: Palgrave Macmillan.
Mershon, Carol, and Olga Shvetsova. 2013. *Party System Change in Legislatures Worldwide.* Cambridge: Cambridge University Press.
Meyer, Thomas. 2013. *Constraints on Party Politics.* Colchester: ECPR Press.
Millard, Frances. 2004. *Elections, Parties, and Representation in Post-Communist Europe.* Basingstoke: Palgrave Macmillan.
Mölder, Martin. 2016. 'The Validity of the RILE Left–Right Index as a Measure of Party Policy'. *Party Politics* 22 (1): pp. 37–48.
Mölder, Martin. 2017. 'Which Measure of Political Difference between Parties Works Better? A Comparison in Predicting Coalition Formation'. *Electoral Studies* 46: pp. 26–38.
Moore, Michael K., and John R. Hibbing. 1998. 'Situational Dissatisfaction in Congress: Explaining Voluntary Departures'. *Journal of Politics* 60 (4): pp. 1088–107.
Morlino, Leonardo. 1996. 'Crisis of Parties and Change of Party System in Italy'. *Party Politics* 2 (1): pp. 5–30.
Musella, Fortunato. 2015. 'Personal Leaders and Party Change: Italy in Comparative Perspective'. *Italian Political Science Review* 45 (3): pp. 227–47.
Musella, Fortunato. 2017. *Political Leaders Beyond Party Politics.* London: Palgrave Macmillan.
Muuli, Kalle. 2013. *Vabariigi sünnimärgid: varjatud murdehetki Eesti poliitikas.* Tallinn: Tulimuld.
Nikolenyi, Csaba. 2004. 'Strategic Co-ordination in the 2002 Hungarian Election'. *Europe-Asia Studies* 56 (7): pp. 1041–58.
Nikolenyi, Csaba. 2014. *Institutional Design and Party Government in Post-Communist Europe.* Oxford: Oxford University Press.
Norris, Pippa. 1995. 'May's Law of Curvilinear Disparity Revisited: Leaders, Officers, Members and Voters in British Political Parties'. *Party Politics* 1 (1): pp. 29–47.
Norris, Pippa. 1997. *Passages to Power: Legislative Recruitment in Advanced Democracies.* Cambridge: Cambridge University Press.
Norris, Pippa, and Joni Lovenduski. 1995. *Political Recruitment: Gender, Race, and Class in the British Parliament.* Cambridge: Cambridge University Press.
O'Brien, Diana Z., and Yael Shomer. 2013. 'A Cross-National Analysis of Party Switching'. *Legislative Studies Quarterly* 38 (1): pp. 111–41.
O'Dwyer, Conor. 2014. 'What Accounts for Party System Stability? Comparing the Dimensions of Party Competition in Postcommunist Europe'. *Europe-Asia Studies* 66 (4): pp. 511–35.
Okasha, Samir. 2020. *Agents and Goals in Evolution.* Oxford: Oxford University Press.
Oltay, Edith. 1995. 'Government and Parties in Hungary (1990–1994)'. *Comparative Southeast European Studies* 44 (11–12): pp. 746–61.
Panebianco, Angelo. 1988. *Political Parties: Organization and Power.* Cambridge: Cambridge University Press.

Passarelli, Gianluca. 2015. *The Presidentialization of Political Parties: Organizations, Institutions and Leaders*. London: Palgrave Macmillan.

Pattie, Charles, and Ron Johnston. 2012. 'The Electoral Impact of the UK 2009 MPs' Expenses Scandal'. *Political Studies* 60 (4): pp. 730–50.

Pedersen, Mogens N. 1979. 'The Dynamics of European Party Systems: Changing Patterns of Electoral Volatility'. *European Journal of Political Research* 7 (1): pp. 1–26.

Pedersen, Mogens N. 1980. 'On Measuring Party System Change: A Methodological Critique and a Suggestion'. *Comparative Political Studies* 12 (4): pp. 387–403.

Peters, John G., and Susan Welch. 1980. 'The Effects of Charges of Corruption on Voting Behavior in Congressional Elections'. *American Political Science Review* 74 (3): pp. 697–708.

Pettai, Vello, and Marcus Kreuzer. 1999. 'Party Politics in the Baltic States: Social Bases and Institutional Context'. *East European Politics and Societies* 13 (1): pp. 148–89.

Pilet, Jean-Benoit, and William P. Cross (eds). 2014. *The Selection of Political Party Leaders in Contemporary Parliamentary Democracies: A Comparative Study*. London: Routledge.

Poguntke, Thomas, Susan E. Scarrow, and Paul D. Webb. 2020. 'Political Party Database'. https://dataverse.harvard.edu/dataverse/Political_Party_Database.

Polish News Bulletin. 2005. 'SLD Undergoes Face Lift and Changes Leader'. *Polish News Bulletin*. 30 May.

Political Risk Services. 2000.'Independent Smallholders Party (FYGP)'. PRS Group/Political Risk Services. 1 September.

Polk, Jonathan, Jan Rovny, Ryan Bakker, Erica Edwards, Liesbet Hooghe, Seth Jolly, Jelle Koedam, Filip Kostelka, Gary Marks, and Gijs Schumacher. 2017. 'Explaining the Salience of Anti-elitism and Reducing Political Corruption for Political Parties in Europe with the 2014 Chapel Hill Expert Survey Data'. *Research & Politics* 4 (1): 2053168016686915.

Pop-Eleches, Grigore. 2010. 'Throwing out the Bums: Protest Voting and Unorthodox Parties after Communism'. *World Politics* 62 (2): pp. 221–60.

Popescu, Marina, and Martin Hannavy. 2001. Political Transformation and the Electoral Process in Post-Communist Europe. https://web.archive.org/web/20140116005942/http://www.essex.ac.uk/elections/.

Powell, Eleanor Neff, and Joshua A. Tucker. 2014. 'Revisiting Electoral Volatility in Post-Communist Countries: New Data, New Results and New Approaches'. *British Journal of Political Science* 44 (1): pp. 123–47.

Powell, Eleanor Neff, and Joshua A. Tucker. 2017. 'Little Is Known about Party System Volatility in Post-Communist Europe, but We Have Interesting New Methods and Data for Studying It'. *British Journal of Political Science* 47 (1): pp. 235–9.

Praino, Rodrigo, Daniel Stockemer, and Vincent G. Moscardelli. 2013. 'The Lingering Effect of Scandals in Congressional Elections: Incumbents, Challengers, and Voters'. *Social Science Quarterly* 94 (4): pp. 1045–61.

Prosser, Christopher. 2014. 'Building Policy Scales from Manifesto Data: A Referential Content Validity Approach'. *Electoral Studies* 35: pp. 88–101.

Protsyk, Oleh, and Marius L. Matichescu. 2011. 'Clientelism and Political Recruitment in Democratic Transition: Evidence from Romania'. *Comparative Politics* 43 (2): pp. 207–24.

Prum, Richard O., Jacob S. Berv, Alex Dornburg, Daniel J. Field, Jeffrey P. Townsend, et al. 2015. 'A Comprehensive Phylogeny of Birds (Aves) Using Targeted Next-Generation DNA Sequencing'. *Nature* 526 (7574): pp. 569–73.

Pytlas, Bartek. 2015. *Radical Right Parties in Central and Eastern Europe: Mainstream Party Competition and Electoral Fortune*. London: Taylor & Francis.

Quinn, Thomas. 2012. *Electing and Ejecting Party Leaders in Britain*. London: Palgrave Macmillan.

Rahat, Gideon. 2007. 'Candidate Selection: The Choice before the Choice'. *Journal of Democracy* 18 (1): pp. 157–70.

Rahat, Gideon, and Ofer Kenig. 2018. *From Party Politics to Personalized Politics? Party Change and Political Personalization in Democracies*. Oxford: Oxford University Press.

Riggs, Fred W. 1968. 'Comparative Politics and the Study of political Parties: A Structural Approach'. In *Approaches to the Study of Party Organization*, edited by William J. Crotty, pp. 45–104. Boston: Allyn & Bacon.

Robbins, Joseph W., and Lance Y. Hunter. 2012. 'Impact of Electoral Volatility and Party Replacement on Voter Turnout Levels'. *Party Politics* 18 (6): pp. 919–39.

Roberts, Andrew. 2008. 'Hyperaccountability: Economic Voting in Central and Eastern Europe'. *Electoral Studies* 27 (3): pp. 533–46.

Rohrschneider, Robert, and Stephen Whitefield. 2012. *The Strain of Representation: How Parties Represent Diverse Voters in Western and Eastern Europe*. Oxford: Oxford University Press.

Rovny, Jan, and Erica E. Edwards. 2012. 'Struggle over Dimensionality: Party Competition in Western and Eastern Europe'. *East European Politics and Societies and Cultures* 26 (1): pp. 56–74.

Royed, Terry J., Kevin M. Leyden, and Stephen A. Borrelli. 2000. 'Is "Clarity of Responsibility" Important for Economic Voting? Revisiting Powell and Whitten's Hypothesis'. *British Journal of Political Science* 30 (4): pp. 669–98.

Salvati, Eugenio, and Michelangelo Vercesi. 2018. 'Party Organizations and Legislative Turnover Signals of an Unstable Parliamentary Class?'. *Italian Political Science* 13 (1): pp. 82–94.

Samuels, David. 2008. 'Political Ambition, Candidate Recruitment, and Legislative Politics in Brazil'. In *Pathways to Power: Political Recruitment and Candidate Selection in Latin America*, edited by Peter M. Siavelis and Scott Morgenstern, pp. 76–91. University Park, PA: Pennsylvania State University Press.

Samuels, David J., and Matthew S. Shugart. 2010. *Presidents, Parties, and Prime Ministers: How the Separation of Powers Affects Party Organization and Behavior*. Cambridge: Cambridge University Press.

Sandri, Giulia, Antonella Seddone, and Fulvio Venturino. 2015. *Party Primaries in Comparative Perspective*. London: Routledge.

Sandri, Giulia, Antonella Seddone, and Fulvio Venturino. 2016. 'Understanding Leadership Profile Renewal'. In *The Politics of Party Leadership*, edited by William Cross and Jean-Benoit Pilet, pp. 90–106. Oxford: Oxford University Press.

Sartori, Giovanni. 1994. *Comparative Constitutional Engineering*. London: Palgrave Macmillan.

Scarrow, Susan. 2014. *Beyond Party Members: Changing Approaches to Partisan Mobilization*. Oxford: Oxford University Press.

Scarrow, Susan E., and Paul D. Webb. 2017. *Organizing Political Parties: Representation, Participation, and Power*. Oxford: Oxford University Press.

Schumacher, Gijs, and Nathalie Giger. 2018. 'Do Leadership-Dominated Parties Change More?' *Journal of Elections, Public Opinion and Parties* 28 (3): pp. 349–60.

Schwindt-Bayer, Leslie A., and Margit Tavits. 2016. *Clarity of Responsibility, Accountability, and Corruption.* Cambridge: Cambridge University Press.

Semenova, Elena. 2015. 'Parliamentary Party Switching: A Specific Feature of Post-Communist Parliamentarism?' *Zeitschrift für Parlamentsfragen* 46 (2): pp. 272–91.

Semenova Elena, Edinger Michael, and Best Heinrich (eds) 2014. *Parliamentary Elites in Central and Eastern Europe: Recruitment and Representation.* London: Routledge.

Shabad, Goldie, and Kazimierz M. Slomczynski. 2004. 'Inter-Party Mobility among Parliamentary Candidates in Post-Communist East Central Europe'. *Party Politics* 10 (2): pp. 151–76.

Siavelis, Peter M., and Scott Morgenstern. 2012. *Pathways to Power: Political Recruitment and Candidate Selection in Latin America.* University Park, PA: Pennsylvania State University Press.

Sikk, Allan. 2005. 'How Unstable? Volatility and the Genuinely New Parties in Eastern Europe'. *European Journal of Political Research* 44 (3): pp. 391–412.

Sikk, Allan. 2006. 'From private Organizations to Democratic Infrastructure: Political Parties and the State in Estonia'. *Journal of Communist Studies and Transition Politics* 22 (3): pp. 341–61.

Sikk, Allan. 2012. 'Newness as a Winning Formula for New Political Parties'. *Party Politics* 18 (4): pp. 465–86.

Sikk, Allan, and Licia Cianetti. 2015. 'Political Mechanics of Smallness: The Baltic States as Small States in the European Parliament'. In *Small States in the Modern World: Vulnerabilities and Opportunities*, edited by Harald Baldersheim and Michael Keating, pp. 91–109. Cheltenham: Edward Elgar.

Sikk, Allan, and Philipp Köker. 2015. 'Candidate Turnover and Party System Change in Central and Eastern Europe'. Paper presented at the ECPR General Conference, Montreal, 26–29 August.

Sikk, Allan, and Philipp Köker. 2016. 'Rejuvenation of renomination? Corruption and candidate turnover in Central and Eastern Europe'. Paper presented at the APSA Annual Meeting. Philadelphia, PA, 1–4 September.

Sikk, Allan, and Philipp Köker. 2019. 'Party Novelty and Congruence: A New Approach to Measuring Party Change and Volatility'. *Party Politics* 25 (6): pp. 759–70.

Singer, Matthew M. 2011. 'Who Says "It's the Economy"? Cross-National and Cross-Individual Variation in the Salience of Economic Performance'. *Comparative Political Studies* 44 (3): pp. 284–312.

Slomczynski, Kazimierz, and Goldie Shabad. 2012. 'Perceptions of Political Party Corruption and Voting Behaviour in Poland'. *Party Politics* 18 (6): pp. 897–917.

Snegovaya, Maria. 2020. 'Voice or Exit? Political Corruption and Voting Intentions in Hungary'. *Democratization* 27 (7): pp. 1162–82.

Somer-Topcu, Zeynep. 2009. 'Timely Decisions: The Effects of Past National Elections on Party Policy Change'. *Journal of Politics* 71 (1): pp. 238–48.

Somer-Topcu, Zeynep. 2016. 'Agree or Disagree: How Do Party Leader Changes Affect the Distribution of Voters' Perceptions'. *Party Politics* 23 (1): pp. 66–75.

Spirova, Maria. 2007. *Political Parties in Post-Communist Societies: Formation, Persistence, and Change.* New York: Palgrave Macmillan.

Stanley, Ben. 2020. 'A Comparison of Two Polish Party Leaders: Jarosław Kaczyński and Donald Tusk'. In *Party Leaders in Eastern Europe: Personality, Behavior and Consequences*, edited by Sergiu Gherghina, pp. 171–95. Cham: Palgrave Macmillan.

Strasser, Bruno J., and Paul N. Edwards. 2017. 'Big Data Is the Answer . . . But What Is the Question?' *Osiris* 32 (1): pp. 328–45.
Strøm, Kaare. 1990. 'A Behavioral Theory of Competitive Political Parties'. *American Journal of Political Science* 34 (2): pp. 565–98.
Strøm, Kaare, and Wolfgang C. Müller. 1999. 'Political Parties and Hard Choices'. In *Policy, Office, or Votes? How Political Parties in Western Europe Make Hard Decisions*, edited by Kaare Strøm and Wolfgang C. Müller, pp. 1–35. Cambridge: Cambridge University Press.
Sykes, Patricia Lee. 1988. *Losing from the Inside: The Cost of Conflict in the British Social Democratic Party*. London: Routledge.
Szczerbiak, Aleks. 2007. 'Electoral Politics in Poland: The Parliamentary Elections of 1997'. *Journal of Communist Studies and Transition Politics* 14 (3): pp. 58–83.
Taagepera, Rein. 1999. 'Ignorance-Based Quantitative Models and their Practical Implications'. *Journal of Theoretical Politics* 11 (3): pp. 421–31.
Tavits, Margit. 2005. 'The Development of Stable Party Support: Electoral Dynamics in Post-Communist Europe'. *American Journal of Political Science* 49 (2): pp. 283–98.
Tavits, Margit. 2007. 'Clarity of Responsibility and Corruption'. *American Journal of Political Science* 51 (1): pp. 218–29.
Tavits, Margit. 2008a. 'On the Linkage between Electoral Volatility and Party System Instability in Central and Eastern Europe'. *European Journal of Political Research* 47 (5): pp. 537–55.
Tavits, Margit. 2008b. 'Party Systems in the Making: The Emergence and Success of New Parties in New Democracies'. *British Journal of Political Science* 38 (1): pp. 113–33.
Tavits, Margit. 2013. *Post-Communist Democracies and Party Organization*. Cambridge: Cambridge University Press.
Tavits, Margit, and Natalia Letki. 2009. 'When Left Is Right: Party Ideology and Policy in Post-Communist Europe'. *American Political Science Review* 103 (4): pp. 555–69.
Tavits, Margit, and Natalia Letki. 2013. 'From Values to Interests? The Evolution of Party Competition in New Democracies'. *The Journal of Politics* 76 (1): pp. 1–13.
Thames, Frank C. 2007. 'Discipline and Party Institutionalization in post-Soviet Legislatures'. *Party Politics* 13 (4): pp. 456–77.
Thomsen, Danielle M. 2017. *Opting Out of Congress: Partisan Polarization and the Decline of Moderate Candidates*. Cambridge: Cambridge University Press.
Tucker, Joshua A., and Kevin Deegan-Krause. 2011. 'It's the Bribe, Stupid! Pocketbook vs. Sociotropic Corruption Voting'. Paper presented at the APSA Annual Meeting, Seattle, WA, 1–4 September.
van Biezen, Ingrid. 2003. *Political Parties in New Democracies: Party Organization in Southern and East-Central Europe*. New York: Palgrave Macmillan.
van Biezen, Ingrid. 2005. 'On the Theory and Practice of Party Formation and Adaptation in New Democracies'. *European Journal of Political Research* 44 (1): pp. 147–74.
van Haute, Emilie, and Anika Gauja (eds). 2015. *Party Members and Activists*. London: Routledge.
van Holsteyn, Joop J. M., Josje M. den Ridder, and Ruud A. Koole. 2017. 'From May's Laws to May's Legacy: On the Opinion Structure within Political Parties'. *Party Politics* 23 (5): pp. 471–86.
Vidra, Zsuzsanna. 2018. 'Hungary's Punitive Turn: The Shift from Welfare to Workfare'. *Communist and Post-Communist Studies* 51 (1): pp. 73–80.

Volkens, Andrea, Tobias Burst, Werner Krause, Pola Lehmann, Theres Matthieß, et al. 2020. The Manifesto Data Collection. Manifesto Project (MRG/CMP/MARPOR). Version 2020a. Berlin: Wissenschaftszentrum Berlin für Sozialforschung (WZB). https://doi.org/10.25522/manifesto.mpds.2020a.

Volpi, Elisa. 2019. 'Ideology and Party Switching: A Comparison of 12 West European Countries'. *Parliamentary Affairs* 72 (1): pp. 1–20.

Webb, Paul, Thomas Poguntke, and Robin Kolodny. 2012. 'The Presidentialization of Party Leadership? Evaluating Party Leadership and Party Government in the Democratic World'. In *Comparative Political Leadership*, edited by Ludger Helms, pp. 77–98. London: Palgrave Macmillan.

Whitten, Guy D., and Harvey D. Palmer. 1999. 'Cross-National Analyses of Economic Voting'. *Electoral Studies* 18 (1): pp. 49–67.

Wiggins, David. 2001. *Sameness and Substance Renewed*. Cambridge: Cambridge University Press.

Willey, Joseph. 1998. 'Institutional Arrangements and the Success of New Parties in Old Democracies'. *Political Studies* 46 (3): pp. 651–68.

Wittenberg, Jason. 2006. *Crucibles of Political Loyalty: Church Institutions and Electoral Continuity in Hungary*. Cambridge: Cambridge University Press.

Yanai, Itai, and Martin Lercher. 2016. *The Society of Genes*. Cambridge: Harvard University Press.

Žeruolis, Darius. 1998. 'Lithuania'. In *Handbook of Political Change in Eastern Europe*, edited by Sten Berglund, Tomas Hellén, and Frank H. Aarebrot, pp. 121–56. Cheltenham: Edward Elgar.

Zittel, Thomas. 2015. 'Constituency Candidates in Comparative Perspective—How Personalized Are Constituency Campaigns, Why, and Does It Matter?' *Electoral Studies* 39: pp. 286–94.

Zuba, Krzysztof. 2020. 'Leaders without Leadership: Surrogate Governments in Poland'. *Europe-Asia Studies* 72 (1): pp. 33–54.

Zuckerkandl, Emile, and Linus Pauling. 1965. 'Evolutionary Divergence and Convergence in Proteins'. In *Evolving Genes and Proteins*, edited by Vernon Bryson and Henry J. Vogel, pp. 97–166. New York: Academic Press.

Index

Āboltiņa, Solvita 187
Action of Dissatisfied Citizens (ANO) 7
agency 11–12, 20, 21, 34
Albatrosses 8, 45
Alliance for the Future of Austria (BZÖ) 3, 90
Alliance of Alenka Bratušek (ZAAB) 168, 197
Alliance of Free Democrats (SZDSZ) 61, 105, 208
Andriukaitis, Vytenis 188
ANO, *see* Action of Dissatisfied Citizens (ANO)
Ansip, Andrus 185
Ataka 209
Australia 182
Austria 3, 26, 90
AWS, *see* Solidarity Electoral Action (AWS)
AWSP, *see* Solidarity Electoral Action of the Right (AWSP)

Babiš, Andrej 7
Balcerowicz, Leszek 188
BDSA, *see* Social-Democratic Coalition of Algirdas Brazauskas (BSDA)
Belka, Marek 187
Berlusconi, Silvio 7, 182
Bērziņš, Gaidis 188
Better Estonia–Estonian Citizen (PE-EK) 61, 122, 125
big data 6, 13–16, 46–7
BITE, *see* Free Choice in People's Europe (BITE)
Borisov, Boyko 185
Bratušek, Alenka, *see* Alliance of Alenka Bratušek (ZAAB)
Brazauskas, Algirdas 97, 196, *see also* Social-Democratic Coalition of Algirdas Brazauskas (BSDA)
Brexit Party 90
Bridge (Most–Híd) 197

BSP, *see* Bulgarian Socialist Party (BSP)
Bugár, Béla 197
Bulgarian Radical Democratic Party/Free Radical Democratic Party 163
Bulgarian Socialist Party (BSP) 56, 108, 133, 165
BZÖ, *see* Alliance for the Future of Austria (BZÖ)

Cameron, David 10
Canada 182
candidate congruence, *see* congruence of slates
candidate dropout 7, 49, 54–6, 69–71, *see also* weighted candidate dropout (WCD)
candidate novelty 7, 49, 54–6, 64, 69–71, *see also* weighted candidate novelty (WCN)
candidate recruitment 20, 34–5, 38, 78, 205
candidate selection 5, 20, 34, 38, 88
candidate turnover
candidate weighting 49–53
  in mixed systems 53
Centre Party (K) 61, 123–5, 131–2, 165, 168, 174, 176
Cerar, Miro, *see* Party of Miro Cerar (SMC)
Čevers, Ziedonis 195
Chapel Hill Expert Survey (CHES) 31, 117, 200–6, 209, 214, 218–19
Christian and Democratic Union–Czechoslovak People's Party (KDU–ČSL) 170, 178
Christian Democracy, Italy 4
Christian Democrat Union (LKDS) 174, 194
Christian Democratic Movement (KDH) 162, 196, 210
Christian Democratic People's Party (KDNP) 177, 203

Christian Party (KP) 168
Citizens for European Development of
    Bulgaria (GERB) 54, 185, 209
Civic Democratic Alliance (ODA) 107
Civic Democratic Party (ODS) 29, 56, 133,
    167, 195
Civic Platform (PO) 3, 61, 90, 108, 112,
    136, 156, 159, 167, 174–5, 186, 201,
    209
cleavages 117
Coalition Party and Country People's
    Union (KMÜ) 61, 104, 123–5, 130,
    165, 173
collective defection 28, 129, 135, 165, 168,
    172–9
Common Choice (SV) 100, 105
Communist Party of Bohemia and Moravia
    (KSČM) 133, 197
Comparative Candidates Survey 16
congruence
    of party leaders 192–97
    of party programmes 215–7
    of slates 8, 34, 56–61, 74, 118, 120, 126,
      130, 157–8, 160–1, 171–72, *see also*
      candidate congruence
Conservative Party, United Kingdom 3,
    10, 22, 26
Conservative People's Party (EKRE),
    Estonia 176
Conservative People's Party (SKL),
    Poland 165
Corbyn, Jeremy 29
corruption 69, 76–79, 86, 88
Corruption Perception Index (CPI) 79, 83,
    86, 88
Csáky, Pál 197
ČSSD, *see* Czech Social Democratic Party
    (ČSSD)
Czech Social Democratic Party
    (ČSSD) 133, 163, 186

David 49–51, 119–20
Dawkins, Richard 11, 19
Dawn (ÚSVIT) 167
de Gaulle, Charles 4
Democratic Left (DL) 133, 165–6
Democratic Left Alliance (SLD) 26, 61,
    105, 170, 182, 187
Democratic Party (DS) 173

Democratic Party of Pensioners
    (DeSuS) 102, 169
Democratic Party Saimnieks (DPS) 164
Democratic Union (UD) 4, 105, 165
Democrats for a Strong Bulgaria (DSB) 195
Denmark 3, 4, 90
DeSuS, *see* Democratic Party of Pensioners
    (DeSuS)
DFP, *see* People's Party (DFP)
Direction-Social Democracy
    (Smer-SD) 56, 210
district magnitude 50–2
DL, *see* Democratic Left (DL)
Dombrovskis, Valdis 196
DP (Latvia), *see* Labour Party (DP),
    Latvia
DP (Lithuania), *see* Labour Party (DP),
    Lithuania
DPS (Bulgaria), *see* Movement for Rights
    and Freedoms (DPS)
DPS (Latvia), *see* Democratic Party
    Saimnieks (DPS)
dropout, *see* candidate dropout
DS, *see* Democratic Party (DS)
DSB, *see* Democrats for a Strong Bulgaria
    (DSB)
Dzurinda, Mikuláš 196

ECCEE, *see* Electoral Candidates
    in Central and Eastern Europe
    (ECCEE)
EKGP, *see* United Smallholders Party
    (EKGP)
EKRE, *see* Conservative People's Party
    (EKRE), Estonia
ELDP, *see* Liberal Democratic Party
    (ELDP), Estonia
Electoral Candidates in Central and
    Eastern Europe (ECCEE) 14, 46–7,
    63, 95, 159, 170
electoral paradigm, *see* genetic paradigm
En Marche 4, 90
Equal Rights (L) 155
ER, *see* Reform Party (ER)
ERSP, *see* National Independence Party
    (ERSP)
European Union 158, 209
evolution
    in genetics 7, 11, 19–20, 39

in party systems 2, 10–1, 61, 140
in political parties 3, 7, 10, 12, 39, 61, 141

Farage, Nigel 90
Farmers' Union (LZS) 174, 194
FDP, *see* Free Democratic Party (FDP)
feasible candidates 41–2, 68, 69–72
Fico, Robert 210
Fidesz 3, 32, 59–61, 163, 175, 177, 182, 200, 203, 209
Fidesz–MDF, *see* Fidesz; Hungarian Democratic Forum (MDF)
fission
  and leadership congruence 195–7
  and programmatic change 216–7
  and slate congruence 157–8, 160–4
  definition of 151–2, 155
  detection based on candidate movement 166–70
  fissionary tendencies 152, 164, 179, 216
  of electoral coalitions 159, 161
Five Star Movement 4, 90, 182
FKGP, *see* Independent Smallholders Party (FKGP)
For a Good Latvia! (PLL) 196, 210
For Fatherland and Freedom/LNNK (TB-LNNK) 173, 188
For Human Rights in a United Latvia (PCTVL) 155, 156
For Latvia from the Heart (NSL) 169
For Order and Justice (UTT) 133, 164, 169
Forza Italia 4, 7
FP, *see* Progress Party (FP)
France 4, 28
Free Choice in People's Europe (BITE) 155–6
Free Democratic Party (FDP) 26
Freedom and Dignity (NPSD) 168
Freedom and Solidarity (SaS) 186
Freedom Party (FPÖ) 3
Freedom Union (US), Czech Republic 61, 136, 165, 170
Freedom Union (UW), Poland 4, 61, 136, 165, 189
Freeholder Party of the Czech Republic (SsČR) 167
fusion
  and leadership congruence 193–4

and programmatic change 216–7
and slate congruence 157–8, 171–4
definition of 151–2, 155
detection based on candidate movement 175–8
fusionary tendencies 152, 164, 176, 179
of electoral coalitions 170, 177

Garden of Eden 92
Gašparovič, Ivan 164
genes/genetics
  in evolutionary biology 11, 19–20, 39
  in political parties 8, 11–2, 19–20
genetic paradigm 19–20, 27, 30, 32, 34, 42, 43–4
genuinely new party, *see* party novelty/newness, genuine novelty
Georgia 97
GERB, *see* Citizens for European Development of Bulgaria (GERB)
German Democratic Republic 10
Germany 3, 10, 26, 181–2
Goliath 49–51, 119–20
Grebeníček, Miroslav 197
Green and Farmers' Union (ZZS) 174, 178
Green Party, Austria 26
Green Party, Germany (Democratic Republic) 10
Green Party, Germany (Federal Republic) 3, 182
Gregor Virant's Civic List (LGV) 107
Gyurcsány, Ferenc 107, 182, 187, 209

Harmony (S) 155–6
Harmony Centre (SC) 156, 169, 209, 210
Head-Up (HV) 167
Hiller, István 187
Homeland Union (TS) 100, 210
Hrušovský, Pavol 196
Hungarian Democratic Forum (MDF) 59–61, 163, 175, 197
Hungarian Democratic People's Party (MDNP) 197
Hungarian Justice and Life Party (MIÉP) 61
Hungarian Socialist Party (MSZP) 48, 61, 104, 107, 182, 187, 209
HV, *see* Head-Up (HV)

HZD, *see* Movement for Democracy (HZD)
HZDS, *see* Movement for a Democratic Slovakia (HZDS)

I, *see* Pro Patria Electoral Coalition (I)
I-ERSP, *see* Pro Patria–National Independence Party (I-ERSP)
IL, *see* Pro Patria (IL)
Independent Smallholders Party (FKGP) 196, 208
IRL, *see* Pro Patria and Res Publica Union (IRL)
Israel 4, 120
Italy 4, 7, 77, 182

Janković, Zoran 185, 197
Janša, Janez 48
Jobbik 53
JP, *see* New Party (JP)
Jurek, Marek 163
Jurkāns, Jānis 194

K, *see* Centre Party (K)
Kaczyński, Jarosław 183
Kadima 4, 120
Kallas, Siim 174, 196
KDH, *see* Christian Democratic Movement (KDH)
KDU–ČSL, *see* Christian and Democratic Union–Czechoslovak People's Party (KDU–ČSL)
Kirkilas, Gediminas 196
KK, *see* Safe Home (KK)
Klaus, Václav 29, 168
KLD, *see* Liberal-Democratic Congress (KLD)
KMÜ, *see* Coalition Party and Country People's Union (KMÜ)
Kostov, Ivan 195
Kovács, István 35–8, 47–8
Kovács, László 187
KP, *see* Christian Party (KP)
Kreituse, Ilga 195
KSČM, *see* Communist Party of Bohemia and Moravia (KSČM)
Kun, *see* Royalists (Kun)

L, *see* Equal Rights (L)
Labour Party (DP), Latvia 164, 195
Labour Party (DP), Lithuania 4, 133, 154, 175, 186
Labour Party (Labourists), Lithuania 4
Labour Party, United Kingdom 3, 10, 29
Labour Union (UP) 61, 170
Labourist Party 4
Latgale Democratic Party (LDP) 174, 194
Latin America 14, 20
Latvia First Party (LPP) 134, 196, 210
Latvia's Way (LC) 164, 174, 187, 194, 196, 210
Latvian Association of Regions (LRA) 168
Latvian Socialist Party (LSP) 155–6, 194
Law and Justice (PiS) 3, 10, 61, 90, 108, 112, 136, 159, 163, 183
LB, *see* Left Bloc (LB)
LC, *see* Latvia's Way (LC)
LD, *see* Liberal Democrats (LD)
LDDP, *see* Lithuanian Democratic Labour Party (LDDP)
LDP (Latvia), *see* Latgale Democratic Party (LDP)
LDP (Lithuania), *see* Liberal Democratic Party (LDP), Lithuania
LDS, *see* Liberal Democracy of Slovenia (LDS)
League of Polish Families (LPR) 61, 112, 136
Left Bloc (LB) 197
Lega Nord 182
legislative switching 24, 35, 166
Lendvai, Ildikó 187
Lezsák, Sándor 197
LGV, *see* Gregor Virant's Civic List (LGV)
Liberal and Centre Union (LICS) 133, 168
Liberal Democracy of Slovenia (LDS) 107, 134–5, 213
Liberal Democratic Party (ELDP), Estonia 100, 123, 131, 161
Liberal Democratic Party (LDP), Lithuania 164
Liberal Democrats (LD) 174
Liberal Democrats (LIDEM) 166
Liberal-Democratic Congress (KLD) 4, 165
LICS, *see* Liberal and Centre Union (LICS)
LIDEM, *see* Liberal Democrats (LIDEM)

Liepaja Party 178
List Pim Fortuyn 4
Lithuanian Democratic Labour Party (LDDP) 164, 188
Lithuanian Liberal Union (LLS) 102, 105, 133, 164
Lithuanian Social Democratic Party (LSDP) 105, 162, 188, 196
LKDS, see Christian Democrat Union (LKDS)
LKRS, see Russian Union (LKRS)
LLS, see Lithuanian Liberal Union (LLS)
LPP, see Latvia First Party (LPP)
LPR, see League of Polish Families (LPR)
LRA, see Latvian Association of Regions (LRA)
LSDP, see Lithuanian Social Democratic Party (LSDP)
LSP, see Latvian Socialist Party (LSP)
LZS, see Farmers' Union (LZS)

Macron, Emmanuel 4, 90
Manifesto Project (MARPOR) 31, 71, 95, 200–6, 214, 218–9
Mazowiecki, Tadeusz 188
MCPP (mean change in party positions) 206–15
MD, see Moderates (MD)
MDNP, see Hungarian Democratic People's Party (MDNP)
Medgyessy, Péter 182, 187
Mesterházy, Attila 187
MIÉP, see Hungarian Justice and Life Party (MIÉP)
Migaš, Joezf 189
Mihaylova, Nadezhda Nikolova 195
Miliband, Ed 29
MKOE, see Our Home is Estonia (MKOE)
Moderates (MD) 28, 125, 131–2, 164, 210
Most–Híd, see Bridge (Most–Híd)
Movement for a Democratic Slovakia (HZDS) 164, 173, 175
Movement for Democracy (HZD) 164
Movement for Rights and Freedoms (DPS) 168, 195
MSZP, see Hungarian Socialist Party (MSZP)

NA, see National Alliance (NA)
National Alliance 'All for Latvia' (PVL) 187
National Alliance 'All for Latvia!'/ For Fatherland and Freedom/LNNK (PVL-TB-LNNK) 187
National Alliance (NA) 168
National Harmony Party (TSP) 155–6, 194
National Independence Party (ERSP) 123–4, 132, 161
National Movement Simeon II (NDSV) 54, 56, 184
National Resurrection Party (TPP) 168
NDSV, see National Movement Simeon II (NDSV)
Nečas, Petr 56
Netherlands 4, 7, 182
New Era (JL) 184, 203, 210
New Party (JP) 134
New Slovenia (NSi) 108
New Union (NS) 133, 162, 164, 175, 196
non-feasible candidates 41–2, 68, 69–72
Non-Partisan Bloc in Support of Reforms (BBWR) 108
novelty, see candidate novelty, party novelty/newness
NPSD, see Freedom and Dignity (NPSD)
NS, see New Union (NS)
NSi, see New Slovenia (NSi)
NSL, see For Latvia from the Heart (NSL)

ODA, see Civic Democratic Alliance (ODA)
ODS (Bulgaria), see United Democratic Forces (ODS)
ODS (Czechia), see Civic Democratic Party (ODS)
OĽaNO, see Ordinary People and Independent Personalities (OĽaNO)
Olechowski, Andrzej 186
Olejniczak, Wojciech 187
Orbán, Viktor 3, 32, 182
Ordinary People and Independent Personalities (OĽaNO) 102, 175
organizational paradigm 18–19, 26, 27, 29, 43, 198
Ortman, Jaroslav 197
Our Home is Estonia (MKOE) 132

252 INDEX

Paksas, Rolandas 133, 164
Palikot, Janusz, *see* Palikot's Movement (RUCHP)
Palikot's Movement (RUCHP) 159, 167, 182, 186
Pantelējevs, Andrejs 187
ParlGov 71, 80, 95, 188–9
Paroubek, Jiří 182, 186
Partido Ecológico Español 10
Parts, Juhan 184
party entry 27, 39
 and candidate novelty 100–5
 and candidate turnover 92–4
 identification of 95–99, 109–13, 115–16
party exit 27, 34, 71, 91
 and candidate dropout 105–8
 and candidate turnover 92–4
 identification of 95–9, 109–13, 115–16
Party for Freedom (PVV) 7, 159
party leaders
 change of 29–30, 180–1
 continuation of 192–7
 novelty of 183–6
 types of 181–3
party logos 10
party novelty/newness
 conceptualization of 5–6
 genuine novelty 4, 16, 27, 38, 54, 63, 71, 74, 90, 91, 104, 157, 172
 partial novelty 90, 105, 112, 115, 126, 129, 189
Party of Civic Rights ('Zemanites') 163
Party of Entrepreneurs and Businessmen (SPŽSR) 173, 175
Party of Miro Cerar (SMC) 54, 90, 184
Party of the Democratic Left (SDĽ) 100, 189
Party of the Hungarian Community (SMK–MKP) 197
party switching 20, 34, 43, 46, 57, 164–5, 174, 179
 by group of politicians, *see* collective defection
 in parliament, *see* legislative switching
Paulauskas, Artūras 196
Pauls, Raimonds 134

PCTVL, *see* For Human Rights in a United Latvia (PCTVL)
PE-EK, *see* Better Estonia-Estonian Citizen (PE-EK)
People of Freedom 182
People's Party (DFP) 3, 4, 90
People's Movement for Latvia (TKL-ZP) 164
People's Party (TP) 100, 102, 134, 174, 185, 194, 196, 210
People's Party for Freedom and Democracy (VVD) 158
People's Union (RL) 175
Philistia 119–20
PiS, *see* Law and Justice (PiS)
PJN, *see* Poland Comes First (PJN)
Plaid Cymru (PC) 26
Płażyński, Maciej 186
PLL, *see* For a Good Latvia! (PLL)
PO, *see* Civic Platform (PO)
Poland Comes First (PJN) 159
Polish Peasant Party (PSL) 61, 167
Political Party Database 182
Popular Front (RR) 105, 123–4, 131–2, 165
Positive Slovenia (PS) 54, 168, 169, 185, 197
PP, *see* Right Wingers (PP)
PR, *see* Right Wing of the Republic (PR)
Prince of Sweden, Carl Philip 124
Pro Patria (IL) 102, 123–24, 126, 131–2, 136, 161, 164, 174, 178, 194, 196
Pro Patria and Res Publica Union (IRL) 102, 156, 173, 194
Pro Patria Electoral Coalition (I) 161, 163, 194, 196
Pro Patria–National Independence Party (I-ERSP) 61, 123–4, 132, 136, 194, 196
Progress Party (FP) 3, 90
PS, *see* Positive Slovenia (PS)
PSL, *see* Polish Peasant Party (PSL)
Public Affairs (VV) 56, 107, 166, 167
PVL, *see* National Alliance 'All for Latvia' (PVL)
PVL–TB–LNNK, *see* National Alliance 'All for Latvia!'/ For Fatherland and Freedom/LNNK (PVL–TB–LNNK)

INDEX 253

Rally for the Republic (RPR), France 4
Rally for the Republic (SPR–RSČ), Czechoslovakia/Czech Republic 102, 133
Rally of the French People (RPF) 4
Reform Party (ER) 61, 100, 102, 123–24, 126, 131–2, 161, 164, 165, 168, 174, 185, 194, 196, 210
rejuvenation 69, 77, 83, 88
relative list position 51, 58, 64–67
renomination 69, 77–78, 80, 88
Representative Audit of Britain 16
Repše, Einars 184
Res Publica (RP) 102, 105, 164, 178, 184, 194
Right Wing of the Republic (PR) 95, 163
Right Wingers (PP) 61, 123–5, 132, 161, 194
RL, see People's Union (RL)
Rõivas, Taavi 185
Royalists (Kun) 122, 124
RP, see Res Publica (RP)
RPF, see Rally of the French People (RPF)
RPR, see Rally for the Republic (RPR), France
RR, see Popular Front (RR)
RUCHP, see Palikot's Movement (RUCHP)
Russian Party (VE) 176, 178
Russian Union (LKRS) 169

S, see Harmony (S)
Safe Home (KK) 104, 123, 130, 173
Sąjūdis (SK) 105, 210
Samoobrona (SRP) 164
SaS, see Freedom and Solidarity (SaS)
Saxe-Coburg-Gotha, Simeon, see National Movement Simeon II (NDSV)
SBC, see volatility, split-by-congruence (SBC) volatility
SC, see Harmony Centre (SC)
SD, see Social Democrats (SD), Slovenia
SDE, see Social Democratic Party (SDE), Estonia
SDK, see Slovak Democratic Coalition (SDK)
SDKÚ, see Slovak Democratic and Christian Union (SDKÚ)
SDL', see Party of the Democratic Left (SDL')

SDP, see Social Democratic Party (SDP), United Kingdom
SDS (Bulgaria), see Union of Democratic Forces (SDS)
SDS (Slovenia), see Slovenian Democratic Party (SDS)
SDSS, see Social-Democratic Party of Slovenia (SDSS)
selfish gene 11, 19, see also genes/genetics in evolutionary biology
Ship of Theseus 1
single-mandate districts, see candidate weighting, in mixed systems
SK, see Sąjūdis (SK)
Šķēle, Andris 100, 174, 185, 194, 196
SKL, see Conservative People's Party (SKL), Poland
slates
 component slates 154
 definition of 8, 33
 joint slates 154, 157, 192
 making of 33–39
 proto-slates 20, 37–9, 76, 124, 166, 199
SLD, see Democratic Left Alliance (SLD)
Śledzińska-Katarasińska, Iwona 136
Slovak Democratic and Christian Union (SDKÚ) 100, 162, 196
Slovak Democratic Coalition (SDK) 100, 105, 157, 161–3, 179, 195, 196
Slovenian Democratic Party (SDS) 102
SMC, see Party of Miro Cerar (SMC)
Smer-SD, see Direction-Social Democracy (Smer-SD)
SMK–MKP, see Party of the Hungarian Community (SMK–MKP)
Social Democratic Party (SDE), Estonia 28, 124, 165, 168, 174, 176, 178, 179, 210
Social Democratic Party (SDP), United Kingdom 3
Social Democratic Party (SPD), Germany 182
Social Democrats (SD), Slovenia 135, 169, 186
Social-Democratic Coalition of Algirdas Brazauskas (BSDA) 133, 188
Social-Democratic Party of Slovenia (SDSS) 105, 165

socio-economic indicators
  economic growth (GDP) 80, 83, 137–40
  unemployment 80, 85
Solidarity Electoral Action (AWS) 3, 61, 90, 108, 133, 135, 165, 173
Solidarity Electoral Action of the Right (AWSP) 108
Spain 10
SPR–RSČ, *see* Rally for the Republic (SPR–RSČ), Czechoslovakia/Czech Republic
SPŽSR, *see* Party of Entrepreneurs and Businessmen (SPŽSR)
SRP, *see* Samoobrona (SRP)
SsČR, *see* Freeholder Party (SsČR)
Straujuma, Laimdota 187
Suchman, Tamás 48
Sulík, Richard 186
SV, see Common Choice (SV)
Sweden 124
Szabó, Iván 197
Szabó, János 196
SZDSZ, *see* Alliance of Free Democrats (SZDSZ)
Szydło, Beata 183

TB–LNNK, *see* For Fatherland and Freedom/LNNK (TB–LNNK)
Team Stronach 3, 90
TKL-ZP, *see* People's Movement for Latvia (TKL-ZP)
TOP09 159
Topolánek, Mirek 29
Torgyán, József 196, 208
TP, *see* People's Party (TP)
TPP, *see* National Resurrection Party (TPP)
TR, *see* Your Movement (TR)
TS, *see* Homeland Union (TS)
TSP, *see* National Harmony Party (TSP)
Turkey 158
Tusk, Donald 186

Ü (index of programmatic similarity) 203–17
UD, *see* Democratic Union (UD)
UdL, *see* Working for Lithuania (UdL)
UKIP, *see* United Kingdom Independence Party (UKIP)
Ukraine 48, 97

Union for a Popular Movement (UMP) 4
Union of Democratic Forces (SDS) 133, 163, 170
United Democratic Forces (ODS) 170, 195
United Kingdom 3, 10, 16, 22, 26, 29, 48, 77, 90, 182
United Kingdom Independence Party (UKIP) 90
United Left (ZL) 167
United Smallholders Party (EKGP) 196
United States of America 20, 31, 77
UP, *see* Labour Union (UP)
US, *see* Freedom Union (US)
Uspaskich, Viktor 186
ÚSVIT, *see* Dawn (ÚSVIT)
UTT, *see* For Order and Justice (UTT)
UW, *see* Freedom Union (UW)

VE, *see* Russian Party (VE)
Vienotība 168, 175, 187, 196, 210
Virant, Gregor *see* Gregor Virant's Civic List (LGV)
Vlaams Belang 4
Vlaams Blok 4
volatility
  as a measure of party system stability/change 2, 117–18
  calculation of 118–19
  determinants of 136–40
  extra-system 138–40
  in Central and Eastern Europe 133–6
  intra-system 138–9
  split-by-congruence (SBC) volatility 126–8
Vona, Gábor 53
VV, *see* Public Affairs (VV)
VVD, *see* People's Party for Freedom and Democracy (VVD)

Wałęsa, Lech 108
WCD, *see* weighted candidate dropout (WCD)
WCN, *see* weighted candidate novelty (WCN)
weighted candidate dropout (WCD) 54–6, 92–4, 105–8, 109–13
weighted candidate novelty (WCN) 54–6, 92–4, 100–5, 109–13
Wilders, Geert 7, 158

Windsor, Elizabeth Alexandra Mary 47
Working for Lithuania (UdL) 105, 114, 133, 162, 164, 196
Your Movement (TR) 167

ZAAB, *see* Alliance of Alenka Bratušek (ZAAB)
Zares–Social Liberals 135
Zatlers's Reform Party (ZRS) 168, 175, 186
Zatlers, Valdis 186, *see also* Zatlers's Reform Party (ZRS)
Zeman, Miloš 133, 163, *see also* Party of Civic Rights ('Zemanites')
ZL, *see* United Left (ZL)
ZRS, *see* Zatlers's Reform Party (ZRS)
ZZS, *see* Green and Farmers' Union (ZZS)